RENZO PIANO BUILDING WORKSHOP

Phaidon Press Limited
2 Kensington Square
London W8 5EZ

First published 1995

ISBN 0 7148 2859 9

A CIP catalogue record for this book is
available from the British Library

Frontispiece illustration: Il Grande Bigo,
Columbus International Exposition, Genoa

Printed in Hong Kong

RENZO PIANO BUILDING WORKSHOP

Complete works

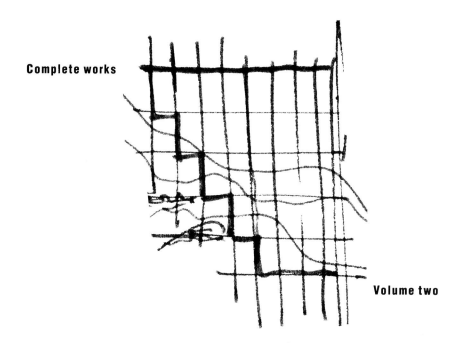

Volume two

Peter Buchanan

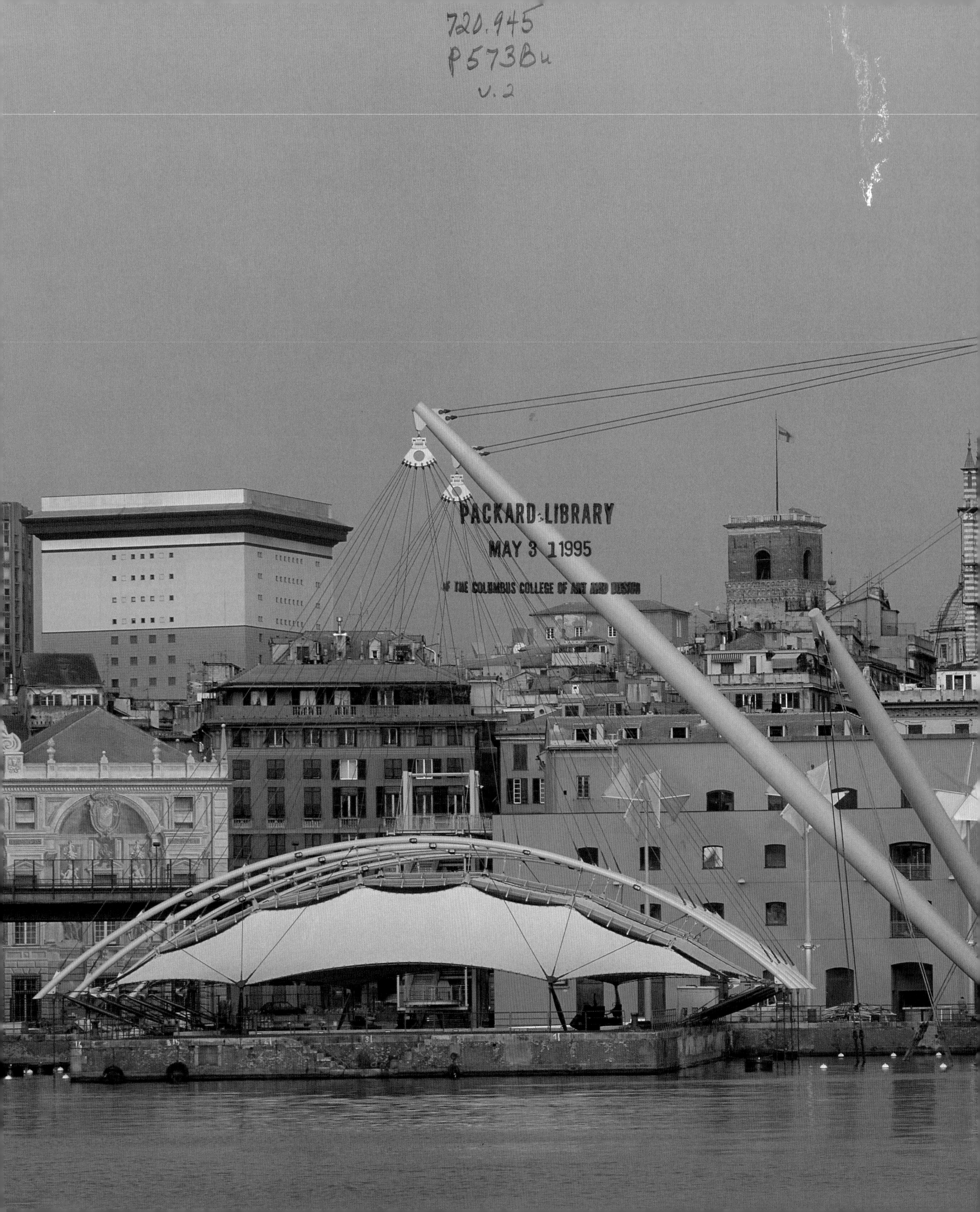

Contents

Further Dimensions of the Organic **6**

Bercy 2 Shopping Centre, Paris **16**

Thomson Optronics Factory, Saint Quentin en Yvelines **34**

Metro Stations, Genoa **46**

Cruise Ships and Yacht **58**

Interview with Renzo Piano **64**

UNESCO Laboratory-workshop, Vesima **76**

Glass Furniture **92**

Columbus International Exposition, Genoa **94**

'Galileo in Padua' Exhibition Project, Padua **130**

National Centre for Science and Technology, Amsterdam **132**

Credito Industriale Sardo, Cagliari **140**

Lingotto Factory Renovation, Turin **150**

'Automobiles in Milan' Exhibition, Milan **168**

Beyeler Foundation Museum, near Basle **170**

Padre Pio Pilgrimage Church, San Giovanni Rotondo **180**

J M Tjibaou Cultural Centre, Nouméa **190**

Potsdamer Platz, Berlin **210**

Kansai International Airport, Osaka **220**

Acknowledgements **228**

Bibliography **230**

Index **236**

Photographic credits **239**

6

Further dimensions of the organic The continuing evolution of a natural architecture

This second volume of the Renzo Piano Building Workshop's complete works illustrates all the practice's buildings completed since those featured in Volume One and includes those schemes under design development which, if not yet finalized, are already strong projects with their own clear intentions and identity. In time, these projects should offer instructive comparison with the built versions, and give useful insight into how work evolves and matures in the collaborative processes of the Building Workshop. Such comparisons should also chart the continuing evolution and maturation of Piano's approach to architecture.

Certainly, seen against the buildings published in Volume One, the recent and current works shown in this book suggest that the Building Workshop is in the process of extending its engagement with what might be thought of as the organic dimensions of the man-made environment. As conjectured in the essay introducing Volume One, the work of Piano and the Building Workshop is the product of an ongoing quest for what is characterized there as a 'natural' architecture. This notion goes beyond an architecture that emulates the forms and efficiencies of nature; and even one that further seeks a harmony with nature by gently accommodating itself to nature, and inviting it within its fabric as an all-pervading presence. It encompasses also an architecture that feels natural to its place and times, that draws on

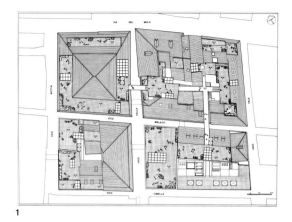

1

8   Recent works in and near Genoa.
1 The Molo urban regeneration project, 1994: this current study returns the Building Workshop to the same area where its ongoing involvement with the harbour area began.
2, **3** Columbus International Exposition, 1984-1992: this reconnects the historic city with the oldest part of the harbour.
4 Brin station, 1983-1991, on Genoa's new metropolitan railway.

2

3

4

the still vital forms and skills of local tradition and yet, in extending the possibilities of the present, helps the future gracefully to unfold. Born in the fluid sensitivities of a honed and receptive instinct rather than in the rigidities of intellect and theory, it is an architecture such as the world itself might bring forth from all the potential offered at a particular place at a particular moment, if it could do so unmediated by style- and self-conscious architects.

The above characterization remains as true of the work in this second volume as it did of that in the first. This introduction considers only how such concerns are being extended into new territories, or at least, those new to the Building Workshop. First though, a few comments on the particular flavour lent to this volume by the work it includes. As in Volume One, the buildings and projects are heterogeneous. Again this reflects how much they are shaped by place and programme rather than a personal design idiom. Nevertheless, it is possible to identify common themes among these recent projects despite their mutual differences. Two obvious and overlapping themes that immediately stand out encompass works built in or near Genoa, Piano's home town and the main base of the Building Workshop, and those close to or actually afloat in the sea. In the heart of Genoa are the setting and structures for the 1992 Columbus International Exposition which have helped to

resurrect and revitalize much of its historic legacy (p 94). These are in the oldest part of the harbour from which Columbus must often have set sail, before seeking Spanish patronage. And they include the floating Italian Pavilion.

The Columbus exposition culminated an involvement with the harbour area that began as long ago as 1981 when the newly formed Renzo Piano Building Workshop was asked to make proposals for the Molo quarter (p 98), applying a process that involved the participation of the local community. Nothing came of the ingenious project that resulted. But with the continuing, if hesitant, regeneration of parts of the old city occasioned by the exposition, the Building Workshop has, more than a decade later, recently been commissioned once more to study and make proposals for the area. Following on from the original Molo project, came another to investigate an area that became part of the exposition site. It was for this project that Piano first proposed to reconnect the old city with its harbour, and so with the sea.

Also in Genoa, the Building Workshop is involved in the construction of a metropolitan railway system. It has already completed three of the eight stations it has been commissioned to build for the first phase of this project (p 46). And at Vesima, some 20 kilometres west of the city, the Building Workshop has built a second Genoese base,

5

5 UNESCO laboratory-workshop, Vesima,
1986-1992: the Building Workshop's own
research base outside the city.
6 *Crown Princess*, 1988-1991: one of a pair of
identical cruise ships.
7 Aquarium of the Columbus International
Exposition.
8 'Automobiles in Milan' exhibition, Ansaldo,
Milan, Italy 1990: conversion intended as the
first stage in founding a design museum.

6

a laboratory-workshop, which it shares with UNESCO (p 76). From the steep slope on which it perches, the building looks down on the sea, the presence of which pervades the building and forms a backdrop to all its activities.

Other works in this volume are for sites surrounded by the sea. The Kansai International Airport Terminal (see Volume One, p 24 for the design) is at an advanced stage of its very rapid construction programme on an artificial island off Osaka, Japan. Site photographs showing progress on the building of this immense masterwork close this volume (p 220). Construction will soon start on the J M Tjibaou Cultural Centre on a site projecting into the sea near Nouméa on the Pacific Island of New Caledonia (p 190). As the design of this project developed, it passed through several variations, each recognizably different from the others. So it is used here to show how any design, even one already acclaimed by other architects when chosen as a competition winner, is continuously reinvestigated and developed yet further in the Building Workshop's intensely exploratory design process.

Destined to rise almost directly from the waters of Amsterdam harbour in the Netherlands is the National Centre for Science and Technology (p 132) which, though its design is still evolving, is already a strong statement. Built to float upon the sea, and included here to elaborate the nautical theme

despite preceding the period covered by this volume, are the last of the four yachts designed by Piano over a 20-year period together with the *Crown Princess* one of two identical cruise ships, on whose design the Building Workshop collaborated (p 58).

Another theme shared by several works in this volume is that they house exhibition, gallery and/or cultural functions. The buildings rehabilitated for the Columbus exposition provided showroom and gallery space, and the floating Italian Pavilion is basically an exhibition hall; the aquarium is also dedicated to exhibition. Those parts of the Fiat Lingotto Factory in Turin, Italy (p 150), that have been refurbished and extended to date are: a large exhibition hall for trade fairs, and a gallery that can serve as an extension of the hall or house independent art exhibitions. Another refurbishment of old industrial premises, for the 'Automobiles in Milan' exhibition, in the Ansaldo district of that city (p 168), was intended to form the embryonic stage of a permanent museum of Italian design. Other projects still under design that serve exhibition purposes are: the Amsterdam centre (p132), the Beyeler Museum outside Basle, Switzerland (p 170), and the cultural centre in Nouméa (p 190). The latter building serves wider cultural purposes in addition to housing exhibitions; so too do the Columbus exposition buildings and the Fiat Lingotto complex, both of which incorporate halls for concerts.

9

8

7

1

1 Bercy 2 Shopping Centre, Paris, 1987-1990: laminated timber elements support the shell.

2 National Centre for Science and Technology, Amsterdam, the Netherlands, 1989-: like the Genoa aquarium it will jut into the harbour and serve exhibition purposes.

3 Thomson Optronics Factory, Saint Quentin en Yvelines, France, 1988-1990: buildings and planting are interwoven on same grid.

4 Padre Pio Pilgrimage Church, San Giovanni Rotondo, Foggia, Italy, 1991-: timber props reach from stone arches to support the roof.

5 J M Tjibaou Cultural Centre, Nouméa, New Caledonia, 1990: each major space is encased in a cage of laminated timber ribs.

6 Columbus International Exhibition: the aquarium seen from under the tent roof that is suspended from the Bigo. Both structures conjure obvious nautical associations.

2

The number of the Building Workshop's projects that are associated with Genoa and/or the sea, or that serve exhibition or cultural functions, lends a particular, and in large degree circumstantial, flavour to this volume. Far more significant is what the comparison of recent and earlier works reveals about the directions in which the Building Workshop is going. Some insight can be gained from exploring further common themes that such comparison highlights in the recent work. Most significant of these is the continuing, and probably increasing, use of natural materials, particularly wood and stone – and not just as cladding or finishes, but as structure too – which emphasizes just how far Piano's work is from the High-Tech movement with which he was once associated.

Of the recently completed buildings, both the Vesima laboratory-workshop and the Bercy 2 Shopping Centre in Paris (p 16) have internally exposed, laminated wood roof structures. At Vesima, laminated-timber beams support the wood frames of the glass roof that slopes above floors of timber and slate, and low walls of stucco and fieldstone. These natural materials have an unassertively down-to-earth quality which tends to reinforce the impression of working under a pergola with ever-responsive mechanical 'foliage'. The feeling of being at one with nature is heightened by the views, plants and ever-changing sunlight that pene-

trate and pervade the building. Like the Thomson Optronics Factory in Saint Quentin en Yvelines in France (p 34) the laboratory-workshop also sets new standards for the Building Workshop in terms of the seamless integration of architecture and surrounding landscape or planting. At Bercy, the laminated-timber beams inside the building come as a surprise after the stainless steel armour of the exterior. But their presence, together with that of the planting and natural light, again provides a reassuringly natural and down-to-earth touch in an enclosed environment that otherwise exalts only the ephemera of consumerism.

Of the projects currently at an advanced stage of design, both the Padre Pio Pilgrimage Church in San Giovanni Rotondo, southern Italy (p 180), and the J M Tjibaou Cultural Centre (p 190) make particularly conspicuous use of timber. The church has a secondary structural system of timber props reaching upward to support a timber roof deck. And the Cultural Centre will have a series of external cage-like structures made primarily of laminated wood, each wrapped like a vegetal husk around one of the major spaces. The architects refer to each of these husks as a 'case'. Together the cases will mediate between the building and its surroundings, evoking the forms of the local vegetation and traditional settlements, and exploiting local climatic conditions to provide natural ventilation.

3

4

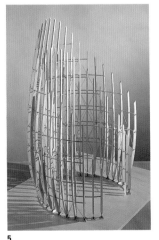

5

12 Natural materials used as claddings.
1 IRCAM Extension, Paris, France, 1988-1989: the facing is panels of terracotta units.
2 Rue de Meaux housing, Paris, France, 1988-1991 has grc facades with terracotta tiles.
3 Credito Industriale Sardo headquarters, Cagliari, Sardinia, Italy, 1985-1992: stone is used as a facing and as slotted screens.
4 Sports Hall, Ravenna, Italy, 1986-.

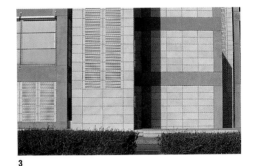

3

The Padre Pio Pilgrimage Church also reintroduces stone as a structural material, capable of virtuoso feats, with what will be the longest-span stone arches ever built. Yet for all their virtuosity these arches will lend the church an earthy and archaic quality, in keeping perhaps with the simple monk the building commemorates and the ancient rituals of the mass it will shelter. More mundanely, the building for the Credito Industriale Sardo in Cagliari in Sardinia (p140) uses stone as a facing material. This follows the use of terracotta as a facing material on the IRCAM extension and Rue de Meaux Housing in Paris (Volume One p 202 and p 214), and more recently on buildings for the Columbus Exposition. At Cagliari the Building Workshop has also used stone for screens with cut-out slots that are rather mechanistic in shape, as if they were in pressed metal not stone. Here, stone is used in a purely contemporary idiom. For the Potsdamer Platz scheme (p 210), a stipulation in the design guidelines, which are being prepared as part of the masterplan and detailed design of the urban spaces, is that most of the buildings must be faced in terracotta. This is intended to achieve some unity despite the contrasting design idioms of the other architects who will be building within the masterplan area beside the Building Workshop.

A major theme revealed in the recent work, when compared with earlier designs, is the increasing use of structural shells comprised of complex curves. A combination of cylindrical and toroidal curves envelop both the Bercy 2 Shopping Centre and the Kansai International Airport Terminal. For the Potsdamer Platz scheme for Berlin, similar forms are being explored to clad the roof and main facade of a huge block containing a theatre and other public facilities. Other kinds of curves will be used for the roofs of the Padre Pio Pilgrimage Church, and a sports hall for Ravenna, Italy (Volume One p 31). The 'cases' of the Cultural Centre for Nouméa also form complex curves. The walls of the museum in Amsterdam are curved but are planned to comply with more simple conical profiles. And the observation lounges of the cruise ships are enclosed by rounded forms shaped in aluminium.

Associated with this adoption of complex curves is the use of cladding systems of repetitive rectangular metal panels, usually of stainless steel, to protect the roof below and give some sense of scale and order to what might otherwise appear to be rather amorphous forms. To achieve this, and keep the number of panel sizes to a minimum, requires a sophisticated geometric discipline, which it is only possible to determine using computers. This line of exploration started with the Bercy 2 Shopping Centre, which is clad in 27 000 panels of 34 different types. It found its ideal expression at Kansai where all 90 000 cladding panels of this immense building are identical.

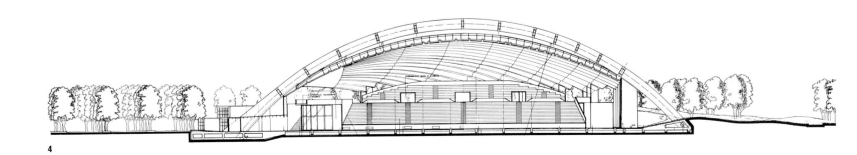

4

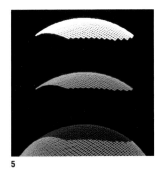

5

Geometrical explorations.

5 Sports Hall, Ravenna, Italy, 1986-.

6 Padre Pio Pilgrimage Church, S Giovanni Rotondo, Foggia, Italy, 1991.

7 National Centre for Science and Technology.

8 Bercy 2 Shopping Centre.

9 Kansai International Airport passenger terminal: 1988-1994.

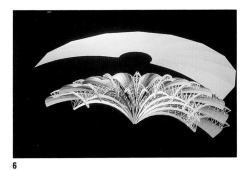

6

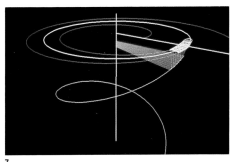

7

The use of repetitive rectangular units to clad complex forms was instigated largely by Peter Rice, the Ove Arup & Partners' engineer on these projects, who drew on his early experience of calculating how to tile the shells of Jørn Utzon's Sydney Opera House. (The input of various Arup engineers is acknowledged as crucial to all the schemes that explore this theme.) Another major spur to these investigations was Rice's interest in fractals and chaos-theory mathematics, and what these reveal about the non-Euclidian geometrical order of nature. None of these volumes or their claddings is actually derived from fractals or chaos-theory mathematics; but their discovery and implications were felt to legitimate the investigation of an architectural order closer to the organic order revealed by recent theoretical explorations. Significantly, both Bercy 2 and Kansai found their solutions in toroidal geometries. As is increasingly appreciated, the torus is the most common geometric figure found in nature, to which such things as magnetic fields, convection currents and the shape of many fruits conform.

The exploration of complex geometries also reflects the Building Workshop's increasing use of computers, which is one of its most important recent trends. Architectural offices are increasingly dependent on computers for drawings, engineering calculations and so on – all uses to which they are put by the Building Workshop; but, with considerable guidance from Ove Arup & Partners, the Building Workshop uses the computer in other ways, thus showing a more profound understanding of its true potential than other architects' practices. It is not a mere time and labour-saving tool, nor simply one that can draw up or control the small batch manufacture of a profligate number of special case components. Instead the computer's potential lies in its capacity to calculate structures in new and more precise ways, and to let the designer enter novel conceptual territories. In particular, the latter includes complex mathematical topologies which can open up a new world of form, bringing with them new disciplines, and so new economies and efficiencies.

Together, these two factors might allow designers to get ever closer to emulating the complex disciplines of nature, rather than superficially imitating its forms. Nature's repetitive elements, such as leaves and fish scales, are grown gradually and so can all be made to the same genetic template yet be different in size and shape. With elements made by industrial processes, a similar organic integrity is found by using only identical components. So it is in its capacity to follow disciplines as stringent as those to which nature complies, not in its capacity to imitate the natural forms that may or may not result, that the computer allows the designer to get closer to nature and the organic. But the bonus of organically suggestive and finite

13

8

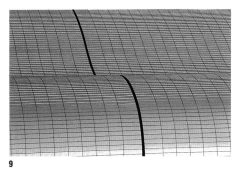

9

1

1 Thomson Optronics Factory: some panels of the spherical head of the testing tower fold together to allow views out.
2 National Centre for Science and Technology, initial design: means are being considered of pivoting the panels to admit light and air.
3 Columbus International Exposition: an urban reconstruction scheme that involved the conversion of historic buildings.

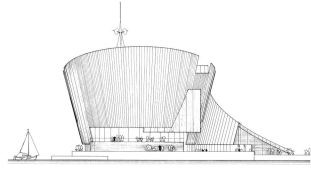

2

form, such as that of the Kansai terminal, is certainly sought too. For Piano and the Building Workshop, the computer need not be seen as opposed to craft, leading to work made at a detached remove and so inhumanely lifeless. Instead, if informed by intentions such as those outlined above, the computer is an essential tool of the modern craftsman. This is especially so if it is used to hone such a precise understanding of structures and materials that they can be pressed to the limits at which their essential aspects are eloquently communicated.

With the latest metal-clad shells now under design, the emulation of nature goes further than before. Shells with parts that move, and open up in various ways, are now being investigated by the Building Workshop, and indeed a small one has already been built as the head of the Thomson factory's testing tower. The Amsterdam museum will be wrapped in curved, outwardly sloping walls, which will be clad in copper-finished metal panels. This skin will compensate for the building's relative geometric simplicity by being able to open up where necessary to ventilate and illuminate some of the spaces behind it. This will probably be achieved by pivoting the panels like vertical louvres. The large building planned to house a theatre and casino in the Potsdamer Platz project was at one stage to be covered by a curving shell clad in stainless steel panels. Despite the complex geometric

discipline of this curved and tapering shell, it was intended that its scaly metallic skin would also open up. Huge sections, each comprised of several panels, were to tilt and swing away, rather like the shields that protect the wings of a beetle, to allow summer sun to stream into an indoor piazza. This device persists in the current, and far from final, scheme; but now the roof shell has been simplified into tilting planes.

Another small but significant group of recent and current works, is that of large-scale urban reconstruction schemes. These deal with the city in a more complex and sophisticated manner than anything the Building Workshop has designed before. The Columbus International Exposition is significant for the continuities it creates and, perhaps more importantly, re-creates across both space and time: reconnecting the old city core with the oldest part of the harbour; bringing to light and back to life important relics of the past, and contributing new civic spaces and other facilities. These will not only enhance life in the city immeasurably, but will provoke its further regeneration.

With the Potsdamer Platz scheme for Berlin there was only a single building left to restore but, even so, continuities are being established across time and space. Here, key parts of the historic street pattern will be re-established, both to resurrect part of Berlin's past and to help reconnect a city that was so brutally separated into East and West. More

3

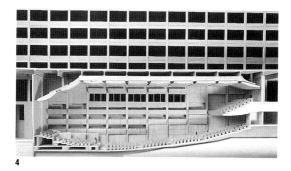

4

5

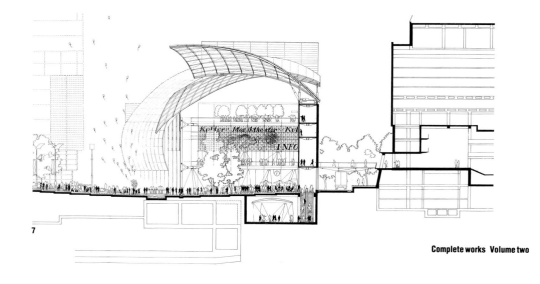

4, 5, 6 Lingotto Factory Renovation, Turin, Italy, 1983-: the conversion of a modern monument into a catalyst for regional regeneration. **4** the concert and congress hall currently nearing completion, **5** the gallery arranged for a show of American art, and **6** a contrasting arrangement for a show of Russian art.

7 Potsdamer Platz, Berlin, 1992-, intermediate scheme: the roof of a block is to open up in summer as an extension of a new piazza.

6

than that, the buildings of Hans Scharoun's Kulturforum (Berlin's cultural quarter), which resemble rocky outcrops rather than conventional buildings, will become a terminating focus for the rebuilt Alte Potsdamerstrasse, and thus newly connected with what was East Berlin. And these existing buildings will be linked by landscaping to the Tiergarten, to integrate them fully into the urban fabric of Berlin.

The Columbus exposition and Potsdamer Platz schemes both show an unprecedented understanding of, or perhaps feeling for, the city as an organic entity, which while always having to cope with change must also retain certain fundamental continuities. This new maturity in Piano's approach is revealed especially in the handling of the urban spaces between buildings. In the Berlin scheme particularly these are no longer residual spaces between dominant buildings. Instead they are elaborated as the vital frame that ties the scheme together and into the context of the larger city, and within which buildings will come and go. So the network of streets and urban spaces, along with their paving and furniture, are being designed so that the other architects who will join the Building Workshop in building there may respond and take their design cues from this frame, ensuring that instead of the city decomposing into fragments, it will retain a sense of cohesiveness and organic integrity throughout future change.

Further dimensions of the organic are explored in that microcosm of the organic city, the multi-functional megastructure that the Fiat Lingotto Factory is becoming. From being a vast single-use factory, emblematic of Modern industrial culture, it is being converted to house a wide range of functions that will interact to mutual benefit as a model of contemporary post-industrial ideals. These new functions are intended each to be big enough and collectively to be sufficiently diverse that the synergystic interactions will give the complex a life of its own. Such a fertile entrepreneurial ecology will not only keep its constituent enterprises continuously changing, up to date and lively, but will also play a revitalizing role in the economy of the whole region.

To help it achieve this, provision is being made to install the electronic equivalent of a central nervous system. This will monitor the servicing and security arrangements in all parts of the building as well as instantaneously connecting the various tenants to one another, to the region and to the world beyond. These dynamic interactions within the building, and between it and the wider world, can be seen as inherently organic. More than that, in the collaborative ventures it is intended to foster, as well as by preserving the legacy of the past, the conversion of the Lingotto complex exemplifies the other quintessential ideals that Piano pursues.

15

7

16

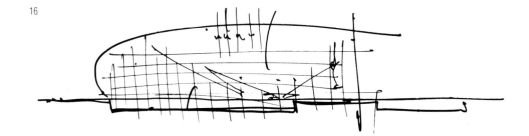

Bercy 2 Shopping Centre Charenton le Pont, Paris, France **1987–90**

A silvery blob bulging into the space defined by the ramps of a motorway interchange, the Bercy 2 Shopping Centre must be one of the strangest structures ever built. Not that it is exotically elaborate: it is understated in the extreme. Indeed, it appears less like a building (with separate walls, roof and windows) and more as a distended metallic-finished bag of space or a flaccid, semi-inflated airship. Yet the shape of this shell is highly, if unconventionally, disciplined geometrically to allow for maximum repetition of components and simplicity of construction. But the sophistication of its geometry is contrasted in an almost unsettling fashion with the deliberate coarseness of some of its constructional detailing, particularly the way in which the cladding is fixed. The random pattern of shiny and matt patches of cladding, and the use of wood with a shrewd yet seemingly almost ingenuous directness inside, reinforce this dichotomy.

As one enters the building a startling lack of correlation between its exterior and interior is revealed. Inside the curving carapace there is not the single open volume that might be expected. Instead there are layers of partitioned concrete floors and a multi-level mall that runs close to and at an angle with the longest edge of the outer shell. Moreover, this shell covers only part of the shopping centre, which extends as a more conventional structure beyond both sides along which the metal-clad curves are summarily terminated. On one of these sides are loading bays, storerooms and plant. On the other, the shopping centre extends towards and beneath an elevated hotel to where its main entrance looks along the axis of a conventional street.

The entrance to the centre, itself a major compositional element in the facade of the hotel, is an obvious compromise arrived at in collaboration with the architect of the hotel. In fact, the design of the whole shopping centre was similarly constrained. The Building Workshop was commissioned after the client had rejected a conventional boxy design by other architects. The legacy of this design remains in many of the basic moves that had previously been agreed with the local planners: the placing of access ramps, servicing and parking; the structural grid, and some of the internal planning. These fixes were accepted by the Building Workshop as

1

a base against which it would juxtapose its contributions. More of a compromise is the treatment of the interior public spaces which resulted from a rather fraught collaboration between the Building Workshop and retail specialist interior designers.

All the above characteristics make Bercy 2 a very difficult building for many, even fans of Piano, to come to terms with. Many high-profile architects might reject such a problematic (and so typically real-world)

commission. And many of them might be too self-conscious to let the intrinsic logic of the project itself take them into such novel and unfamiliar territory, as does the shell used here, even though such a way of working is the only way to achieve the originality they crave. But Piano believes in both 'looking into the dark' in this manner, and in extending past achievements. So, for all its strangeness, Bercy 2 is a seminal design. Although shaped by very particular conditions, the concepts pioneered here, and the experience gained with this shell, formed an essential background to the design (for what is, by comparison, an almost unconstrained situation) of the Kansai International Airport Terminal (p 220) – a building that none will demur at deeming a masterpiece.

The shopping centre is

located to the east of central Paris, where the suburbs of Charenton begin, in an area undergoing considerable redevelopment. Visually prominent, its shell is something of a landmark on its corner between the A4 that leads out of the city and the Boulevard Périphérique which rings Paris, and along this stretch is elevated to cross railway marshalling yards. Because of its accessible location, the general area was zoned for regionally oriented uses: offices, hotel and shopping centre. The hotel, which now straddles the entrance to the shopping centre, was designed by the architect who prepared the area masterplan, which zoned the corner for a shopping centre. All this was approved by the local borough, but without co-ordination with the City of Paris in whose jurisdiction the Périphérique falls. The result, which should one day be rectified, is that only minimal signage has been allowed to indicate access to the shopping centre. It is virtually impossible for a first-time visitor simultaneously to negotiate the motorway interchange and find the entrance to the shopping centre's car park.

18 **Bercy 2 Shopping Centre**
References and context.
1 Zeppelin airship: an image the designers kept in mind.
2 Aerial view of context and site, prior to demolition of the old buildings on it, nestled against ramp of motorway interchange close to the Seine.
3, **4** Seen from a distance the shiny shell of the shopping centre resembles an airship.

2

3

4

The shell and its form are a response to the shape of the site, and especially to the arcs traced by speeding cars on the motorway ramps that hem this corner. Chosen as a defensive armour against this aggressive, dystopian setting, the metal cladding reinforces the association with the cars whipping by. The intention was to make something distinct and memorable that would be grasped in an instant from a passing car, and yet, as always with Piano, it would also be generated by the forces felt to be at work on the site and so devoid of any gratuitous gesturing. It is a building simultaneously and paradoxically of its place and an alien intruder. The shell is indeed a shield, both shaped by, and a defence against, the context. And although not emblazoned with heraldic symbols, it performs the same historic function as did shields on the battlefield in that it gives immediate identity to the building.

To give some scale and geometric discipline to the shell, and so to help passers-by understand and relate to it, it was sheathed in repetitive cladding panels. These are formed from satin-finished stainless steel so that their varying angles reflect different parts of the sky, while some seem to be of matt finish. Together, these turn the shell into a patchwork of different colours and tones, in places grading into each other, and in others strongly contrasted. The effect is to etherealize the shell as much as to give a more tangible presence.

Whatever one makes of this shell, it is a compelling object. But views of it are marred by the sign that rises above one edge of it as a long horizontal which, among other visual infe-

licities such as crude lettering, sits uneasily with the sloping roof. Although a horizontal sign might be more legible, the architect's proposal for a mast of signs and banners would have set off the building better. This mast, which would have served its heraldic function in a suitably exuberant manner, was designed by RFR (Rice Francis Ritchie) the small specialist architectural-engineering firm in which Peter Rice, also structural engineer with Ove Arup & Partners for the shopping centre, was a partner. But the client considered it insufficiently legible and the local planners thought it too tall.

Closer to the shell, and viewing it from the adjacent pavement where few people other than architects usually have reason to go, gives quite a different impression from that gained at a distance. Instead of being struck by the sensual form of the double-curved shell and the geometric sophistication necessary to clad it in repetitive rectangular units, what is remarkable is a very pragmatic crudity – which some admire and others abhor. Where the slightly sloping bottom edge of a row of stainless-steel panels would have intercepted the pavement, panels are not cut but simply omitted from the row from this point onwards. This allows a view behind the panels, of their fixings and so on. A similar

19

Bercy 2 Shopping Centre

5, **6** From above, the shell can be seen as a shield against the hostile setting and the cars that speed past.

7 Unrealized design by RFR for signage mast.

8 The entrance facade protrudes below a hotel designed by another architect.

9 Beyond where a row of cladding panels would have intercepted the ground, the bottoms of the panels are not trimmed. Instead, further panels are omitted, revealing structure, escape doors etc.

10 Facetted curve of the shell bulges into the arc of the motorway ramp.

5

6

7

8

9

10

1

Bercy 2 Shopping Centre

Stainless steel cladding panels.

1 Panels placed over rooflights and smoke vents are made of perforated steel.

2 Detail section through both layers of outer shell: **a** cladding panel, **b** nylon hook, **c** 50mm diameter tubular steel fixing rail, **d** steel prop, **e** purlin **f** 22mm chipboard decking, **g** 60mm polyurethane insulation, **h** pvc waterproofing membrane.

3 Panels with nylon hooks in foreground await clipping into position.

rational, yet untidy, nonchalance pertains along the near-horizontal edges of the top of the shell where ragged edges of uncut panels oversail the roofs below.

The stainless steel panels have no weather-excluding role. But they are not just a decorative and contextual gesture. Instead, the panels are protective, reflecting the sun to create a shaded, ventilated roof. This extends immensely the life of the waterproofing membrane by protecting it from the extremes of temperature and, to a degree, from dust and pollution too. The water-excluding membrane and the insulated shell that it seals are some distance behind the panels. These are clipped on very simply to steel tubes propped away from the membrane with large nylon hooks that are clearly visible in places. The panels are revealed

not even to discharge rainwater onto those of the row below them. Instead, they channel the water behind the lower panels where it washes down the waterproof membrane. Here, unseen, it is gathered at intervals by gutters welded to this membrane.

Piano's buildings typically let water flow over only a short stretch of metallic or glass roof before it is conducted away out of sight, usually in a gutter. Grime is not washed long distances over visible surfaces, and so is less likely to disfigure them. There is an obvious rationale for this approach, yet even here, the outward step of the top of each tier of panels from that above, the water running behind them, the simplicity of the fixings, and the raggedly-stepped edges of uncut panels leave some people uneasy. This particularly offends fastidious fans of British High-Tech, architects of which have an almost fetishistic propensity to over-detail and to seek a sleek and organic closure of form, tendencies which are simply unquestioned stylistic prejudices that Piano refreshingly transcends.

In essence, the shell is wrapped around a corner and roofs the top floor of a concrete frame that takes its structural grid from that supporting the elevated hotel rooms. As usual with this building type, retail accommodation is arranged along a mall, although in this case there are some atypical features. Because the placing of the entrance has pushed the mall to one side of the building, all the large-space users and the foodcourt are displaced to one side. The mall not only has more levels than is usual in developments of this kind, but surprisingly has only a limited amount of retail space on the ground floor entrance level, and none on its lowest, first-basement level. The main shopping levels are the first floor, occupied by the foodcourt and some large-space users, and the second floor, on which there is a hypermarket behind a row of small shops. A second-floor shop which terminates the mall, extends upwards to fill a large area on the third floor. A restaurant was originally intended for this level, which would have opened out onto the terrace between it and the hotel.

The building's two basement levels are entirely given over to parking, as is most of the ground floor. From the top two levels of parking (first basement and ground floor), there are views and access through glazed entrance lobbies directly

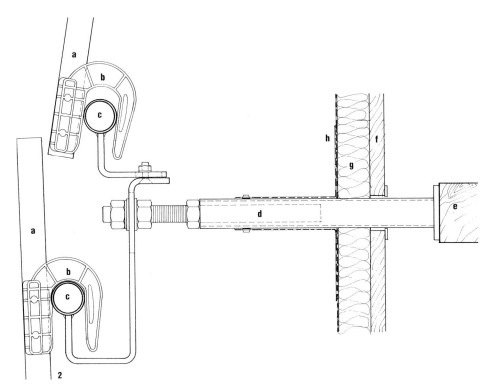

2

3

4 The mall seen from its top-most level and looking back towards the entrance. Note how the laminated timber beams span on the diagonal and become trusses with the addition of steel ties and props.

into the lower levels of the mall. Hence the parking is experienced as a much more integral part of the building than is usual, with prominent and pleasant connections right into the heart of the mall, where one arrives at the central of three closely-spaced wells.

Together, these wells rise through the mall almost as a single atrium linking its various levels visually. They also link the levels with inclined travelators in the two outer wells and a pair of glass-sided lifts at one end of the central well. These vertical connections are empha-

sized by the bright daylight that floods from above: two of the wells are lit by clouds of circular roof lights in the shell, and the remaining one by a large roof light set in the terrace between the shell and the hotel. The bottom of the central well is planted with *ficus benjamina* (weeping fig) trees and other evergreens that reach up to provide a soft green focus to the shopping mall and to the views in from the parking. And in the outer well beyond the glass-sided lifts, water cascades down towards the central well.

Responsibility for the handrails, floor patterns and finishes, pastel colours and other interior details of the public spaces rests with a now-defunct British design consultancy, suddenly appointed by the client during design development. But its input was subject to advice and approval by Piano, a condition that was insisted upon by the client's representative, Jean Renaud, who was immensely supportive of the Building Workshop throughout the project. Despite, or perhaps because of, this partial control, these visually crucial elements, which are

restrained yet awkward, are the least satisfactory aspect of the building – most especially because they blur the distinction between what is designed by the Building Workshop and what by the commercial tenants. Except for the roof overhead, the interior detailing has a stilted feel, neither exuberant nor elegant, and even the shops seem subdued in presence. Structure, atria and galleries all seem too rigidly rectilinear without splays or setbacks to open up views, catch the eye and cajole and cosset the movement of shoppers.

Above this stilted rectilinearity floats the weird and wonderful roof. Its laminated-timber beams span the mall at an angle, and on one side curve steeply downwards, signalling the mall's proximity to the side of the shell. Although the roof deck/ceiling is painted white, the laminated-wood structural elements, which include the purlins that curve to follow the horizontal contours, are all natural-coloured and exposed. Together with the curve of the shell, this gives some sense of being beneath an upturned ship's hull, punctured by the swathes of circular roof lights and by rectangular spring-shutter smoke vents.

Over the third-floor shops, the laminated beams simply span the diagonal between the heads of concrete columns, which extend up from the concrete structure below. To

21

Bercy 2 Shopping Centre

5, 6 Computer perspectives of shell **5** in context, and **6** alone.

7 Elevation of shopping centre and hotel.

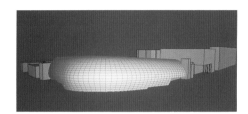

5

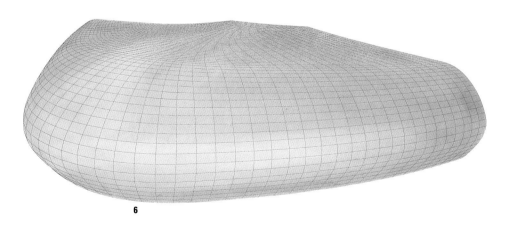

6

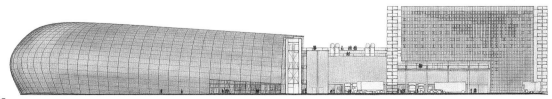

7

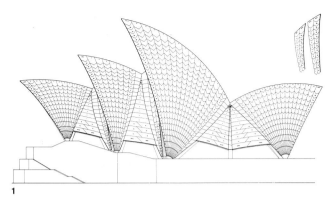

1

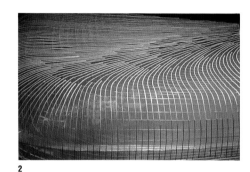

achieve the larger spans over the mall, steel ties and props were added below these beams so that, for this part of their length, they become the top chords of trusses. Originally steel was considered for the structure. But laminated wood was adopted for its lower cost, superior fire resistance and evocative nautical associations. Like the props and ties added to the laminated-wood beams to span the mall, all joints are steel and detailed with a straightforwardness typical

Bercy 2 Shopping Centre
Geometric discipline of cladding.
1 Elevation of shells of Sydney Opera House: a precedent in cladding curves with repetitive rectangular units.
2 Model study of lines of joints between panels, which though rectangular are designed to take up irregularities of alignment.
3 Plan, perspective and elevational computer studies of arrangement of cladding panels.

22

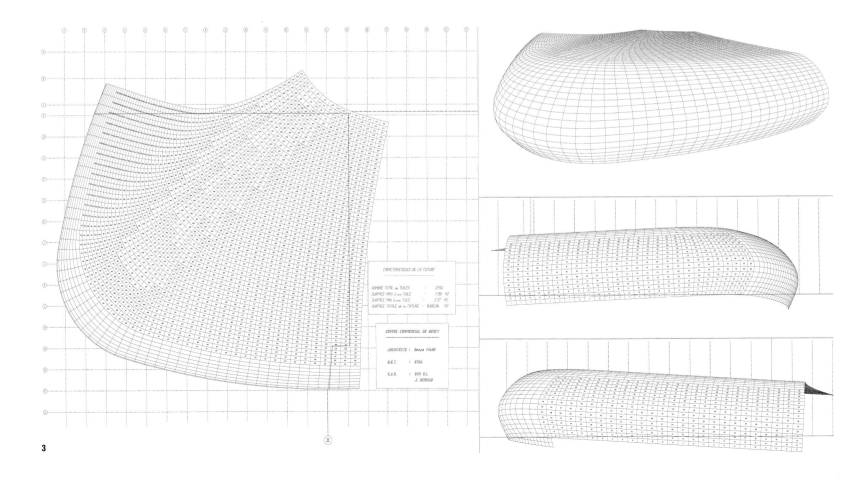

2

of the Building Workshop. On the outside of the decking, which depending on the curvature is chipboard or plywood, is the thermal insulation of 60mm polyurethane tiles and then the pvc waterproofing membrane. Fixed to the structure below, and penetrating all these layers, are the posts that support the tubular-steel cladding rails. Over the smoke vents and the perspex domes of the roof lights, the cladding panels are of perforated stainless steel. These form the patches on the shell that, when seen from a distance, are slightly matt in comparison with the other panels.

As eventually resolved and built, the structure and cladding are extraordinarily simple. The difficult and innovative part was in conceiving and working out the geometry that made this possible. Originally the Building Workshop had considered cladding the shell in the zinc sheet that is familiar

from Paris' mansard roofs and can be dressed to any shape. But Peter Rice, drawing on his early experience of devising the tiling on the shells of Jørn Utzon's Sydney Opera House (1973), advocated seeking some geometric discipline that would allow modular panels to be used.

After defining the shape of the shell subjectively with Piano, responding to site shape and the other factors described above, the geometric discipline was sought by the associate-in-charge, Noriaki Okabe, and his assistant Jean-François Blassel, who worked in collaboration with Rice and members of his engineering team, particularly Henry Bardsley. The plan shape of the outer limits of the shell was quickly and simply arrived at: it conforms to the arcs of three circles of different

3

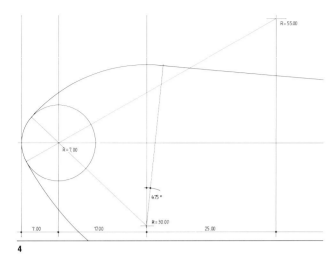

4

cicumference and centre. The disciplines of the section and the cladding layout were much more difficult and were determined after trial-and-error.

The initial idea was that the three-dimensional form could be derived from a revolving paraboloid. But this proved impossible to cover with panels of identical shape. Eventually, a way was found to generate a suitable form by using a constant section but shifting it both horizontally and vertically. This approach was tested and refined using a perspex model that combined the arcs of two circles with a straight line. The result was a form that achieved two crucial objectives: that all primary structural components could be made in the same jig, to be trimmed only as necessary; and that the surface of the shell could be clad entirely in repetitive rectangular panels. These are designed so that discrepancies in the geometry are absorbed accumulatively along both the sides and the ends of each panel; only 34 sizes were required for the 27 000 panels. This represents an admirable degree of standardization, though not the extraordinary achievement realized later with the Kansai airport where all 90 000 cladding panels are identical. But then such things are only possible on a building as enormous as the terminal, where the curves are absorbed in tiny increments.

Bercy 2 served, then, as a test bed for many ideas that are now being more perfectly realized at Kansai. Yet its importance for the Building Workshop, and for architecture generally, goes further than that. Both Okabe and Rice had been fascinated for years by fractal geometry and its significance in giving new insights into the laws of natural form. Neither Bercy nor Kansai apply fractal geometries, but for the design teams of both buildings fractals were felt to legitimate the search for post-Euclidean architectural forms. The Bercy Shopping Centre, then, is a design that is exemplary of the Renzo Piano Building Workshop. This is not just because it is shaped by context and research into new constructional disciplines. It is also because, by exploring new laws of form, the design gets closer to emulating nature than if it adopted forms that merely looked organic.

23

Bercy 2 Shopping Centre
Geometric discipline of section and plan.
4, 6 Studies for setting out of sections of the shell. The outline of the roof section remains constant, but is also projected progressively backwards and downwards; the lower part, a tangent of a constantly-sized circle that is also slid backwards and downwards, pivots progressively towards vertical.
5, 7, 8 Models for studying geometry of outer shell. **7** shows how outer edge conforms in plan to arcs of circles of three different radii.
8 illustrates similar principle as diagram **6**.

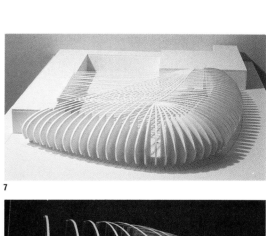

7

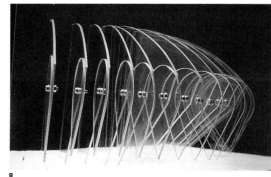

8

6

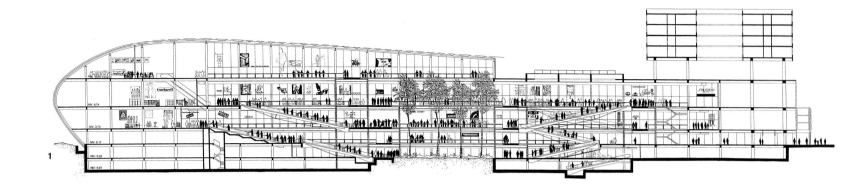

24 **Bercy 2 Shopping Centre**

1 Longitudinal section through mall and entrance below elevated hotel rooms.

2 Location plan: **a** boulevard Périphérique, **b** A1 motorway, **c** ramp to parking, **d** hotel, **e** housing, **f** light industry.

3 Partial cross section. Note how bottom levels of central well are visible and entered directly from the car parking garage.

4 Central well of mall seen from second floor level. Light flooding down from the cloud of rooflights above and the trees reaching up from below create a focus to the whole centre. On the far side of well are the glass-sided lifts.

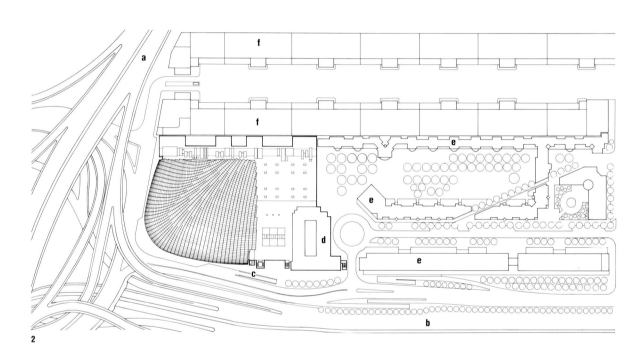

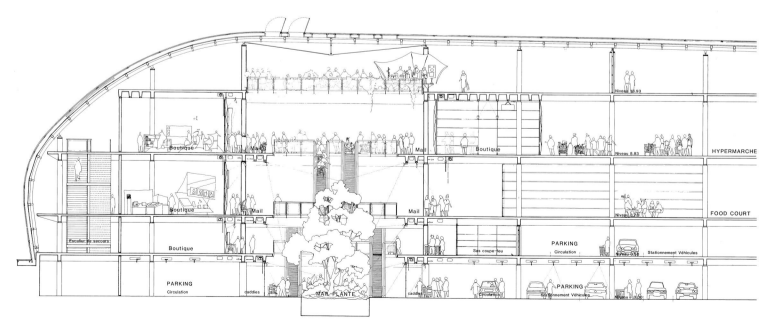

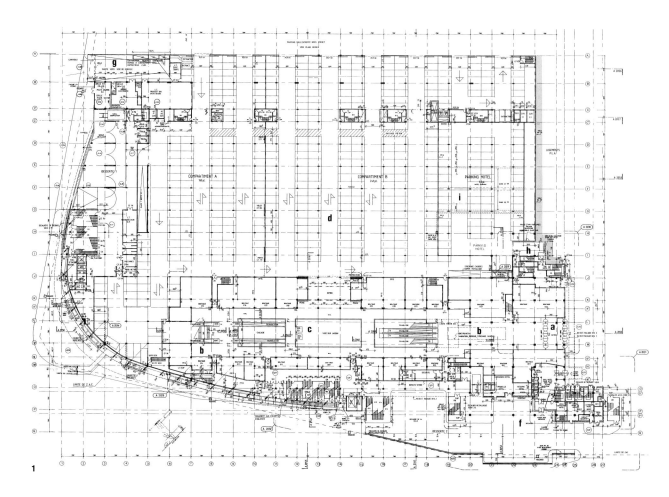

26 **Bercy 2 Shopping Centre**
Plans

1 Ground floor: **a** main entrance, **b** mall, **c** central well, **d** parking garage, **e** entrance to mall from parking, **f** car entrance, **g** service entrance, **h** entrance to hotel parking, **i** hotel parking.
2 First basement: **a** bottom level of mall, **b** parking garage, **c** entrance from parking to mall.

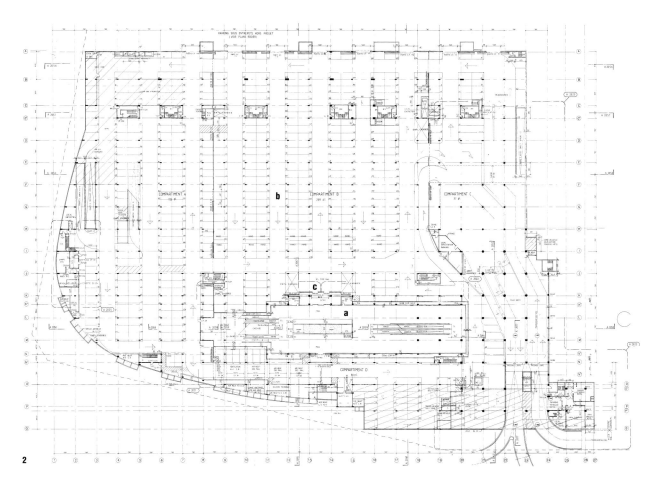

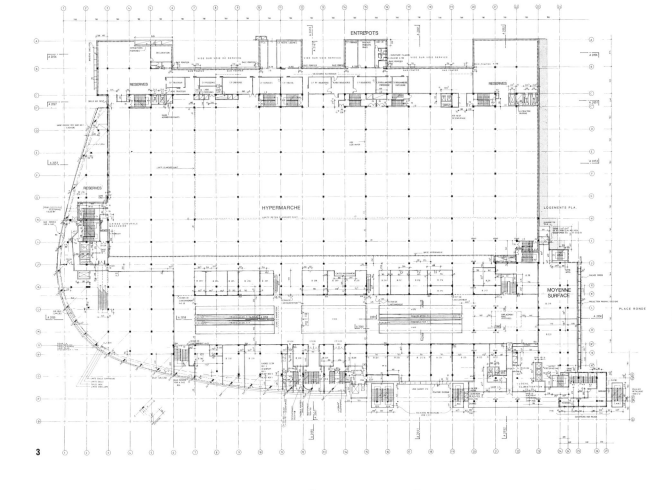

3

Bercy 2 Shopping Centre

Plans

3 Second floor.

4 First floor.

5, **6** Views of roof-lit wells and inclined
travelators.

5

6

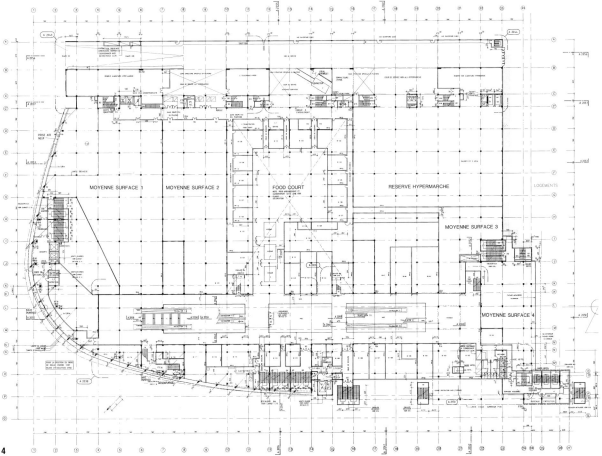

4

MOYENNE SURFACE 1   MOYENNE SURFACE 2   FOOD COURT   RESERVE HYPERMARCHE   LOGEMENTS

MOYENNE SURFACE 3

MOYENNE SURFACE 4

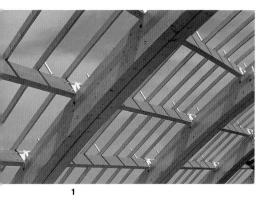

1

2

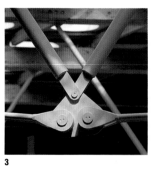

3

4

5

28   **Bercy 2 Shopping Centre**

Construction views and details of shell roof structure.

1, **2** The hierarchy of laminated timber elements is made up of main beams, purlins and joists.

3, **4**, **5** Views of the joints between the steel props and ties that transform part of the laminated timber beams into trusses.

6 Erecting the main beams.

7 Escape stair adjacent west end of mall.

8 Reflected ceiling plan. Note how the main beams span the concrete column grid on the diagonal, and how the purlins curve with the horizontal contours.

9 View also shows how main beams span diagonally across the heads of the concrete columns and the purlins curve with the horizontal contour.

10 Detail elevation and section of junction that connects elements of main beam to each other and to head of column, and that also secures ends of ties that form bottom chord of truss over mall.

11, **12** Close up views of junctions of elements of main beams to each other and, via pin-joint, to column head, and of pin-jointed junctions of purlins to main beams.

6

7

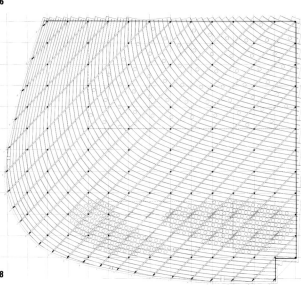

8

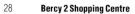

9

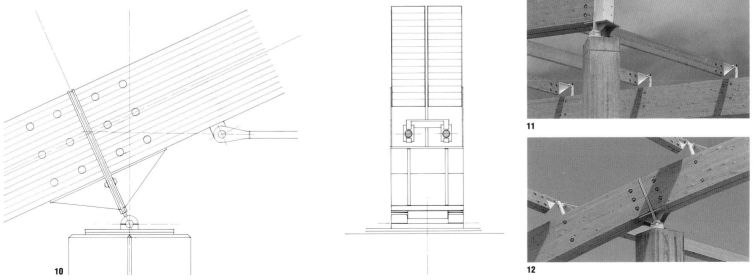

10

11

12

1

2

3

5

30

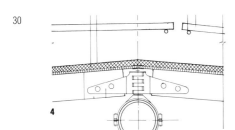

4

6

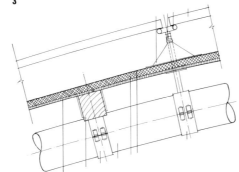

Bercy 2 Shopping Centre

Constructing and cladding the shell.

1, 2, 3 Views showing how the cladding panels are clipped to the tubular cladding rails.

4 Details of earlier version of roof with tubular steel structure.

5 Attaching the purlins to the main beams.

6, 7, 10 Fixing the cladding rails in position and clipping on the cladding panels.

8 View from above shows how main beams span on the diagonal of the concrete column grid.

9 Short posts rising through the pvc waterproofing membrane will support the cladding rails.

7

9

10

8

11

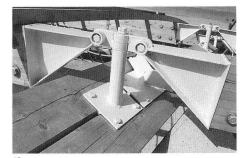

12

14

15

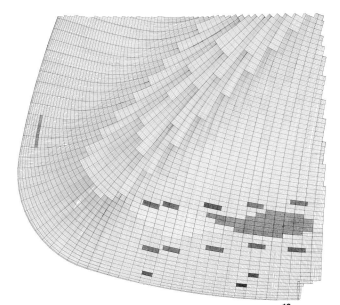

13

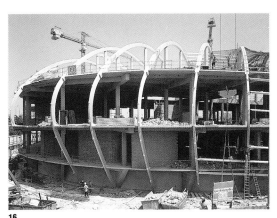

16

17

18

Bercy 2 Shopping Centre   31

11, 12 Views of junctions of main beams and purlins.

13 Roof plan. The non-Euclidian geometrical disciplines and sense of organic order seen here is unparalled in the work of any other architect – as also is the nonchalance of the ragged edges left by not cutting cladding panels.

14 Domed rooflights seen from above awaiting cover of perforated steel panels that will be clipped to the tubular cladding rails.

15 Rooflights seen from mall below.

16, 17, 18 Construction sequence shows:
16 main beams in place and purlins being erected, **17** joists being fixed, and **18** decking, insulation and waterproof membrane in place and cladding panels being clipped to tubular rails.

Renzo Piano Building Workshop

Bercy 2 Shopping Centre
Client GRC
Design team R Piano, N Okabe (associate in charge), J F Blassel (architect in charge), S Dunne, M Henry, K McBryde, A O'Carrol, B Plattner (associate), R Rolland, M Salerno, N Westphal
Assisted by M Bojovic, D Illoul, P Senne
Model makers Y Chapelain, O Doizy, J Y Richard
Structural engineers Ove Arup & Partners (P Rice, A Lenczner) OTRA (J P Rigail)

Collaborating local engineer J L Sarf
Services engineers OTH S I (J Herman)
Bureau d'étude OTRA (J P Rigail)
Bureau de control Veritas
Clerk of works Copibat
Interiors Crighton Design Management
Landscape architects M Desvigne, C Dalnoky
Contractors:
concrete Tondela Nord France
roof Cosylva, Enterprise Industrial, S P P R

32 **Bercy 2 Shopping Centre**

The completed stainless steel panel-clad exterior.
1 The shell has a defensive and very enigmatic presence.
2,3,4 The cladding viewed from different distances.
5 View over the roof to the city beyond clearly reveals the different types and sizes of cladding panels.

1

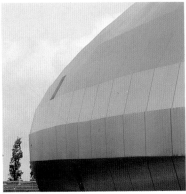

2

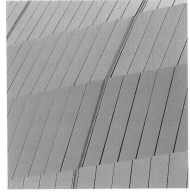

3

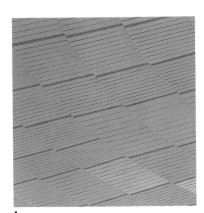

4

34

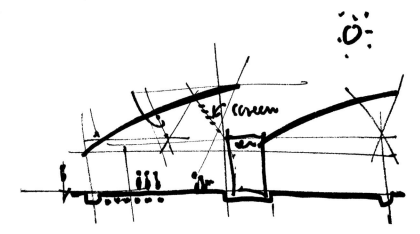

Thomson Optronics Factory   Guyancourt, Saint Quentin en Yvelines, France **1988–91**

Like the well-established laboratory-workshop at Vesima (p 76) and the planned J M Tjibaou Cultural Centre at Nouméa (p 190) the Thomson Optronics Factory is integrated seamlessly into its immediate natural surroundings. But the buildings at Vesima and Nouméa nestle into pre-existing settings of distinctive topography and vegetation. The Thomson Factory, on the outskirts of Saint Quentin en Yvelines, a satellite new town of Paris, interlocks instead with new landscaping on what had been a flat and featureless site; and architecture and 'nature' are integrated by being subordinated to the same formal and dimensional discipline.

For the moment though, while the landscaping is still taking hold and establishing its equality with the architecture, the curves of the building's profile, like those of the Bercy 2 Shopping Centre (p 16), present a striking view from a distance. From where it can be seen, until it is hidden by the new trees planted around it and the sprawl of little houses to the south, its big curving north-light roofs appear almost like closely-packed breakers rolling amid seas of waving grass.

Also like Bercy 2, this research and manufacturing facility was a highly compromised commission which other high-profile architects might have shied away from. If Bercy 2 is tainted in the eyes of some because it is too exclusively commercial, then the Thomson Factory is problematic because it develops and makes sighting devices not only for the navigation of civilian aircraft but also for military use. Bercy 2 was especially problematic because so much of the design was defined before the Building Workshop was appointed; but the major problem with the Thomson Factory, besides very limited time and money, was the contrary one of there being few stable fixes such as a specific brief and an exact schedule of accommodation to guide the design. The client was in a state of flux and had little time to clarify its needs before construction had to begin, so what could be called a loose-fit design was adopted. The common discipline that unites building and landscaping allows considerable flexibility in the location and expansion of the various uses, both across the site and within each bay of building; yet, no matter how this flexibility is exploited, a loose-fit design also ensures pleasant working conditions, with most workplaces having

1

36   **Thomson Optronics Factory**

1 Oblique view of southernmost wing, the closest part of which houses the staff dining room.

2 Site and roof plan. Phase one is on east of central north-south road and phase two on its west.

3–7 Diagrams showing progressive planting and maturing of landscaping.

2

bright daylight and many of them overlooking planted courts. It is this design strategy, and how it operates at different levels, that give this building its very contemporary significance.

By the time it was ready to appoint the Building Workshop as architect for the new factory, Thomson had already committed itself to handing over its former premises in Paris to a developer within 18 months. Then, after complaints from some employees who thought that such a commission should be subject to competition, one was organized. By the time the Building Workshop had won this with a hastily prepared and sketchy design, only 15 months remained to finalize a thorough and detailed design with proper client consultation, and to complete construction and fitting out. The client's changing requirements compounded the

time problem. This was partly because it was in the throes of reorganization, which entailed hiving off the manufacture of some product components to subcontractors. It was due also to the accelerating miniaturization of electronics which has led to the manufacturing space becoming ever smaller and of necessity 'cleaner' in relation to research and administration areas. As a result, it was difficult to be sure how big the building should be, either initially or after the company's reorganization, nor how much of it should be allocated to what functions. It was to enable the postponement of such decisions and to allow continuing flexibility, as well as to help achieve speedy and cheap construction, that the loose-fit design strategy was developed. Asserting a clear, fixed order that facilitates yet controls change, this strategy operates at three levels: in informing the design of the site plan, in the cross-section of the repetitive bays of which the building is composed and in the kit of components with which it is clad.

The site-planning strategy plays fixity against fluidity; these characteristics being marked by arcs of a circle and bands of straight lines respectively. The elements that define the arcs give a sense of containment, and so of place, as well as providing the concealment

preferred by high-security research establishments. Along the southern boundary are grassy mounds formed from the earth which was excavated to create a pair of ponds that collect the rain water from the factory's large roof area. These mounds hug the curved outer edge of the ponds, hiding the little houses and factory from each other. The entrance drive passes through a gap in the mounds, which frame a sort of forecourt to the factory, and then between the ponds. Together, these elements provide a contained outlook for those parts of the complex that face them. Along the eastern boundary, the arc of the ponds and mounds extends as a high wall, which shuts out the road that runs along this side. Into this curve nestles a shallow segment of bunker-like space in which storerooms and such installations as electricity substations and generators are located.

The straight, inner edge of the ponds, and that of the service bunker, are at right angles to each other and establish the rectilinearity of the rest of the site plan. This is banded conceptually by a grid of east–west lines, parallel to the inner edge of the ponds, and 3.6 metres apart. Much of this grid is defined by lines of trees and other planting. The grid defines the positions of the buildings within this frame of vegetation;

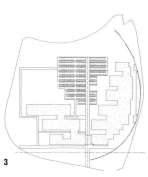

3

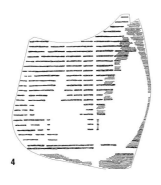

4

5

6

7

8

Thomson Optronics Factory

8 View from south-east corner of site.

9 Axonometric sketch of structure.

10 Rows of trees extend out from the building that will in time extend out new wings between the trees.

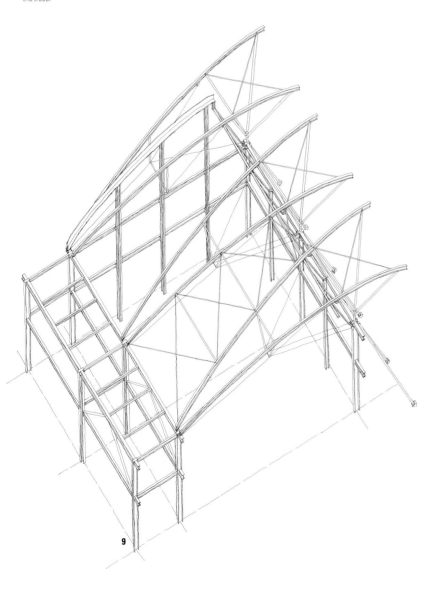

9

buildings and vegetation interlock and the former can be deployed and extended, almost as if they were pieces conforming to the rules of a board game. In contrast to the confining closure of the arcs of mounds and wall, the grid of lines suggests fluidity and open-endedness. This will be especially true when the lines of trees eventually extend outside the closing circle and across adjoining sites. At the insistence of the local planning department, more recent arrivals in the area, such as a gigantic Renault factory, must extend Thomson's landscaping principles, which the Building Workshop developed in collaboration with landscape architect Michel Desvigne. The concept is that this whole area will be gridded by lines of trees that will thicken into woods between the major developments but thin out as they approach the building complexes.

For the buildings, a standard structural bay was devised. It is generously scaled to allow considerable variation in internal use and layout, and is shaped always to ensure pleasant brightly-lit conditions. Again, arcs of circles (the north-light roofs, or umbrellas as the design team calls them) provide a sense of sheltering enclosure and define a certain fixity, a zone overhead that will always remain uncluttered, bright and

airy; while the rectilinear frame below offers flexibility, accommodating a changing variety of machines and partitions, mezzanines and even full first floors. Between each of these tall, 14.4 metre-wide bays, in which services are laid out on a 3.6-metre grid, are lower 3.6 metre-wide bays for circulation and services. North-south sections through the complex either alternate the larger bays and corridors or, if taken through the fingers of building that interlock with the garden, consist of pairs of such north-lit volumes with a central corridor.

The structure is designed for flexibility of both cladding and internal arrangement as well as for economy. The steel frame consists of standard I-sections clearly expressed inside and out, with the cladding slotted between their flanges. This cladding consists of a pre-designed or selected catalogue of components, which includes the elegant glazing system developed for the IRCAM Extension in Paris (Volume One, p 202). These components are applied to suit uses within the building and can be changed later as the accommodation is rearranged. To restrict as little as possible the placing of internal partitions and equipment, the wide, structural bays are free from secondary structure and services below wall height. There

37

10

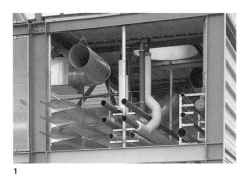

1

Thomson Optronics Factory

1 The duct above the corridor in the narrow structural bay is packed with service runs.

2 Close up view of the corner of one of the major bays shows the extreme delicacy of the structure and the glazing.

3 Night view: transparent ends of short bays interlock architecture and landscaping.

4, 5, 9 Sectional diagrams show, from left to right: **4** natural lighting, **5** artificial lighting and **9** air-conditioning.

3

is no internal cross-bracing for lateral stability, this being provided by the relative stiffness of the corridor frames and by props that lean in from the gardens. The structure also supports and accommodates air-conditioning and other service runs in big horizontal ducts above the corridors, while outside those walls that edge gardens, air-conditioning ducts are suspended beneath the sloping props. The need to keep the horizontal air ducts within a reasonable size was the critical

factor limiting the length of any bay.

To keep costs down, as well as to pursue a constant theme in Piano's architecture, the roof structure is designed to be, and to look, as light as possible. To diminish their span and to carry the roof outwards to shade the sloping clerestory, the northern ends of each arched rafter are supported by a pair of sloping props. Together with another pair to the adjoining rafter, these props branch from the head of a post. Where these posts form part of an external wall they are in turn braced by a pair of props leaning in from the garden. But along these northern edges, rafters propped from the same post are closer together than those that do not share a post. To average out the spans of the roofing they support, the rafters are not parallel but splay at angles so as to be almost equidistant at midspan and alternately closer together and further apart along both edges.

As originally designed by the engineers, Ove Arup & Partners, the rafters were to have been curved metal tubes. These would not have taxed the capabilities of British manufacturers, but apparently would have been difficult for the French building industry to produce. The contractor proposed a cheaper solution that was readily adopted: the rafter is a curved standard I-section stiffened by a single

prop and suspension ties. Originally, there were to have been no purlins either, the roof being formed from two layers of corrugated steel sheet laid cross-wise to each other and self-supported. But this was unacceptable to the local authority; it insisted on purlins, which are now concealed within the corrugations of the inner sheet. This forms the ceiling and hides the insulation over the interior volumes, but it does not extend outwards where the roof overhangs the clerestory, or the porches at the ends of some bays. If anything, these compromises to the original design further accentuate the extraordinary sense of lightness achieved by these umbrella roofs.

To date, two phases of the factory have been built, one on either side of a road that extends the entrance drive towards pockets of car-parking space in the centre of the site. The first phase edges a wide service yard beside the service bunker. It consists of paired umbrella-roofed bays that thrust into the garden towards the centre of the site, linked by somewhat shorter single bays extending between the service yard and the planted court. From the south, these units of paired bays contain:

4

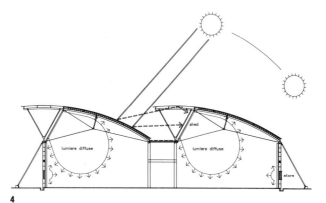

5

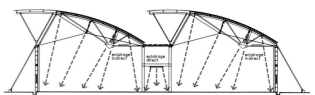

6

Thomson Optronics Factory

6 The Pompidou Centre with its external structure and ducts and its bright colours is an obvious precedent to the Thomson Factory.

7, 8, 10 Interiors of double-height volumes:
8 bare shell prior to fitting out, and **7** as fitted out as laboratories. **10** the dining room with its full height windows and mezzanine gallery that is a more pleasant solution than a complete first floor.

8

7

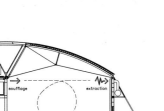

9

administration, information centre (technical library, data-base etc), research and then manufacturing. The individual plantrooms for each pair of bays are placed alongside the service yard, where they are easily accessible and close to the service bunker. Immediately adjacent to the plantrooms, in the research and manufacturing bays, are the highly- serviced, sealed and dust-free 'clean' rooms used for the research and assembly of electronic components. Beyond these

are the halls for larger-scale assembly and experimentation. The individual cubicles and offices for engineers are usually located in those parts of the building that have windows overlooking the gardens with which they interlock.

In addition to the very wide corridors between the major bays, there are equally generous passageways which branch off at right angles to connect the different departments; these always pass through the western ends of the shorter bays. Here they open up into double-volume halls that look out, through glass walls, onto the porches under the extensions of the umbrella roofs, and terminate each finger-like garden court. Piano insisted on the corridors being generous in scale so as to give people plenty of room to meet and chat without blocking the passage of passers-by; and he conceived the halls as places for both spontaneous and more planned socializing in this relatively isolated complex. The halls have proved popular and

are now affectionately known as 'Renzo rooms'.

The second-phase building contains additional administrative offices, including those for directors, and social facilities such as a large canteen. As with phase one, the roof of the southernmost bay faces south instead of north to present a proper front to people arriving. But, despite the overhang over the sloping clerestory, this results in excessive solar gain problems in these bays. This roof also extends to link these two blocks and create a generous gateway over the road that divides the phases. Also built in the second phase is a tower that rises beside the south-east corner of phase one: a concrete lift shaft holds aloft a spherical head, clad in aluminium panels, which are supported on the inside by vertical ribs of laminated wood. Designed and made with rigorous attention to the resultant complex geometric alignments, these panels slide and fold on curving vertical tracks to open up and allow views out in different directions and at varying upward angles. It is from this vantage point that the sighting devices are tested.

If distant views of the factory are impressive, so are those on approaching it, particularly

39

10

1

Thomson Optronics Factory

1 Test tower peeping around south-east
corner.

2 Section of test tower.

3 Distant view from the west with test tower
visible above northlight roofs.

when passing through the
mounds to the south and across
the ponds which are edged with
willows. Ahead, the building
spreads wide on either side of
the gateway between the first
and second phases. The long
facades are articulated by the
props that lean against the
building and by those that
branch out to support the over-
hanging roof which shades the
big clerestory windows. These
props, like the building's other
structural elements, are painted
a fiery orange-red that stands
out from the crisp white
cladding panels; the service
ducts are blue and the window
frames a vivid green. This is
Piano's most colourful building
since the 1973 Pompidou
Centre in Paris (Volume One,
p 52). The colours are well
chosen, although in places
there seems to be too much
of the ductwork blue. But, for

all their cheerful freshness,
these colours, together with
the external structure and
ducts and the further associations these conjure with the
Pompidou and the buildings
it inspired, inevitably provoke
some feeling of *déjà vu*, and
so perhaps of the design being
somewhat *passé*.

The loose-fit strategy, however, might be a model of how
to build in a time of ever-accel-
erating change. It works successfully in different ways for
the Thomson Factory at the
scales of site plan, section and
cladding, while guaranteeing
a sense of contact with nature –
interiors basked in an ever-
changing natural light and
enjoying a lush natural outlook. But this looseness of fit,
and the speed and low cost of
construction, have resulted in
a building that is somewhat
better in its broad brush strokes
than it is in all its details. This
is especially true in respect of
the messy external ducts visible
on some roofs and the way in
which the building has been
occupied by the client. The generous scale of the major structural bays has allowed the
building to be more densely
occupied than intended.
Several bays have been filled
in entirely with a first floor so
that ground-floor rooms do

not benefit from the sense of
lofty top-lit space. More
pleasant is the solution used
in the canteen where a first-
floor gallery projects only partially into the tall volume.

Perhaps the looseness of fit is
too tolerant, and the generosity
of the architectural frame
should have been counter-
balanced by a greater assertive-
ness so that, while liberating
options for choice and change,
it also prevented alterations
that would compromise the
sense of airy spaciousness.
Nevertheless, the interweaving
of architecture and land-
scaping, appreciated especially
from the fingers of building
that interlock with the garden
and make the factory so different to the standard 'factory
in a box', will no doubt become
yet more pronounced as the
planting grows. In this way the
building will advance yet again
Piano's continuing quest for a
rapprochement between technology and nature.

2

3

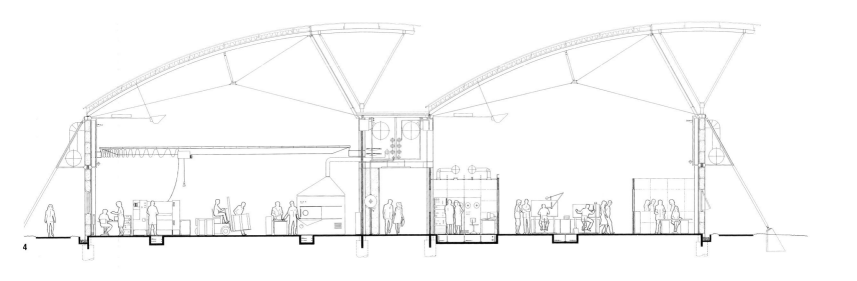

4

Thomson Optronics Factory

4 Typical section between two garden courts.
It consists of two tall volumes separated by a
lower circulation and service strip.

5–10 Erecting the structural frame.

11 Detail section of opening light of window.

7

8

9

10

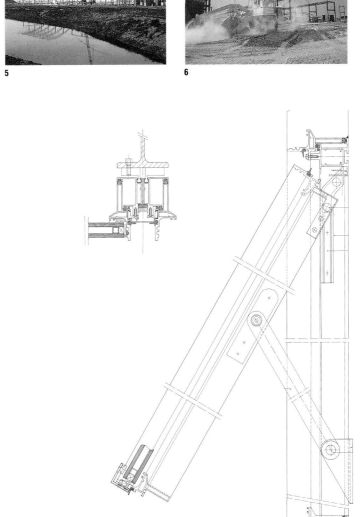

11

1

Thomson Optronics Factory

1 Part of west elevation of first phase of factory shows typical configuration of alternating large and small structural bays, and of garden courts recessed between wings consisting of two large bays and a central small bay. Also shown is how landscape and architecture are laid out to the same grid.

2 North-south section.

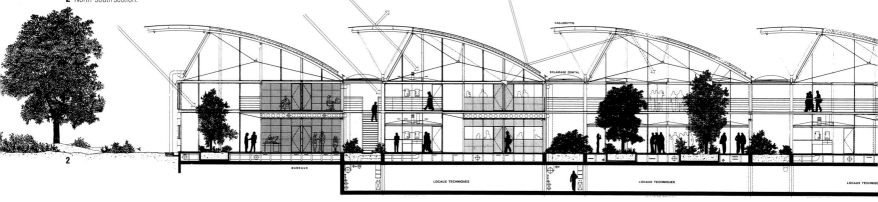

2

Thomson Optronics Factory

Client Thomson CSF

Design team R Piano, P Vincent, A Vincent (associates in charge), A Gallissian (Phase 1), M Henry (test tower), A el Jerari, L Le Voyer, A O'Carrol, D Rat (Phase 2) A H Téménidès

Assisted by C Ardilley, C Bartz, M Bojovic, F Canal, G Fourel, A Guez, B Kurtz

Model makers O Doizy, C d'Ovidio

Structural engineers Ove Arup & Partners (P Rice, R Hough)

Services engineers and cost control GEC Ingéniérie (F Petit, F Thouvenin, C Baché)

Clerk of works Copitec (C Knezovic) Planitec (M Lopez)

Acoustician Peutz & Associés bv

Landscape architects M Desvigne, C Dalnoky with P Convercey

Contractors Durand, Danto Rogeat, Savoie, Villequin

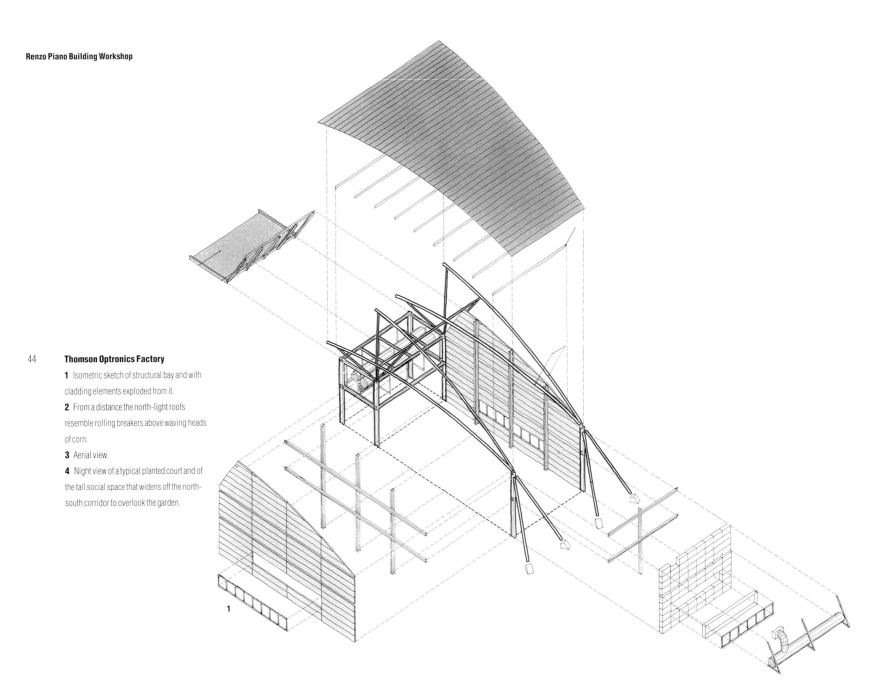

44 **Thomson Optronics Factory**

1 Isometric sketch of structural bay and with cladding elements exploded from it.

2 From a distance the north-light roofs resemble rolling breakers above waving heads of corn.

3 Aerial view.

4 Night view of a typical planted court and of the tall social space that widens off the north-south corridor to overlook the garden.

1

2   3

46

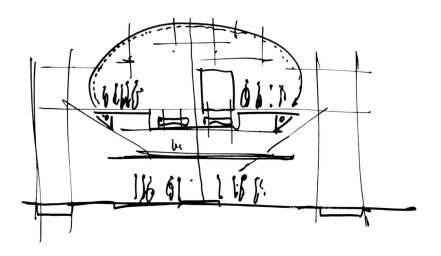

Metro stations Genoa, Italy 1983–91

As part of Genoa's long-overdue programme of renewal that was initiated, at least in part, by the 1992 Columbus International Exposition, some improvements were made to the city's transport infrastructure. These included opening the first section of the metropolitan railway, the Metropolitana. The first of the two routes planned for this rapid-transit system runs partly underground, much of it through existing tunnels, and partly on new tracks elevated above existing roads and railway lines.

The Building Workshop has been involved in the feasibility studies and planning of some of these stations since 1983. It has now built two stations, the semi-underground Dinegro station and the elevated Brin station, and has nearly finished a third, the subterranean Principe station, beside the main railway station. Two more stations are under detailed design development, at Darsena, beside the docks, and Caricamento, beside the entrance to the dockside facilities that accommodated the Columbus exposition. The tracks of this latter station are located beneath the tunnel which was built to take traffic away from a newly created piazza around the historic Palazzo San Giorgio. Further stations are to be built by the Renzo Piano Building Workshop at Piazza de Ferrari, Canepari and Sarzano.

A metropolitan railway was proposed for Genoa as long ago as 1913 by the City Engineer, the far-sighted Renzo Picasso. The author and illustrator of, among other things, a remarkable book comparing developments in the world's leading metropolises, Picasso was aware of the various proposals being made for these cities. He advocated equally ambitious undertakings in Genoa. In particular he proposed an underground railway integrated with the architecture of the streets above. Its platforms were to be beneath street-level arcades. Between the platform and the tracks, an enclosed trench was to carry water, gas and electricity mains, and another was to be a sewer. Such highly integrated designs were not unique in those times, but none was ever built anywhere.

Then, in 1914, the first monorail in Italy, and one of the first in the world, was built to provide public transport just outside of the perimeter of the docks. In 1961, long after this monorail had been demolished a larger system was proposed,

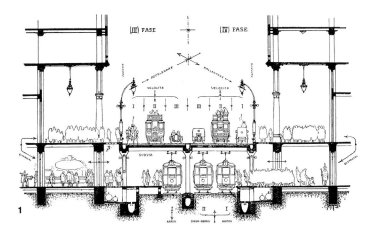

1

but nothing came of it. In 1965, instead of investing in public transport, an elevated road, the *sopraelevata*, was built around the harbour, separating the port from the old city. The light-rail system now adopted uses a single long, narrow, coach articulated at mid-length, thus keeping down infrastructural costs by requiring only narrow tunnels and short station platforms. Similarly pragmatic is the strategy of using existing tunnels and structures where possible. Thus the track between the Dinegro and Brin stations runs through a tunnel built early in the century for trams.

The strategy adopted for the design and construction of the stations is not uncommon, and is virtually the norm for the Building Workshop. A kit was developed, the elements of which can be made in sufficient quantity to achieve high quality at reasonable cost. It can be assembled to create stations adapted to the unique constraints of each site, yet invested with a recognizable common identity. The underground and overground stations proposed for Genoa are vaulted structures, the sectional form of both vaults comprising more than half the geometric figure from which they are derived. The stations below ground are located in a concrete-lined circular-sectional tunnel section. Those above ground have steel arches that form part of an approximate ellipse. Although these vaults are autonomous abstract forms, the way in which access to them is provided copes with the particulars of each situation, and helps integrate the stations into their settings.

48 **Metro stations**

1 Renzo Picasso's 1913 proposal for a metropolitan railway under Genoa's Via Vente Septembre.

2 Cross section of Principe station adjacent to Genoa's main railway station.

3 Cross section of Darsena station adjacent to the harbour.

4 Map of Genoa showing route and stations of first line of metropolitan railway.

5, **6**, **7** Location plans of stations: **5** Canepari, **6** Principe and **7** Darsena.

8, **10** Caricamento station: **8** section through Piazza Caricamento with metropolitan railway and station below new road tunnel in front of the Palazzo San Giorgio, **10** plan.

9 Cross section of generic underground section made of standardized kit of parts.

11 Cross section of Sarzano station.

12 Cross section of Piazza de Ferrari station under Genoa's main square.

13, **14**, **15** Location plans of stations: **13** Caricamento, **14** Sarzano and **15** Piazza de Ferrari.

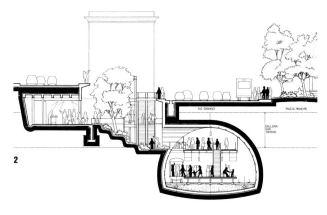

2

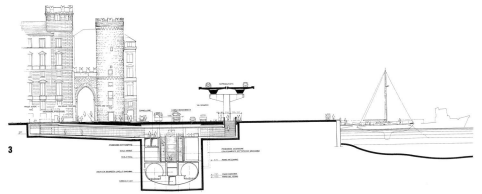

3

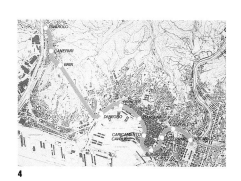

4

5

6

7

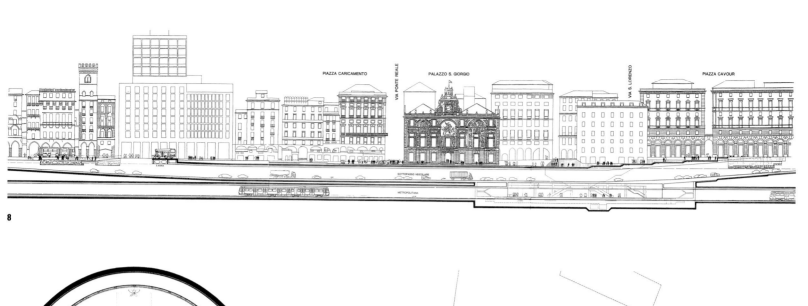

8

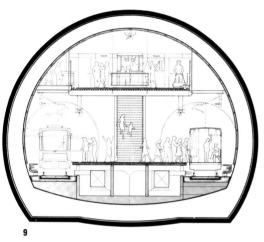

9

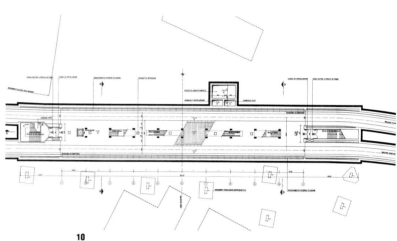

10

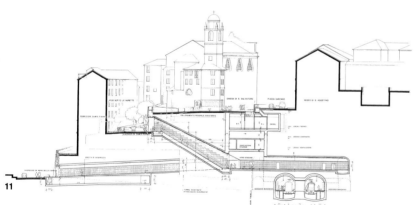

11

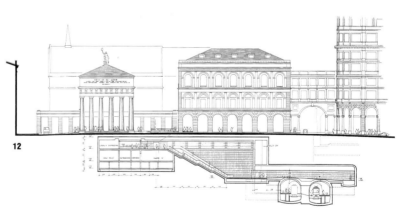

12

13

14

15

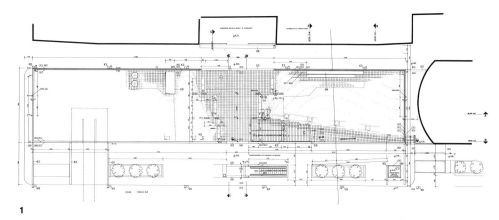

1

Metro stations

Dinegro station.

1 Plan at street level showing sunken and landscaped entrance to station.

2 The entrance appears simply as a stark horizontal slot in the stone-faced wall.

3 Location plan.

4 Cross section: tracks and platforms are under existing road structure.

2

The Dinegro station conforms to neither of the above types. Instead, the tracks and platforms occupy part of what was once a semi-subterranean warehouse. This was built beneath the broad via Buozzi where it edges the docks as part of the construction and road-works that accompanied the erection of the *sopraelevata*. Overhead in these parts of the station are haunched concrete beams that support the road-bed and span between broad columns, all of which are part of the original structure. In the newly constructed parts, such as the ticket hall, there is a flat, suspended ceiling and new walls faced in an artificial stone, devised to resemble the *pietra de Verazzi* once commonly used in Genoa. The Dinegro station also differs from the other stations in having three rather than two tracks. The island platform between two of these tracks is reached via a tunnel from the platform adjacent to the entrance hall.

Despite the utilitarian nature of the building, Piano's typically unelaborated entrance portal arguably does not suffice here, mainly because of its position. Neatly minimalist but too discreet, it is largely invisible from the pavements above. Reached by a broad stair that descends between a stone-faced wall and a bank of bamboo, it appears simply as a stark horizontal slot. Some sort of canopy and sign to signal the presence of the entrance to first-time users would be welcome. The exit is either by the same route or by an escalator that climbs in its own vertical slot to the pavement above. On stairs, platforms and elsewhere, detailing and colour are generally restrained.

Brin station is closer to one of the prototypes and very different to Dinegro. It is an elevated transparent tube, airy and brightly coloured. Flanked on both sides by tall tenements, it is set in a residential area that, together with industry, occupies a flattish valley bottom extending between steep mountains a little way in from the sea. As prominent in

3

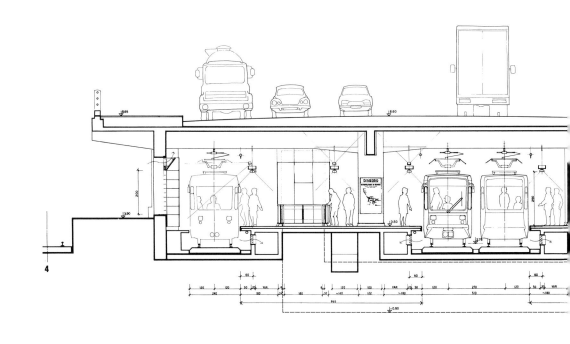

4

5

Metro stations

Dinegro station.

5 Entrance hall with ticket office and escalator up to street.

6 Stairs descend to entrance between wall faced in reconstituted stone and bank of dense planting.

6

presence as Dinegro is discreet, it is, nevertheless, well integrated into its setting in one important way.

The station is set a short distance from where the tracks to the city centre emerge from the old tram tunnel, and where what is now a pedestrian-only street, drops away below the horizontal tracks. Downhill from the station, the old street ends in a minor bus terminus, from where pedestrian access is gained below the elevated tracks, via a sloping pavement that leads straight to the glass entrance doors. Alongside the broad pavement are planted beds with trees that rise between tracks and tenements. The result is a shady and pleasant hybrid of garden and semi-covered piazza that looks likely to become a well-used public space, especially if such things as kiosks, market stalls and benches were to be added. This reflects Piano's increasing sensitivity and sophistication in handling urban spaces.

The ticket hall and automatic barriers controlling admission are located in a glazed hall directly beneath the tracks. On either side of this hall, a lift rises and a pair of stairs reach up and away from each other to the platform above. The stairs are suspended from deep beams parallel to the platform structure. The roughly semi-elliptical arches span at regular intervals between the back edges of the platforms and are formed from I-sectioned steel with the usual, now almost too familiar, circular holes cut in the flanges to lighten their weight. These arches support the framed glass sheets, lapped like tiles but with a ventilation gap, which span between them to shelter the platforms. Running on rails over the unglazed centre of the span is a machine to clean the glass.

These arches, and the structure supporting the tracks, are both painted blue, while the chassis supporting the platforms is painted a complementary yellow, as are the steel of stairs and lift shaft. The sides of the lift shaft are clad in the

51

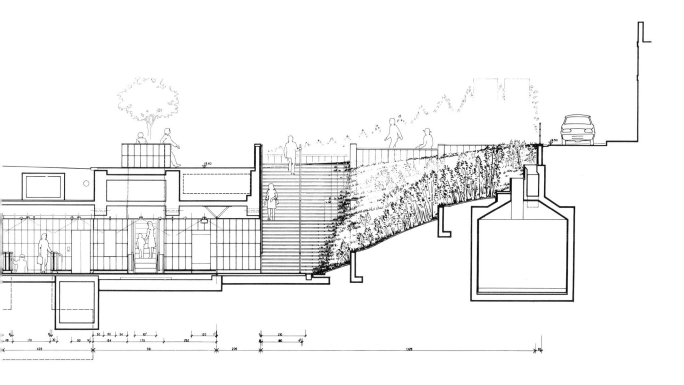

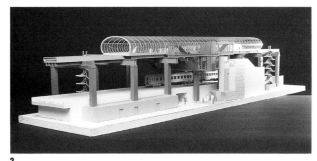

52 **Metro stations**

Brin station.

1 Location plan.

2 Model of generic elevated station.

3 Completed station with machine for
washing the glass.

4,**5** Construction views showing the station
in context above old street.

6 Elevation.

7 Roof plan.

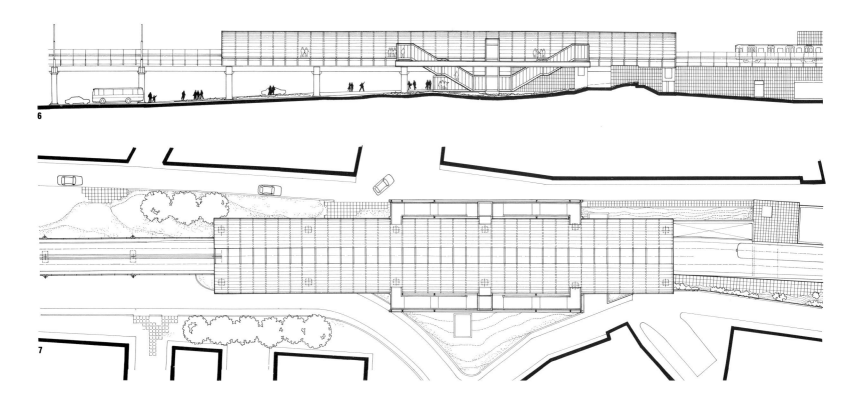

8

9

10

11

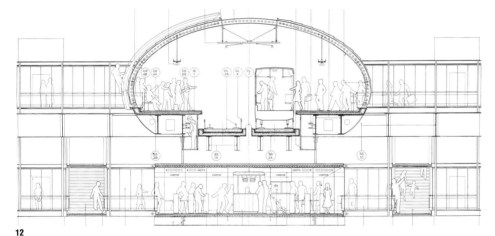

12

13

14

15

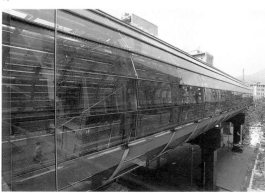

16

17

Metro stations 53

8, **9** Construction views.

10 Stairs and lifts to platform.

11 Close-up of stair up to platform.

12 Cross section through generic elevated station with ticket hall below platforms.

13, **14** Approaches to station: **13** From side street showing lift and stair to elevated platforms, **14** The main approach to the entrance is under the cover of the elevated tracks.

15, **16** Views in both directions from head of stair up to platform.

17 Passengers leaving train and platform.

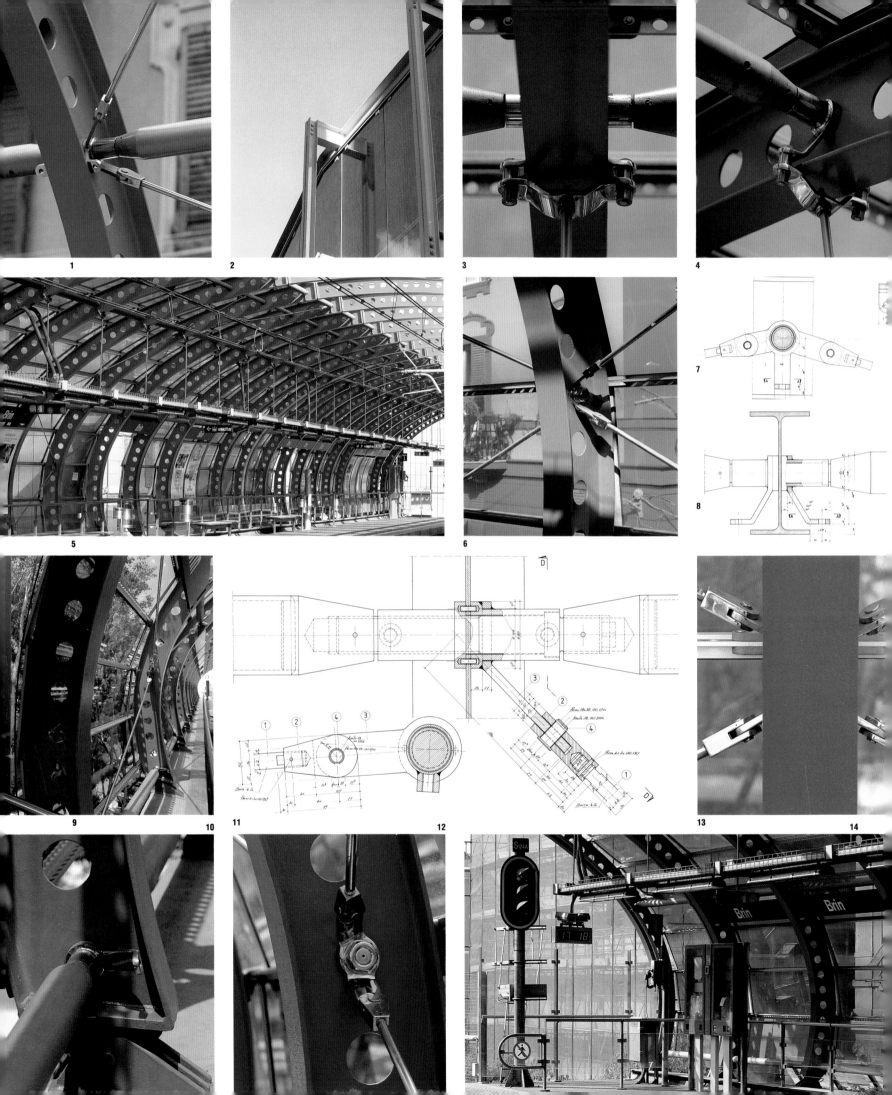

1

2

3

4

5

6

7

8

9

10

11

12

13

14

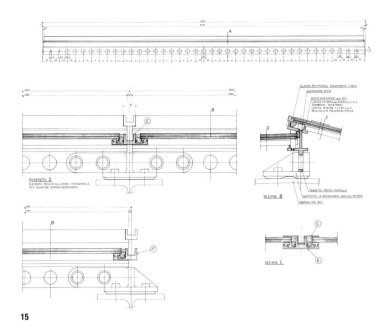

15

same reconstituted stone that Piano used to face the walls of the Dinegro station. Although the stone is used to give some consistent identity to all the stations, it might seem a little gratuitous here. But the use of 'natural' materials as a protective/decorative cladding to steel or concrete-framed structures is becoming a recurrent theme in Piano's work. As well as the terracotta elements used on the IRCAM Extension in Paris (Volume One, p 202), and parts of the new buildings for the Columbus Exposition (p 94), stone has also been used as cladding material on the Credito Industriale Sardo building in Sardinia (p 140). Even with such a simple functional structure as an elevated rapid-transit station, Piano softens technology by introducing nature. This nature is not in the shape of the pretty, but contrived, and high-maintenance flower tubs and hanging baskets of Victorian tradition. Instead, it takes the form of stone cladding, as well as trees and sky conspicuous outside through the glass, and the ever-changing light this admits.

Metro stations

Details.

1, **6–8**, **11–13**, **16**, **18** Junctions between I-sectioned arches, tubular props and ties.

2 External structure at head of stair.

3, **4** Junction to arch of tie for suspended cable tray seen in **5** and **14**

9, **10** Views of the pin-jointed junction at the foot of each arch.

15, **17** Glazing details.

Following pages Brin station is an elevated transparent tube, airy and brightly coloured, through which the surrounding tenements are clearly visible.

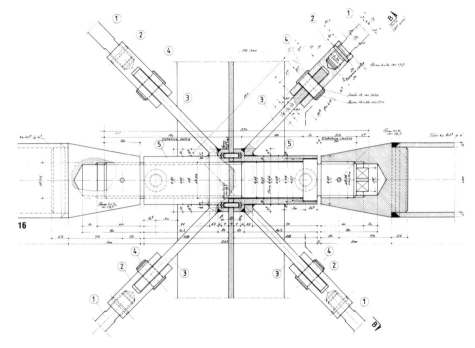

16

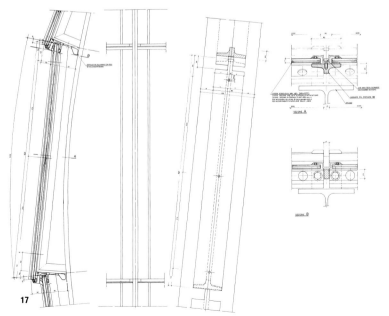

17

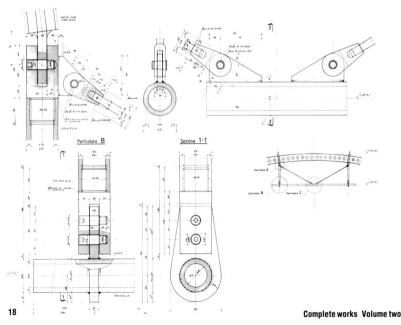

18

Complete works Volume two

Client City of Genoa

Design team R Piano, D L Hart (Dinegro,
Caricamento, Darsena, De Ferrari, Principe
and Sarzano stations, 1983-1994) S Ishida
(associate architect), C Manfreddo
(Caricamento and Darsena stations, 1983),
F Marano (associate engineer), V Tolu
(Canepari and Principe stations, 1983-94), M
Varratta (Brin Station, 1983-90), M Carroll, O
Di Blasi, E Frigerio

Assisted by A Alborghetti, E Baglietto,
K Cussoneau, G Fascioli, N Freedman,
P Maggiora, M Mallamaci, M Mattei,
B Merello, D Peluffo

Model makers D Cavagna, E Miola

Structural engineers:

stations Mageco Srl (L Mascia, D Mascia)

rail track Inco Spa, Reico Spa

Services engineers Aerimpianti Spa

Landscape architect M Desvigne

Contract management Ansaldo
Trasporti Spa

Contractor Imprese Riunite Genova

58

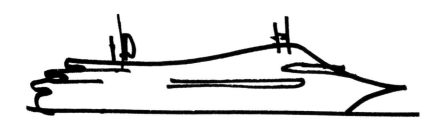

Cruise ships and yacht built in Trieste **1987–90**, Genoa **1984**

Renzo Piano has always been fascinated by the sea and by boats. Shaped by the flow of water past them, the hulls of boats are immensely strong and efficient structures. To those who look inside their hulls, they reveal both how they were made and how they withstand the sometimes immense stresses they must endure. Together, these characteristics give them the sense of organic vitality that Piano has always sought in his architectural structures.

A keen sailor, Piano built four yachts for himself between 1962 and 1984, each time experimenting with a different material and construction method. The first he built in his garage using plywood. The second was built with a thinner plywood, the third in ferro-cement and the fourth of wooden rods embedded in adhesive. With this back-ground, as well as his experi-ence in vehicle design (the Flying Carpet and Fiat vss Experimental Car – see Volume One p 64-5), adding relevant dimensions to his architectural expertise, it is perhaps not sur-prising that Piano was asked to contribute to the design of the cruise ship, the *Crown Princess*. After all, for a modern shipping line, a cruise ship is a floating hotel in which the challenge to the designer is to provide com-fort and a sense of luxury in compact conditions.

Compactness of course is rel-ative. Here, it is a consequence of the enormous amount that is accommodated in the available volume; and it is the sheer size of the *Crown Princess* and its other statistics that first impress. Weighing 70 000 tons, the ship is 246 metres in length, 32 metres in beam and 53 metres from the keel to the roof of the observation lounge. It has a draught (the depth of the ship beneath the water-line) of 7.8 metres. Thirteen decks provide a total floor area of 50 000 square metres accom-modating 1 750 passengers in 798 cabins. There is a crew of 656 and the ship can cruise at 22 knots. Most of these factors were determined and designed by naval architects. The brief to the Building Workshop was to create a distinctive profile, and to contribute to the design of the public rooms and other key areas throughout the ship. The *Crown Princess*, and its later identical sister ship, the *Regal Princess*, were built by the shipbuilders, Fincantieri, in the Monfalcone shipyards near Trieste in Italy.

Italian liners of the 1960s such as the *Leonardo da Vinci* were among the last ships to be

1

2

3

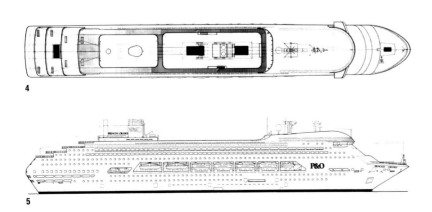

5

60 **Cruise ships and yacht**

1 Wooden model seen in elevation.

2,3 Construction of the *Crown Princess* in the Monfalcone shipyards.

4 Plan.

5 Elevation.

6 Silhouette contrasted with those of older ships.

7 General view shows how the addition of the domed observation lounge invests the slab-sided ship with some sense of organic integrity.

8 Plan of observation lounge with reflected ceiling.

9 Section of observation lounge.

built with a graceful and continuously curving sheerline. Since then the economies of repetitive construction have led to all ships' hulls being built as slab-sided extrusions, with a rectangular plan and flat sheerline, to which are appended a curving bow and stern. The result is quite devoid of the organic integrity and grace that characterized the design of older ships. The *Crown Princess* has just such a typical modern hull. Although he could shape only the top of the superstructure, Piano's challenge was to invest the ship with a sense of that missing organic wholeness, and even of a certain vitality. To this end, he decided that the top and front of the superstructure, which forms the roof of the observation lounge, should be shaped as an elongated dome, 30 metres wide and 60 metres long. This gives the ship's profile a fluid forward-moving emphasis and integrative focus.

Adding to the height of the ship in this manner, without unduly raising its centre of gravity, meant that this part of the superstructure had to be made in aluminium. This led to research into how to cold-form the sheets into the requisite curves and how to bond aluminium directly to steel – something achieved by introducing to the shipyard a new process of controlled explosion in which the metals were made to interpenetrate each other to a depth of a millimetre and more.

Considerable research also went into the improved aerodynamics brought about by the domed form. These were studied in a wind-tunnel at the Danish Naval Institute near Copenhagen. Here, a solution was also devised to the problem of efficiently drawing away from the ship's funnel the smoke which the superior streamlining had initially caused to cling to the stern.

6

7

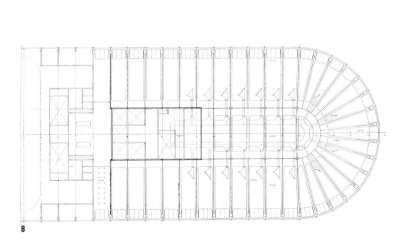

8

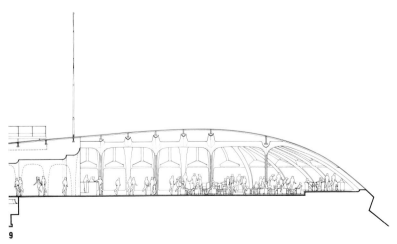

9

1

62   **Cruise ships and yacht**

1 External scaffolding and service ducts used
during construction.

2 Bow of nearly completed ship.

Observation lounge.

3 Cross section.

4 Aluminium shell being lifted into position.

5 Looking up at front of completed observation lounge above the counter-slanted
windows of the captain's bridge.

6 Unfinished interior showing the bare
aluminium structure.

7 Interior nearing completion with sculpted
fibrous plaster ceiling that expresses the
structure and conceals the air-conditioning
ducts and sources of artificial light.

2

3

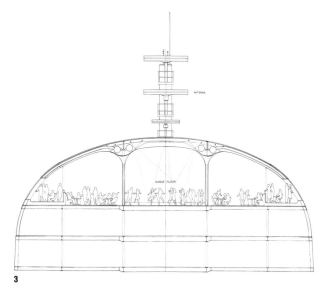

4

5

7

Also contributing to the final
smooth profile were studies
made on clustering the ship's
13 antennae. This is something
to which proper attention is
often not paid, hence the messy
silhouettes of many contemporary vessels.

Only once this profile had
been resolved, was it noticed
that it resembled that of a dolphin, with the domed roof of
the observation lounge as its
forehead. Although this might
not be entirely logical, since
a dolphin is shaped to slip at
speed through the water rather
than float above it, the Building
Workshop was happy to play
up such touching associations.
Now, Piano feels that too much
is made of such resemblances
so that people tend to misunderstand and take too far the
idea that his design literally
is inspired by and emulates
nature.

Inside the observation
lounge, a structure was sought
that would give character to the
space without need for further
decoration beyond the installation of a fibrous plaster ceiling.

Here, the structural ribs, high-
lighted by concealed lighting,
give some impression of being
inside a whale. But the gently
enveloping form is extrovert
too, thanks to the big windows.
Looking forward through these
and over the bow of the ship as
it slices through the sea adds to
the impression of being inside
the creature's forehead and
looking out through its eyes.

For the Building Workshop,
the profile and roof of the
observation lounge constitute
the project's limited successes.
Despite protracted and frus-
trating battles with marketing
men and shipping executives,
Piano feels that the gap
between the original dream of
what the design could be, and
the final result, is a dismayingly
large chasm. Stringent insur-
ance conditions made it
difficult to innovate in engineering terms, and the
marketing view that a cruise
ship is only a floating hotel
made it impossible to invest
the interior with any of the
majestic grace that once characterized ship design.

8

9

10

Resolute Lady

8 Hull under construction.

9 Deck being laid.

10 Under sail.

11, 12 Views over the deck that is uncluttered by any protruding cabin.

13, 14, 15 Details of teak hatches and decking.

16 Early elevational sketch.

17 Section of final design.

11

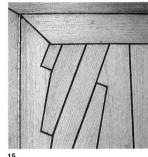
12

Cruise ships and yacht   63

Client P&O, Fincantieri

Design team R Piano, S Ishida, N Okabe (associates in charge), K McBryde, M Carroll, R Costa, M Cucinella, R J Van Santen, F Santolini, R Self, S Smith, O Touraine

Assisted by G G Bianchi, G Grandi, N Freedman, D L Hart, P Maggiora, C Manfreddo, F R Ludewig

Model maker D Cavagna

Local supervisors studio Architetti Associati, Venice

Wind tunnel tests Danish Maritime Institute, Lyngby

Ship builder Fincantieri Monfalcone, Trieste

13

14

15

16

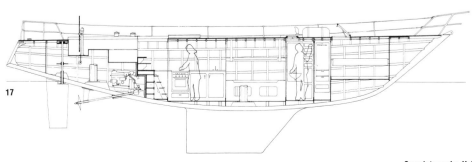
17

The following excerpts are from an interview conducted by the author in English in the UNESCO Laboratory-workshop at Vesima, Genoa, towards the end of 1993.

Interview Excerpts from a conversation with Renzo Piano

PB You have talked in the past of wanting architecture to be thought of as merely a service profession like baking bread. Yet bakers do not feel compelled to invent a new loaf each time as you do.

RP Talking about baking bread is more about behaviour, it is a provocation against the pompous attitude of the 'real artist' or artist *manqué*. Some members of the architectural community are so pompous. They see themselves as belonging to an old and important past. They are like ancient nobles with no more money. I instinctively react against that. The idea of architecture being like baking bread is intended as the opposite, that, instead, architecture is day-to-day patient work. But I totally agree that architecture is not baking bread, every day doing the same thing. The baker is proud to do his job correctly, but every day is a repetition. Every day in architecture, though, is a new adventure. But baking bread is about reality, normality, and that is important for an architect not to lose touch with. Yet for an architect, routine and cliché are dangerous and must be avoided, like style and a rubber-stamp vocabulary. But spare us the trumpet fanfares. This is what I wanted to imply.

PB You fiercely resist being pigeon-holed, particularly as a High-Tech architect. You are wary even of having too much emphasis laid on the way your buildings are constructed in case people see this, which is obviously a major concern for you, as an exclusive one. How would you define your approach to architecture?

RP That my works show the way they are constructed comes from my personal history. I was born to a family of builders, and grew up in an atmosphere of fervour about making. As a young man I grew up in a time that was given rhythm by buildings going up, and new buildings being planned. Making is biologically imprinted into me. Designing buildings that express that making might be very naive, very primitive, but it is absolutely natural to me.

Of course, it is more complicated than that, because the work is not only about making. There has been an evolution, a continuous evolution both in the office and in myself. If in discussion I stress the making part of architecture, it is not because it is the most important, but because this is the origin. When talking about one's life it is natural to talk about the early years.

We have to be careful not to make a mistake of interpretation. When you sit down and talk, you are not talking about reality, but about what you love to talk about. Normally this is about youth, sources, origins. You go automatically to adolescence, to when your character was formed, when sensations were fresh and you were forming your approach to life. This happens to me. I instinctively and constantly refer to this period. But this gives a false impression because I have moved on from there.

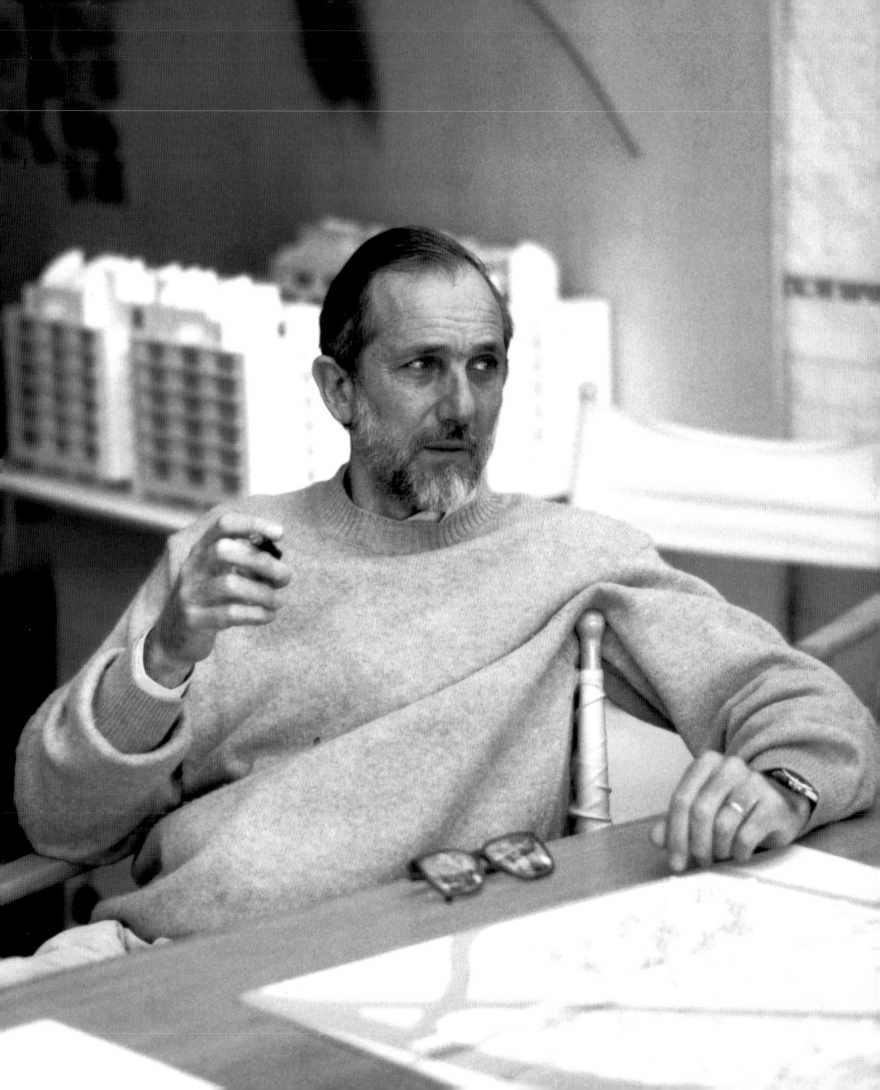

1

2

3

Building Workshop Team Members

1 Renzo Piano and Peter Buchanan
2 Shelley Comer
3 Misha Cramer
4 Noriko Takiguchi
5 Carla Garbato
6 Claudio Manfreddo (*left*) and Stefano D'Atri
7 Ronnie Self
8 Ronan Phelan
9 Giovanna Langasco (*left*) and
Susanna Scarabicchi
10 Stefan Schäfer
11 Dante Cavagna

4

5

6

7

8

9

10   11

So, how would I define what we do now? When I will go shortly to speak to people at the drawing board, it is not going to be about making. The Berlin Potsdamer Platz project is not about making – though of course it will become so. For instance, we will start to work this afternoon on the construction of the shell roof over the theatre and casino, on the problem of how to interconnect the rigid individual components of the roof so that it becomes the curving shell. The components are like leaves, fixed only at points, and how do these interconnect to form the roof surface? But you cannot say that this is the most important aspect of Potsdamer Platz which is very much about space, especially outdoor urban living space.

The same is true for the Cité Internationale for Lyons, another scheme I must work on today. Joining the others in a minute, I may talk a bit about the brick walls and structure of the main hall. But we will probably talk much more about the relationship to nature, to the Parc de la Tête d'Or on one side of the building and to the River Rhône on the other. When developing a design we move constantly from the detail to the general, and back again.

Making has now become part of a much bigger vision in our work, that now includes as equally important such things as history and space. I surprise myself, finding that I am talking more and more about space, the character of space. Kansai airport is very

12

13

Building Workshop Team Members

12 Yasmin Surti

13 Flavio Marano

14 Charlotte Jackman and Ahmed El Jerari

15 Alain Vincent

16 Taichi Tomuro

17 Alessandro Gortan (*left*) and
Maurizio Varratta

18 Lukas Epprecht

19 Michele Ras

20 Michelle Howard

21 William Vassal, Maire Henry and
Dominique Rat (*left to right*)

14

15

16

17

18

19

20

21

much about space. When I was on site last week it was absolutely clear to me that the building is about space, not structure, or construction.

How do I define myself in relation to other architects? I do not know. Maybe this is laziness, or Genoese introversion. But I do not like the idea of placing myself somewhere, and so I place myself where I was at the beginning of my careér, when I was excommunicated. This is true by the way: ten or more years ago someone published a book on the 100 leading architects in Italy. I was not there. In the circumstances you are almost pleased to be excluded. But this was a long time ago and I should rethink my position, yet I cannot be bothered. Besides, I find it impossible to define myself intellectually, I just feel instinctively that I belong to this long stream of people.

In the essay introducing Volume One when you talk about things like evolution, it makes it very clear that we do not depend on the world of architectural critics, on academic history or trends such as Post-Modernism or Neo-Modernism. We do not depend in any way on such intellectual discussion. We belong, and are happy to belong because this gives us the fresh perceptions of a child, simply to that big stream of people who in various ways manipulate material to organize life. This was reflected nicely in the title you proposed for our current touring exhibition, 'A Manipulable Universe'.

67

1

2

68   **Building Workshop Team Members**

1 Paola Maggiora

2 Isabella Carpiceci

3 Bruno Tonfoni (*left*) and Ahmed El Jerari

4 Kenneth Fraser, Charles Hussey, Renzo
Piano, Alberto Giordano, Jane Wernick and
Tom Barker (*left to right*)

5 Gianni Modolo

6 Alberto Giordano

3

As a man, and particularly as one who is an architect, you balance your biological sterility by making things with your hands. You do not make life, so you create things, buildings. It is instinctive, or at least I feel it must be for a number of men around the world. For me, this is as basic to the world as fire and water.

But because we are not animals, we experiment with and elaborate our making. We think about it and look carefully at what has been done by predecessors over the last five centuries. So as I said, we belong to that vast family of people who know how to make things. But because one has been lucky and has had a lot of opportunities, because one can fly around the world and have a fax and so on, because one has a very good team built up over 20 years and has had the opportunity over that period to communicate with very creative people, one inevitably becomes more sophisticated. One starts to understand things about society, anthropology and so on. But what has this to do with architectural critics, Deconstructivism et cetera?

If you work in this way, you then realize that your best works made with your hands feel almost natural. For instance, the structure of the Nouméa cultural centre is getting to be almost what we want, it has almost the same feeling, vibration, richness as the trees that will be around it. We must be careful here because there is room for a lot of misunderstanding of our intentions. But it is true

that the most advanced technological products do often seem almost natural.

This is understandable, because in the end you as a man with your small hands are left with this immense duty of competing with nature. And it is a constant competition. We talk about harmony because we seek a sense of harmony in the objects we create. But there is almost no harmony between you and the making of that object, because this is a fight. People get confused about harmony, they seek it everywhere. In the creative process, harmony is in the final product: in the text – when it is complete; in the building – when it is complete. But it may not be in the doing of it, which maybe tragic, a fierce and continuous fight.

The Arcadian vision of harmony is ridiculous. As is well known, when you are in an ideal position, you do nothing, you are lost. Many people spend a lot of time creating ideal, serene conditions, and then lose all capacity for creativity.

I explain all this because in the end if what we do is well done, then it becomes, as you explained in the introductory essay in Volume One, part of the evolution of the world. Man is part of this larger view of evolution, at the most basic level by making things with his hands. In the end, being an architect is one of the most instinctive jobs on the planet. Creating shelter is an immediate reflex, as immediate and as natural as hunting. I like it when you say in your essay that

4

5

6

7

8

Building Workshop Team Members

7 Hiroko Nishikawa (*left*) and Noriaki Okabe

8 Carla Garbato and Dante Cavagna

9 Geoffrey Cohen

10 Sylvie Milanesi

11 Domenico Guerrisi

12 Paul Vincent

13 Patrick Charles, Joost Moolhuijzen and
 Roger Baumgarten (*left to right*)

14 Renzo Piano and Milly Rossato

15 Stefania Canta

16 Alain Gallissian

9

10

11

12

13

14

15

16

the evolutionary vision which you speculate lies behind our architecture is for me unconscious. Because it is, just as the hunter was unconscious of the role he was playing in the larger adventure of evolution.

Nevertheless the vision you elaborate of architecture as part of the world evolving is so important that I wish that you had given it more emphasis and had not dealt with it so quickly at the end of the essay. Especially as I do not want lazy readers to misunderstand the point about emulating nature and think of me as the man who makes buildings with structures that look like dinosaur skeletons. What we do, as you said in dreaming up a title for our exhibition, is to manipulate the universe to ends that are human yet compatible with the planet.

I will never call on another architect to discuss architecture. We will talk of other things. The Building Workshop swims in a somewhat different world to most other architects. We want to swim in life, not architecture. And the best moments are when by swimming in life we catch exactly what we need to take back and make our buildings.

PB The Anglo-Saxon cast to your ideas and sympathies is striking. Is this part of a lingering legacy of Genoa's contacts with Britain that remained strong at least until the late nineteenth century, and which continued in people like your early mentor, Franco Albini? Would you comment on this and

69

1

Building Workshop Team Members

1 Loïc Couton (*left*) and Pascal Hendier

2 Maurizio Varratta

3 Tetsuya Kimura

4 Renzo Piano (*left*) and Tom Barker

5 Anne Hélène Téménides

6 Junya Fujita

7 Fabrizio Pierandrei (*left*) and Donald L Hart

8 Milly Rossato Piano

9 Lorraine Lin

10 Maria Salerno (*left*) and Stacy Eisenberg

2

3

4

5

6

7

8

9

10

your many continuing links with Britain, with Peter Rice and the whole institution of Ove Arup & Partners, as well as other British consultants?

RP I was never so cultivated as to be really conscious of English culture. The links might be partly because of Albini, but more because for me England sets the example for a high level of professionalism, a detached professionalism with a sense of humour. As a small boy during the war, I learnt that England was the civilized place that was saving Europe. The voice everyone said was the voice of a friend was that on the radio from London. It was the one my parents hushed us to listen to. All this is deep in my past, deep within me.

Later I understood that there were two kinds of professionalism, those of Germany and England. England was the friendly, detached one of people who do things very well, but distanced by humour. I'm not sure it is still like that, and working on the projects for Germany has led me to appreciate their way of doing things. But this is what mainly interested me to begin with. Life is a short adventure, so these feelings about England and its importance for me will always remain.

PB Would you like to explain or comment on any of the buildings included in this volume?

RP I want to say something about Vesima, the laboratory-workshop we are sitting in, something that is equally true for the offices

11

12

14

15

16

17

13

18

19

where the designs are developed in Genoa, Paris and Osaka.

When we started to work in Paris on building a replica of Brancusi's studio, I talked to Pontus Hulten (who amongst other things had been curator of the collection of Modern Art at the Pompidou). From this I started to understand more and more about art as a continually evolving landscape, or 'interiorscape'. Brancusi had wanted his atelier to be kept with all the sculptures and everything else in place because he felt all these different objects – sculptures, pieces of stone and wood that were yet to become sculptures – were part of a larger work in process. Everything lying around was potentially a sculpture. I can picture him sitting and smoking in the corner of his studio, looking at this exploded work of art made of some 30 pieces in different stages.

It was the whole thing that was the artwork. That is why he invented machines that turned the sculptures so slowly that you only noticed when you looked again after some minutes and saw something afresh. He could also make them turn more quickly. But the movement was mainly introduced because he wanted this landscape, or interiorscape, to change gently and slowly. For me this is beautiful. I can imagine the tragedy for him to die just as the bulldozers start to demolish the building. This is the spirit of the studio which we need to understand when we are re-creating it.

71

20

1

2

3

72 **Building Workshop Team Members**

1 Yoshiko Ueno (*left*) and Aki Shimizu
2 Jean Philippe Allain
3 Stacy Eissenberg
4 Richard Librizzi (*left*) and Stefano Arecco
5 Daniele Piano
6 Lionel Penisson
7 Ivan Corte (*left*) and Olaf De Nooyer
8 Kenneth Fraser
9 Philippe Cloudet and Hélène Teboul

4

5

6

7

8

9

When I thought about this I started to realize that, in a much more modest way, my offices, and especially the Vesima workshop, are like that for me. Take that 'piece' over there. That is not a bit of structure, but a promise. I'm talking about a bamboo truss, but the same applies to the tools in Dante Cavagna's workshop, to that drawing bleaching in the sunlight over there, marking the passage of time. We work immersed in this environment made of all these different things, these promises to become other things.

Of course it is more immaterial here than in Brancusi's studio: it is not his collection of actual works which is here, but objects that call to mind other things spread all around the world. This is not just a workshop, but where we collect everything together from the different offices. It is a place where you can be in touch with all sorts of things that are not actually present. In here I can travel around the world. As I walk from level to level, between the work being done on each level, I am speeding around the world.

I feel all this best early on Saturday mornings when nobody else is here. Then I can literally distil everything. I can look at one of these material objects, and then it evaporates as it causes me to think of other things, and then it returns as a physical object before me. In here when designing, we are not in a hurry to come to conclusions too soon. Here, I can distance myself from things, and so the final work acquires that lighter touch.

10

Building Workshop Team Members

10 Alessandra Alborchetti and Vittorio Di Turi

11 Gianfranco Biggi

12 Eva Kruse

13 Bernard Plattner

14 Giorgio Bianchi

15 Pascal Hendier (*left*) and William Matthews

16 Venanzio Truffelli and Emanuela Baglietto

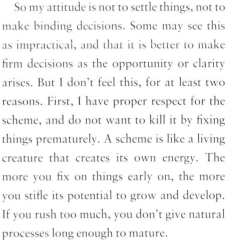

11

12

13

14

PB Can you say a bit more about your design process?

RP Though I sketch prolifically when reconsidering schemes, particularly at weekends or when travelling, I feel guilty sometimes about not always sitting down and quietly designing by myself. But I prefer never to go too far at any moment with a scheme. I prefer to advance through 20 light steps rather than two big ones. Maybe it is part of my shyness. For me, design is like navigation, when you constantly have to correct your course. I'm almost frightened of any other way. This is why I say creative work is made up of unannounced moments. These are ordinary moments, you do not recognize magic moments. You may recognize later that they were magic, but not at the time. When you take 20 steps in a scheme, and each one adds something, there is no moment that seems at the time historically decisive, when you ring bells and announce your triumph to the world.

For instance, in the last few days I have come to this feeling about the Padre Pio Pilgrimage Church, that we should maybe slide things in the radial sections, that there is too much symmetry. Now I haven't told anybody about this yet, and when I do, it might in retrospect have been a fundamental moment – or maybe not. So I don't want to impose this. But I can only work like this when I walk around, see things, distance myself, fly above the scheme and discuss with people.

So my attitude is not to settle things, not to make binding decisions. Some may see this as impractical, and that it is better to make firm decisions as the opportunity or clarity arises. But I don't feel this, for at least two reasons. First, I have proper respect for the scheme, and do not want to kill it by fixing things prematurely. A scheme is like a living creature that creates its own energy. The more you fix on things early on, the more you stifle its potential to grow and develop. If you rush too much, you don't give natural processes long enough to mature.

Second, my reluctance to fix things firmly comes from respect for people working on the job. If you wait, people come forward bringing up more and more fresh ideas. Design is almost like a very patient application of the Socratic method. Le Corbusier's idea of design as a patient search is correct. It is not patience as in just waiting, but rather of every day letting something happen so that the scheme grows that little bit.

My attitude also comes from working for many years with people like Peter Rice. I knew with him that if we settled something too quickly, the germ of an idea coming out of our meeting would never have the chance to flower in a week or so's time. Because as I said, the important moments are not recognizable. We can only keep up the daily ritual of work, of slow advance. Of course this does not go on for ever. You eventually come to a stop because it becomes clear to everybody

15

16

7

9

1

2

74 **Building Workshop Team Members**

1 Antoine Chaaya

2 Katheryne McLone

3 Vittorio Tolu and Claudia Leoncini

4 Daniela Capuzzo

5 Shin Kanoo

6 Maria Cattanneo

7 Mark Carroll

8 Rosella Biondo

9 Marjoline Boudry

10 Michael Palmore

11 Joachim Ruoff, Roger Baumgarten and Joost Moolhuijzen (*left to right*)

4

5

3

7

6

8

9

10

11

in the team that you have got there. You start to feel happy. You start to detect the echoes between the scheme and the world at large.

For me, lack of decision is not indecision, but a power to keep things alive. The process of design is a little like watching a bacterial culture grow under a microscope. Design is also a continous process of slow advance.

PB It is evident that you are in the process of restructuring the Building Workshop. You, yourself, have always been on the move between the offices. And there has always been a lot of coming and going of others between the different bases. But this now seems to have intensified. For instance, the design development of Potsdamer Platz is going on in both Paris and Genoa with members of both teams regularly visiting the other office. Can you explain this?

RP What you say is true. And seeing how projects are credited in Volume One to particular offices of the Building Workshop, made me realize that this gives an impression that is no longer true, nor ever was really. It is especially not true of the vision I have always had. The Building Workshop is a single group, based in different countries.

The special quality of the Building Workshop lies not only in it being a good group of people, who collaborate well, have a particular attitude to craft and so on; it is because as a group we are genuinely international. You could say we are the only genuinely international architectural practice. Most major

12

13

Building Workshop Team Members

12 Eric Verstrepen
13 Cathy Bassière
14 François Bertolero and Elisabeth Nodinot
15 Shunji Ishida
16 Susan Baggs
17 Marie Pimmel
18 Olaf De Nooyer
19 Akira Ikegami
20 Dominique Putz
21 Matteo Piano
22 Christopher Hight
23 Jean Bernard Mothes
24 Eric Novel

15

14

19

20

16

17

18

21

22

architects clearly belong in their approach to their own country. Tadao Ando is very Japanese, Norman Foster is very English, Richard Meier is very American, Rafael Moneo is very Spanish... to name only some of the architects I respect. But nobody could say we are Italian, French or Japanese. And the Paris office is not the French branch of what is an Italian office, as are the equivalent offices in other other countries of other so-called international practices. If architecture is a mirror of life, including the lives of those who make it, then our unique make-up and way of working is one with great relevance.

Our internationalism is not opportunistic or cynical, a way to get more business. Rather it is a way to a richer, more humane point of view. It is like being part of a big family rather than a small one. With a big family, the house may be a chaotic mess. But relationships are rich. Or you could use nationality as a metaphor. Some countries are guarded and defensive. Italy is a mess, but in that messiness and openness to life and influence, comes Italy's historic capacity to develop ideas that become international.

Note: The points Piano makes in his last answer are reflected in the detailed layout of this volume. Projects are no longer credited to a particular branch of the Building Workshop. Although in the past many projects had input from both Paris and Genoa, this has become increasingly the rule.

75

23   **24**

76

UNESCO Laboratory-workshop Vesima, Genoa, Italy **1989-91**

Perched inconspicuously on a steep, verdant and terraced mountainside overlooking the Gulf of Genoa is a glass roof which hugs the slope. The space enclosed by glass walls beneath the roof is, for the most part, a single volume whose floor simply steps with the slope, almost as continuations of the terracing outside. A sophisticated, highly-serviced, version of the agricultural greenhouses found on these slopes, and reached only by a funicular from the coast road below, this is a laboratory and workshop shared by the Building Workshop and UNESCO. Here, among the plants that surround and penetrate the building, and in the bright and ever-changing light admitted through the roof, research and seminars go on, alongside other functions of the Building Workshop. Out of town and withdrawn, yet extrovertly transparent and instantaneously connected by electronics to other branches of the Building Workshop as well as to its far-flung building sites, this new satellite is almost the antithesis of the Building Workshop's other Genoa base, the Gothic palazzo prominent on the little Piazza San Matteo in the heart of the dense and introverted historic city.

The land at Vesima, west of Genoa, and the farmhouse on it have for generations belonged to Piano's family and he had long wanted to put them to suitable use. But it was Peter Rice who provided some of the impetus to use the site as a base for research into the constructional applications of natural materials, in particular the structural potential of such vegetal matter as stalks and fibres – a project close to the hearts of both men. The Building Workshop paid for the building, which has always been seen as something of a research project in itself. UNESCO funds much of this research. It was the nature of this enterprise and the partly horticultural use of the building, as well as its resemblance to the local greenhouses, that made it permissable to build in this coastal area. Research specimens are grown in the building and on much of the site where there are bamboos and reeds, agave and so on. One day, marine specimens might also be grown in the sea, next to the road that edges the bottom of the site.

Alongside the UNESCO-sponsored research it was always intended that the building be used to research matters of immediate application to designs under development

1

UNESCO Laboratory-workshop

Context.

1 The site as it was, with old farmhouse in foreground and view of Genoa in the distance.

2 The Ligurian coast.

3 The terraced hillsides.

4,5 Construction views emphasize sense of building being merely a transparent roof over paved terraces.

2

3

4

5

by the Building Workshop. Recently, substantial funding has been awarded by the European Community for some of this research, which will be of general benefit to other architects and the building industry at large. At the moment there are two such projects underway, both concerned with multi-layered claddings that could contribute to the lower energy consumption and increased longevity of buildings.

With the multi-disciplinary German engineering consultants, Drees & Sommer, the Building Workshop is researching the construction of double-skinned glass walls that will allow light to penetrate deep into the offices of the Potsdamer Platz project (p 210), and yet will also have a high degree of thermal inertia. This will save on energy for lighting, heating and cooling. Research is also being undertaken with Ove Arup & Partners into double-roof construction that includes a buffer zone of air between external and internal temperatures. Such roofs have become a recurrent theme in the Building Workshop's architecture. Two very different examples included in this volume are the shell of the Bercy 2 Shopping Centre (p 16) and the

monitor roof under development for the Beyeler Foundation Museum (p 170).

The laboratory-workshop is constructed to one side of the old farmhouse and follows the slope below it. Its dominant elements are the glazed roof (with its wood-framed panes, laminated-wood beams and automatically controlled external louvres) and tiered levels of workspace. The slender steel posts that support the roof, and the frameless glass walls, which are set a greater or lesser distance behind the roof's oversailing edge, have only a minimal presence. One such glass wall, the only one not shaded by automatic blinds, climbs parallel to the funicular rail. Beside this glass wall, an internal stair connects all the tiered levels. The opposite side of the building is stepped in plan (Piano's analogy for the shape of the diaphanous roof is a butterfly's wing) so opening up views through the corners to the sea or the lushly vegetated gulley that edges the site. From all but the lowest levels, views straight ahead of the sea are restricted to a low, narrow, gap below the louvred roof. But an additional seaward view is gained diagonally in the direction of Genoa and its new harbour,

6

UNESCO Laboratory-workshop
Response to context.
6 Aerial view shows glass-roofed building
clinging to slope between deep and densely
vegetated gulley and funicular rail.
7 Site and location plan.
8 Internal stairs that climb parallel to
funicular rail.

7

through the glazing beside the internal stair.

Reached by an external stair from the laboratory-workshop, the farmhouse now provides overnight accommodation for visitors. Running along the contour from here, against a beautiful fieldstone-faced retaining wall, are spaces for study and socializing. The plane of the glass roof has been extended from that of the laboratory-workshop below, except where a terrace overlooking the sea has been created between the sloping beams to serve these spaces. This has resulted in a flat, opaque ceiling to the upper tier of workspace below, which is consequently the only part of the laboratory-workshop that seems somewhat mundane – apart from the fact that it enjoys a view over the rest of the space.

Except for the predominance of section over plan and the magical top-lit ambience inside (the first studio-workshop that Piano built for himself in Genoa in 1968-9 was also top-lit, like so many of his buildings), this fairly modest structure is not what some might immediately associate with Piano. The only conspicuous 'technological' elements are the solar-cell controlled louvres and blinds. It even takes time to detect the characteristic 'piece' (the repetitive component developed especially for, and intrinsic to the identity of, the building). This is because there is nothing 'technological' about the repetitive and butt-jointed, wood-framed, glazed roof panels – other than an optimistic dependence on modern sealants, which is necessary because the frames are not lapped to allow for movement. The original transparent roofing material, still in place where the roof oversails the glass wall below, was a new high-performance membrane. This was wrapped right around these frames to create a large air pocket between its two skins. But, because the sound of rain on the membrane was intrusive, it was exchanged for conventional double glazing, which also offers

8

increased transparency. Similar substitutions of materials might continue to be made to parts of the roof as future research projects generate new possibilities.

The frameless glazing of the walls is quite virtuoso. The very tall side-panes rely only on extremely slender glass fins for lateral restraint. But these are handled with such understatement (the lack of deflection in the laminated timber beams obviates the need for sliding joints at the heads of panes) that few might notice how daringly the material is pushed to its limits. Elsewhere, construction is very straightforward. Laminated beams are connected to each other, and to the heads of the steel posts, by a steel element with finger joints. But the square-sectioned posts are given a subtle refinement by rubbing down their corners to an arris that stops some 150mm short of their heads, thus giving the slightest suggestion of shaft and capital. And the few walls that are not glass echo the local tradition of pink-painted stucco and fieldstone. The artificial lighting is also dealt with simply. Light from semi-industrial, cantilevered uplighters (which the architects designed for the Lingotto renovation) is here reflected from a row of fabric panels set below the roof.

Although devoid of technological exhibitionism, indeed in part because of this lack, the building exemplifies Piano's evolving architectural ideals. And it certainly confirms the criticisms of his Italian colleagues. It is non-urban, has no conventional (and, for these critics, culturally and psychologically crucial) architectural elements such as rooms, articulated spatial sequences, framed

79

1

UNESCO Laboratory-workshop

Materials and textures.

1 Light is directed onto fabric panels that are set against the roof to act as reflectors.

2 Corner at which fieldstone meets stucco.

3 The rough textures of Mediterranean plants and fieldstone walls edge the steps that climb alongside the funicular rail.

4 The fieldstone wall in the seminar room.

5 Stone facing of external retaining wall.

6 Black slate paves all steps and caps all low walls, both inside and outside.

2

3

4

5

6

doorways and fenestrated facades. It even lacks any real architectural presence. Yet the building lacks nothing in resonance nor relevance; it simply achieves these through different means.

If the transition between outside and inside is deliberately played down and blurred (as is typical of Piano), the entrance sequence is nevertheless drawn out. Here, it takes the form of a funicular ride. With spectacular sea views and flanked by planting, it is a very affecting and memorable experience. And although the building lacks conventional windows, the sense of being exposed to the ever-changing moods of nature is surely as resonant as any framed view. What the building offers is not the sense of secure withdrawal once offered by buildings, but rather an openness to, and participation in, as many aspects of the world and nature as possible.

This is arguably where Piano's ecological sensibilities show, although this is not really a low-energy, low-maintenance 'green' building: its low thermal inertia makes it more dependent on power-consuming air conditioning than would a building of high thermal inertia such as is traditionally found around the Mediterranean. The building was originally conceived in this way so that it could serve as a test-bed for research; for instance, into how to achieve high thermal inertia through the layering of lightweight elements. This is exactly the research now being undertaken here and funded by the European Community.

It is the many ways in which it offers a sense of participation with the world, and current realities, that makes the Vesima building so exemplary of Piano's mature work. To participate in the world, the Building Workshop's architecture does not impose itself upon, but rather responds to and settles gently into a place. Here, the Laboratory-workshop nestles against the sloping site, as if merely sheltering and 'squaring up' the existing terracing. It resembles the local greenhouses and defers to the much smaller farmhouse in the

way in which it extends and adopts some of its finishes, specifically the pink stucco. Thus the building is rooted in both its place and in local tradition, yet modifies these in line with the selective introduction of contemporary materials and technology in order better to face the future.

Participation with nature, or at least some sense of it, is achieved in a number of ways. Not only does the building settle into and shelter luxuriant vegetation but these plants are also studied so that their properties might be exploited or emulated in the Building Workshop's architecture. The interior is also permeated by the presence and changing moods of sky and sea, the latter an especial love of Piano. And from sky, sea and sun comes the light that floods in everywhere and changes with the cycles of day, and season, as well as with the vagaries of the weather. As the automatic louvres and blinds respond to these shifts of sun and light, they draw attention to, and intensify awareness of, these various changes. Although

7

8

UNESCO Laboratory-workshop

The funicular.

7,8 Views of the cabin with its all-glass sides and roof climbing from the coastal road.

9,10 The cabin arrives at the reception.

11 Elevation of the cabin and its bogey which adjusts automatically to the two different slopes it encounters.

12 Looking down along funicular rail from outside entrance to Laboratory-workshop.

13 Vertiginous view over point beyond which funicular plunges steeply to the coast road.

9

10

protected by, and dependent on, modern technology (by solar cell-regulated shading devices and air conditioning), one is conscious of nature and feels at one with its cycles and moods.

For those working under this roof, there is a feeling of being only minimally enclosed beneath a pergola, albeit one covered by responsive mechanisms rather than deciduous vines. But beside this sense of the building emulating aspects of nature, it also fosters a strong spirit of participation, of people working with each other in a communal and collaborative enterprise. The Building Workshop ethos is explicit here: various professionals, such as the architects and researchers, back-up staff and visiting consultants, are mutually exposed to view on their respective levels and united under the embrace of the single sloping roof.

More than that, this outpost-in-nature participates world-wide through instantaneous electronic communications with other branches of the Building Workshop, as well as with consultants and construction sites. To participate fully in our electronic and information age there is no longer any necessity to be embedded in the city and its urban culture: the advantages and contacts once only available at the centre can now be enjoyed everywhere. So the Vesima Laboratory-workshop might be seen as post-urban rather than anti-urban, a now viable alternative to, rather than negation of, life in the city.

Alongside the research being done at Vesima to develop special aspects of particular projects (such as the double-layered walls of the Potsdamer Platz buildings), the space is used for seminars. At these, members of the various

81

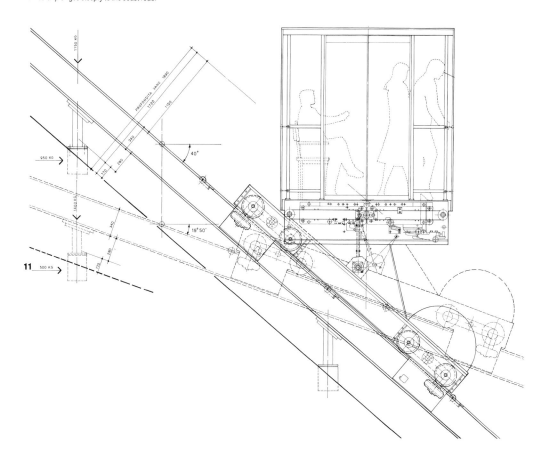

11

12

13

1

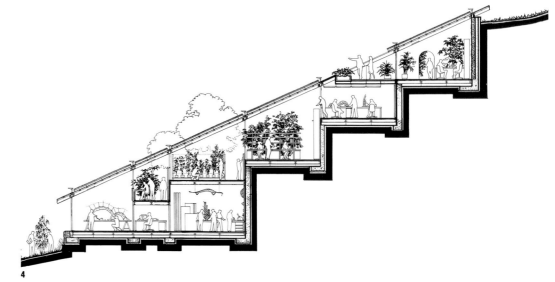

4

82 **UNESCO Laboratory-workshop**

Interiors.

1 The topmost level with chairs laid out for a seminar.

2 An intermediate level.

3 The lowest level that looks out on the sea. On right is a large model of a 'case' of the competition scheme of the J M Tjibaou Cultural Centre.

4 Section.

5 Plan.

6 Evening view of the middle/entrance level as the natural top light begins to be supplemented by reflected artificial light. Beyond the *ficus benjamina* is the reception area.

2

3

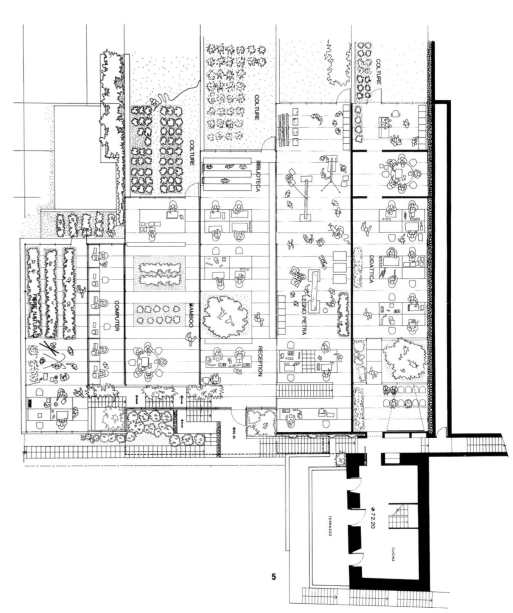

5

84 **UNESCO Laboratory-workshop**

Admitting and controlling the presence of nature.

1, 2 Nature in the form of planting and ever-changing light pervades the space.

3, 4 The entirely-glazed lowest face that looks down the site to the sea.

5, 6 Erecting a temporary framework so as to experiment with secondary internal skins as part of ongoing research for the Potsdamer Platz project.

members of the various branches of the Building Workshop come together with consultants and other specialists to check progress on research programmes and quietly reassess every aspect of an ongoing design. So, for Piano and his collaborators, the building offers another form of participation, a sense of continuous and continuing engagement with the various works by the Building Workshop. Displayed on the different levels, and encountered when moving around, are drawings and models of schemes in design development, construction or long-since completed. These include examples of everything currently being developed in the Building Workshop's other bases. In the contemplative calm that is enhanced by a sense of expansive communion with nature, Piano and others can ponder these works as part of some organic and ever-evolving whole, discovering fresh connections between them and new potentials to explore further.

Much the same process is to be found at work in the Building Workshop's other premises. But the special atmosphere of the Vesima Laboratory-workshop is particularly conducive to such reverie and speculation. Piano's understanding of this experience was brought home to him by a recent commission, now being worked on in the Paris office, to build a replica of Brancusi's studio in which to exhibit appropriately the sculptor's work. Brancusi was emphatic that his studio and sculpture were parts of an integral whole. The presence of earlier pieces inspired and guided the birth of new works. And the sculpture was always being rearranged, so that the dialogue between the pieces, and between them and the studio, its other contents and differing conditions of light and display, sparked new insights and deeper understanding as well as fresh possibilities for other works. At Vesima, the sense of tangible contact with the cycles of nature, and so of its cyclical time, is very different to the compulsions of linear time that dominates contemporary life. This might facilitate the regeneration afforded by always being able to dig and reinterpret contemplatively the roots of the present in the humus of one's own creative past.

Despite exploiting and exploring emergent technologies, the laboratory-workshop seems to grow so inevitably

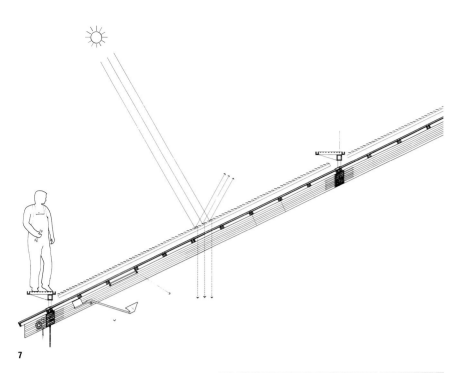

7

UNESCO Laboratory-workshop

7 Section of roof with external louvres and catwalks for maintenance.

8 The opening and closing of the louvres and the movement of the shafts of light they admit draw attention to the movement of the sun.

9 Below the protection of the oversailing roof, electrically-operated external blinds provide shade from the westerly sun.

10 The presence of planting, both inside and out, is felt everywhere.

11, **12**, **13** The changing patterns of the waves and of the light on the sea are further aspects of nature that pervade the building.

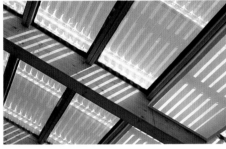

8

9

from its place and programme as to achieve a marvellous freshness and naturalness. Because of that, it is not apparent at first that the building has strong roots in Piano's formative period in the 1960s, or that it exemplifies prime ideals of the Modern Movement. The section inevitably recalls that of the Graduate School of Design studios at Harvard University, by John Andrews (1968), in which studio space steps below a single sloping roof to foster a similar sense of participation in a common educational and research experience. The Vesima plan can be seen to come from the 1960s too. Entry is on a corner from which two axes stretch at right angles (one along the contour and out to a terrace, the other down the internal stair), with accommodation located between them in a rough triangle whose hypotenuse is stepped to give views in two directions. Such plans almost became clichés in some circles in the 1960s, though this one is utterly lacking any sense of contrivance.

Mostly, though, the building calls to mind some of the writings of this period by Reyner Banham. With automatically adjusting shading and natural convection currents up along the slope of the glass aiding the air conditioning, it reveals something of 'the well-tempered environment'. And the sense of being only minimally enclosed in an enveloping nature recalls Banham's article 'Home is not a House'. This was illustrated with a drawing of a man sitting naked in a forest glade enclosed in an air-conditioned bubble with his needs served by a central robot, the many arms of which held out all sorts of electronic devices. Here, paradise was regained in a technologically mediated Eden for an Adam who was at once both a hermit and plugged into the world. At Vesima, this dream has become both realistic and communal. Yet it is also touched by some of the spirit of a contemporaneous antithesis, the rustic homes of the woodbutcher's art in which hand-hewn natural materials added a tactile immediacy to the visual enjoyment of the surrounding nature.

But, perhaps more than this the ideal best realized at Vesima is unlikely to come to mind immediately because this building is so different from the modern architecture usually associated with that most potently pervasive of inspirational visions, Le Corbusier's trinity of *soleil, espace et verdure*.

85

10

11

12

13

1

2

86   **UNESCO Laboratory-workshop**

Elements and details of construction.

1, 2 Oblique views over the roof with its adjustable louvres and maintenance catwalks.

1 Looking up to the old farmhouse.

2 Looking down to the sea prior to installation of louvres and when roof was shaded by reed matting.

3 Axonometric of a corner bay with exploded cladding elements.

4 Junctions of laminated timber beams to each other and to the steel posts that support them.

5 Wall of tall glass sheets stiffened by very slender glass ribs.

6 Close-up of junction of steel joists to each other and to steel post that supports roof. The joists support the timber floor.

7 Looking down from the uppermost work level onto the levels below and the terraces they open out to. Note the flow of space and the sense of all the levels being open to each other and united by the embrace of the single sloping roof, and also the simplicity of the constructional elements and the minimalism of the detail.

8 Exploded isometric of elements that make up junction between beams and head of supporting post.

9 Isometric views: of beams and supporting steel post; of beams, glass stiffening rib and glazing.

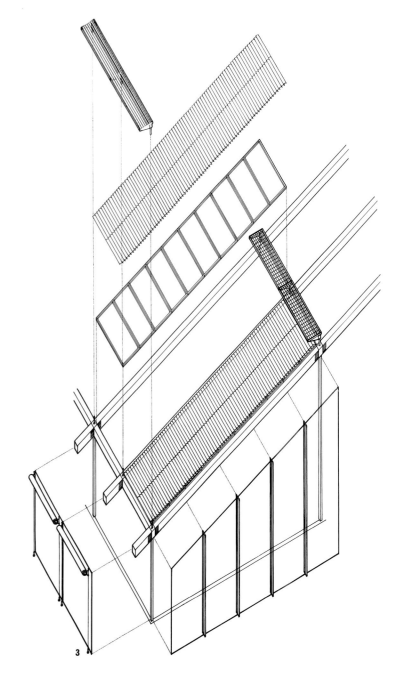

3

4

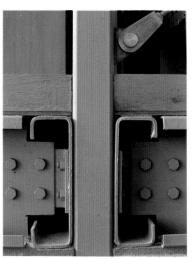

5

6

7

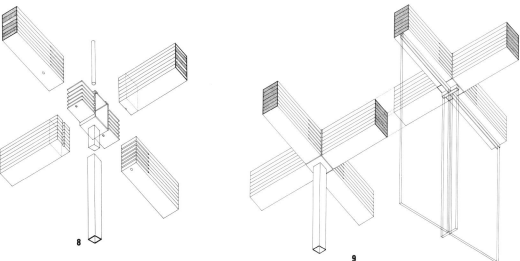

8

9

1

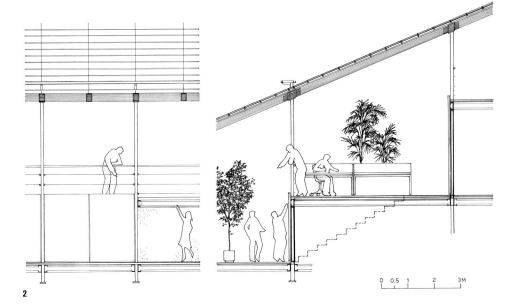

2

88   **UNESCO Laboratory-workshop**

1 Planted terrace on west.

2 Cross and longitudinal sections through bay.

3 Details of typical bay: **a** section of roof, **b** plan of external glazed wall, **c** section of floor **d** section of roof and elevation of post and floor joists **e** section of external glazed wall.

4 The ever-changing play of light on the sea is reflected on the glass wall of the south-east corner. The perspex discs on the ribs restrain the tall glass sheets.

5 Night view from east emphasizes the transparency and lightness that Piano always seeks.

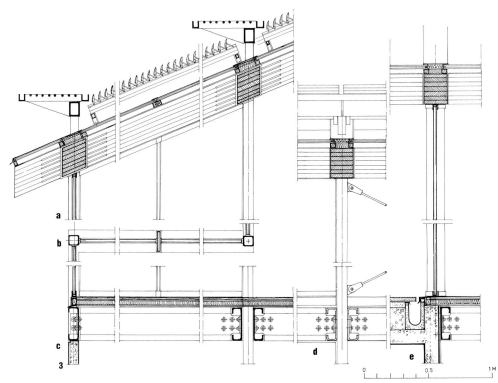

a

b

c

3   d   e

4

5

UNESCO Laboratory-workshop

6 View down onto lowest level and test structures for research into the use of bamboo.

Following page Night view from above sums up all the key aspects of the design: how the building is perched above the sea and reached only by funicular, the cabin of which is docked outside the entrance; how the surrounding vegetation extends through the glass roofs and walls, and the sense of transparency and ethereality.

UNESCO Laboratory-workshop 91

Client Renzo Piano Building Workshop
Design team R Piano, M Cattaneo (architect in charge), F Marano (associate in charge) S Ishida (associate), M Lusetti, M Nouvion
Assisted by M Carroll, O Di Blasi, R V Trufelli, M Varratta
Model maker D Cavagna
Structural engineer P Costa
Soil engineer A Bellini, L Gattroronchieri
Bionic research CRSN (C Di Bartolo)
Landscape architect M Desvigne
Contractor Edilindustria Spa
Sub contractors:
glass walls and roof Focchi, Siv
wood structure and floors Habitat Legno
roofing Pati, Montefluos
solar controlled louvres and blinds Model System Italia
funicular Maspero Elevatori
furniture and fittings Gruppo Bodino
landscaping Nuovo Verde, Ratti Serra

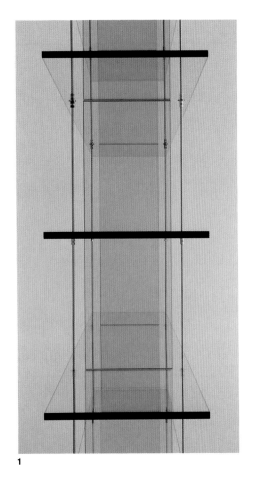

In the reception area of the UNESCO Laboratory-workshop, visitors are confronted by tables and shelves made almost entirely in glass, and therefore sympathetic in character to the understated yet virtuoso frameless glass walls of the building. The furniture comes from a range designed by the Building Workshop for the manufacturer, Fontanarte of Milan.

For Piano, the appeal of using glass for furniture is twofold: although, very heavy, the pieces have the visual lightness and transparency he often seeks, and so these large and solid objects have a very discreet presence. Secondly, a familiar material is being put to a new use that is at odds with its perceived fragility.

Although vulnerable to impact damage, glass is five to ten times as strong as concrete in compression. This characteristic has been exploited by adopting the same principle as post-tensioned concrete: steel rods are tensioned to compress the glass so that it can absorb non-compressive forces. This solution has proved necessary only with the vertical elements. The table tops and shelves are simply thick glass slabs that cantilever past their vertical supports sufficiently to introduce contraflexure and minimize deflection.

In the case of the tables, which come with circular or rectangular tops, the glass legs are secured by the same steel tension rods that pass down their centres to compress the glass. These rods are secured at their top by female-threaded elements countersunk flush with the table-top. At the foot, a similar element secures a steel plate that matches and protects the rectangular leg. When assembled and the rods are tensioned, the table is extremely rigid.

The shelving is even more simple in that the steel rods do not pass inside the verticals. Instead they pass through holes in the shelves and are exposed beside the glass verticals. These are held in place only by the compressive forces introduced by post-tensioning.

The system is elegant, clever and consistent with Piano's architectural approach, except in one crucial way. The table, with which people might enjoy prolonged close contact, lacks the sensual tactility that Piano often seeks in the warmth of wood and the subtly sculpted forms it can take.

1

Glass furniture system 1986–90

2

3

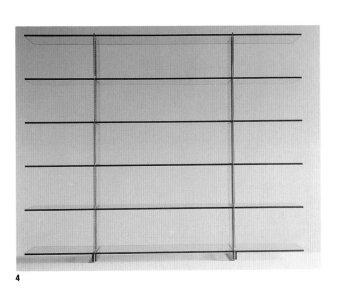

4

92

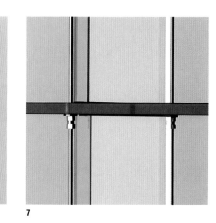

6

7

5

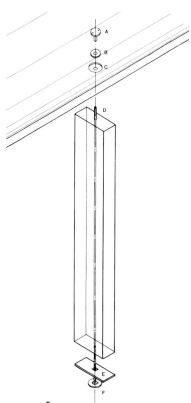

Glass furniture system

1 End-on view of bookcase.

2, **3** Alternative versions of the
rectangular-topped table.

4 Bookcase seen in elevation.

5 Exploded isometric of assembly of table leg.

6, **7** Close-up views of bookcase.

8, **9** Bookcase being assembled.

10 Elevation, section and details of steel
components of table leg.

Client Fontanarte

Design team R Piano, S Ishida (associate
architect), O Di Blasi

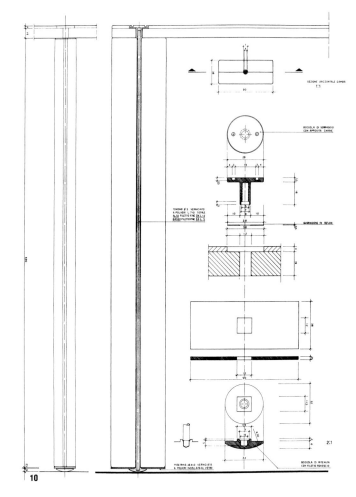

93

10

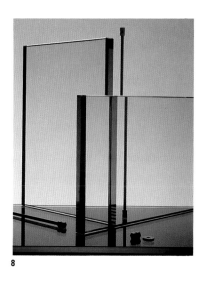

8

9

Columbus International Exposition Genoa, Italy 1984–92

Set in the very heart of Genoa, in the oldest part of its harbour, the Columbus International Exposition scheme served both a short-term event, celebrating the five-hundreth anniversary of the first voyage to America by the city's most famous son, and is a permanent enhancement of the city. It also initiated the much-needed regeneration of Genoa by contributing new facilities for the future, and regrounding the city in its past. The old city is now reconnected to the docks where new leisure and other facilities have been built, historic buildings restored and other long-hidden historic features returned to the view and awareness of the citizens. The scheme also provides a public place with a sense of openness and release that is so welcome in contrast to the claustrophobic confinement of the old city. When once again in regular use, it will add a whole new dimension to the life of the city and the way in which it is experienced.

Although it is a very important scheme for Genoa (and Piano's first, and long overdue, major work built in his native city) this mix of new construction with rehabilitation, conversion and archaeological revelation is not, for Piano and the Building Workshop, a particu-

larly seminal scheme that breaks much new ground. Instead it is one of summation and consolidation where previously developed approaches are brought together. For instance, renovated old buildings and tensile structures had already been used together for the Schlumberger Renovation in Paris (Volume One, p 90). And the terracotta cladding panels used on a new service spine and Harbour Master's office block are clearly derived from those used on the IRCAM Extension in Paris (Volume One, p 202). Yet the application of these different approaches in Genoa is particularly apt, as are the precisely judged hierarchies of visual prominence and reticence between the resulting parts. This scheme also deepens Piano's experience of handling a complex and many-layered historical legacy, and concludes an involvement in the harbour area that started with proposals to regenerate the adjacent Molo quarter.

The scheme was also consolidatory in another important way: it forged the Genoa branch of the Building Workshop into a larger yet tighter unity than in the past. Previously, small teams had worked on projects smaller than this one; but here,

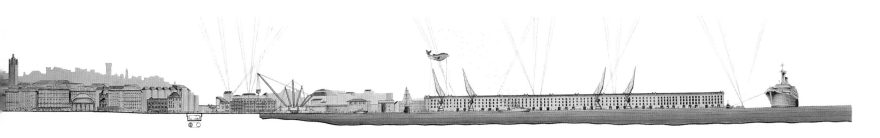

1

Columbus International Exposition

Historic city, harbour and *sopraelevata*.

1 Map of Genoa and harbour in 1766.

2 View over historic city to the sea.

3 Historic city and harbour severed from each other by the *sopraelevata*.

4 The *sopraelevata* blights the outlook of the *palazzata* of the Ripa on the left and isolates the Molo quarter, the first buildings of which protrude into bottom edge of photograph.

5, 6, 8 Narrow high-sided streets of the introverted historic city.

2

3

everybody collaborated on this large and complex scheme, executed only a few hundred metres from the office in Piazza San Matteo. Not only did it enable the Building Workshop to create a rich new synthesis of architectural approaches reintegrating the heart of its home city, but it gave all its members a chance to work together and to keep in constant touch with progress on site. Besides Piano and Shunji Ishida, those playing a major role in this project included Venanzio Truffelli, Mark Carroll, Musci Baglietto, Giorgio Bianchi, Giorgio Grandi, Donald Hart, Claudio Manfreddo and Olaf de Nooyer. More than that, this project also brought the Building Workshop back together with past collaborators, such as Giulio Macchi who had directed Piano's 'Open Site' television programmes.

A new and important collaborator was Mario Semino, Genoa's ex-Superintendent of Historic Monuments, who became a consultant for the restoration of the historic buildings.

Adding quite another dimension during the most intense latter part of this project was the presence in Genoa of another large team which was working up and preparing the construction drawings for the Kansai International Airport Terminal in Osaka (Volume One, p 24). Several key members of this team came over from the Paris office and others were recruited from abroad. So the contrasts between this local project, with its thorough enmeshment in history, and the distant all-new airport on its artificial island, was paralleled in the make-up of their respective project teams. Those working on the exposition project were mainly Italian or foreigners long-resident in Genoa; the Kansai team was thoroughly international. To the excitement stirred by such contrasts, and also by the pressure and long hours endured by the international team developing so quickly such a large and innovative project as the airport terminal, were added the continual comings and

goings of clients, consultants and sub-contractors. These experiences established a new phase in the evolution of the Building Workshop. For the first time, perhaps, the Genoa base entirely realized the spirit that Piano always had envisioned for it.

Embraced by encircling mountains, Genoa has always been close-packed against its harbour. From its beginnings in the eastern corner of the bay, the site of Expo '92, the harbour and city expanded together slowly westwards. Today, the Porto Vecchio fills the whole bay front, its western half still busy with ferries to Corsica and Sardinia and the occasional cruise ship. Farther west, and outside the bay, the Porto Nuovo serves the adjacent heavy industry. But with containerization, most cargo has moved to a new harbour away from the city and some distance still farther west. With this progressive western movement, the eastern part of the Porto Vecchio fell into disuse. Yet this was the historic heart of the port, where some of the city's most important monuments, the Ripa and the Palazzo San Giorgio, once confronted the sea.

In 1133, the Consuls of the Commune of Genoa decreed

4

5

6

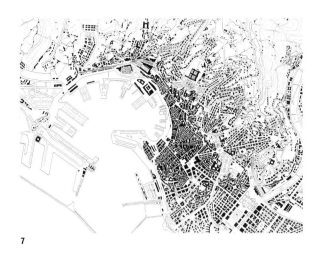

7

the building of the Ripa, so as to return the waterfront to public ownership. This consists of a 900-metre long public portico that merchants were required to construct and maintain along the edge of the quayside before they were allowed to build above it their *palazzata*, which formed such a fine frontage to the city. Then, in 1260, the dictator Gugliemo Boccanegra started construction of the Palazzo San Giorgio as the seat of government, originally the only freestanding building in front of this facade. Later, this Gothic structure became the customs house and then, in 1408, the seat of the Bank of San Giorgio, the main financial institution of Genoa, the original city of international finance. The palace was extended seawards over landfill in the sixteenth century and the new facades decorated with the

trompe-l'oeil frescoes typical of the region. Although repainted earlier this century, these frescoes had disappeared again, partly due to the wartime bombing that destroyed much of the docks, before being repainted for the Exposition.

The once wonderfully direct relationship between the city and its harbour was progressively eroded as the quayside was built outwards in several stages and new buildings were built on the landfill, especially south of the Palazzo San Giorgio. And then this direct contact was abruptly severed altogether in 1835 when, as one of a series of ambitious infrastructure improvements, the occupying Kingdom of Sardinia started construction on what became known as the 'marble terraces'. Built directly in front of the Palazzo San Giorgio and extending northwards from it, these consisted of a high, deep wall containing customs offices and warehouses. On top was a broad promenade that offered fine views of the city and the sea which it served to keep apart.

Barely 50 years later this enormous edifice was demolished to make way for a less formidable barrier, the railway. But what really separated the harbour from the city and the

daily life of its citizens was the reorganization of the whole length of the docks with new quays and piers, warehouses and industrial buildings, and no less than three railway stations. In 1965 this separation was brutally reinforced by the construction of an elevated motorway, the *sopraelevata*, a piece of staggering vandalism, even by the destructive standards of that environmentally benighted decade. Although the railway lines have now gone, the *sopraelevata* remains, whizzing by right in front of the *palazzata* of the Ripa and the Palazzo San Giorgio. It even slices through some very fine seventeenth-century buildings that are now part of the Exposition site. And although the *sopraelevata* enjoys views of the docks, below it walls and fences and a busy road continued to sever city from harbour.

On taking its present name in 1981, one of the first commissions the Renzo Piano Building Workshop received was from the municipality of Genoa. It was asked to apply to a project of physical and community regeneration an approach similar to that pioneered by Piano & Rice Associates at Otranto (Volume One, p 68). This had involved

97

9

8

10

11

12

1

98   **Columbus International Exposition**

Molo urban regeneration project.

1 Only the rooftop of this dense and decrepid quarter get sun and fresh air.

2, **3** Proposals from current study: **2** section, and **3** roof-level plan of public facilities.

4, **5** Inclined mirrors lean into narrow streets to reflect skylight into the buildings.

6, **7** South-east corner of old harbour with the old city behind in **6** and Molo in **7**.

8 Cranes adjacent Magazzini del Cotone, and

9 base of old crane, restored and relocated.

10 Site plan of Exposition: **a** the Molo, **b** Palazzo San Giorgio, **c** Piazza Caricamento, **d** aquarium, **e** Italian Pavilion, **f** Via del Mare, **e** Bigo, **g** Millo, **h** bonded warehouses, **i** exposed edge of old wharf, **j** Harbour Master's office, **k** parking garage, **l** service spine, **m** Magazzini del Cotone.

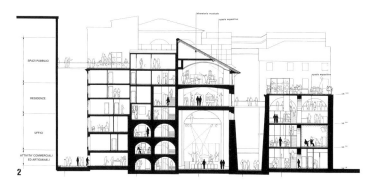

2

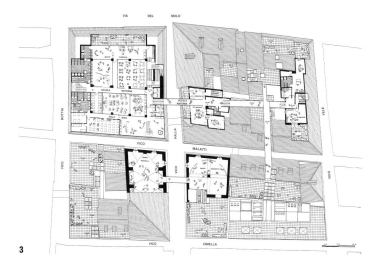

3

the participation of the local community and craftsmen to regenerate a historic town with minimal disruption of its social and physical fabric. The quarter to be regenerated in Genoa was the Molo, a pocket of development on a promontory that juts out into the eastern end of the bay.

One of the oldest quarters of Genoa, in the thirteenth century the Molo became an area of silos and depots for the harbour as well as a residential district. Its state of neglect grew worse after being cut off from the rest of the city by the *sopra-elevata*. Here, as is typical of Genoa, lack of land had forced the expansion of original buildings upwards so that they now rise to seven or eight storeys and the streets between them are very narrow so that little light or fresh air can penetrate. The resulting damp and fetid conditions were already notoriously unhealthy in the seventeenth and eighteenth centuries.

Despite these problems, the Building Workshop's unrealized scheme proposed that the old fabric be kept but rezoned in vertical strata and that some simple devices be introduced which were updated versions of those traditionally used in Genoa. Apart from some cultural uses, such as the conversion of an acoustically-apt salt silo into a concert hall, the lower two floors of the build-

ings would have been given over to commercial uses. The middle levels would have been upgraded as housing, and the upper levels and roof tops converted to such public uses as nursery schools and playgrounds, bars and pedestrian circulation.

The traditional device of using white boards, which lean into the street outside windows and reflect light from above into the buildings, was to be updated. Roof-top mirrors were to reflect more light down into the streets, onto the now mirrored tops of the boards and so into the buildings. And black glass solar chimneys were to be inserted into light wells to induce convection currents that would suck up stale air, thus introducing some natural ventilation. At roof level, circulation routes were to be formed using elevated walkways and bridges that would be the contemporary equivalents of those giving roof-top access to many buildings on Genoa's steeper slopes. These contiguous upper-level routes would have allowed all main vertical circulation up to them, and so also to the upper levels of the apartments below, to be concentrated at only three cores. This would have obviated the need for constructing lift shafts in such places as the already tiny light-wells.

It is a pity that this Molo

4

5

6

7

10

scheme was not implemented, as it was among the most interesting of such schemes by Piano. But, as part of the continuing regeneration of the old city sparked by the Columbus Exposition, the Building Workshop has been commissioned to reappraise and make new proposals for the Molo. These continue the spirit of the earlier plans but are somewhat simplified and more pragmatic, and so rather less exuberant.

Later in 1981, the Building Workshop was asked by the municipality to make a brief study of the much larger area between the Molo and the Palazzo San Giorgio, much of which eventually became part of the Exposition site. Central to this undeveloped project were emphases which continue in the Exposition scheme, on relinking the city with the sea, and providing uses and urban experiences absent from the existing city. Missing, however, was the rediscovery, reuse and restoration of the historic city fabric that is an equally important aspect of the design process and final form of the more recent and executed Exposition scheme.

To reconnect the city and the sea, the 'Axis of Services', as this unrealized 1981 study was known, proposed burying the *sopraelevata* in a tunnel below a broad landscaped piazza that reached from the Ripa to the water's edge. Submerged alongside the road was to be a metro line and station and, between these and the sea, a parking garage for 2 000 cars. Above this, the piazza would have accommodated various outdoor leisure facilities and events. Built over existing wharves, and then extending inland over part of the piazza, were to be new commercial buildings. From an inland end of much the same height as the cornices of the Ripa *palazzata*, whose porticoes they would have addressed with open porches between tall *pilotis*, the roof terraces of these new buildings would have stepped progressively downwards as they approached and projected into the sea. Again, nothing came of this study. Piano now feels this is just as well because these rushed proposals did not deal with the full complexities of the situation.

Because of its long-term involvement in the area, and its status as the region's most internationally illustrious architectural practice, the Building Workshop was the obvious choice to masterplan and design the buildings for the 1992 Columbus International Exposition. The theme proposed and developed for the Exposition was (in contradistinction from Seville's simultaneous exposition) the sea, and the history of ships and

8

9

99

1

Previous page Aerial view clearly shows the Exposition site and its structures and their relationship with the historic city in the foreground.

3

4

5

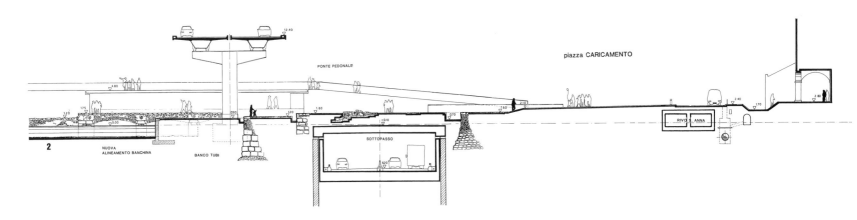

2

piazza CARICAMENTO

PONTE PEDONALE

NUOVA
ALINEAMENTO BANCHINA

BANCO TUBI

SOTTOPASSO

RIVO S. ANNA

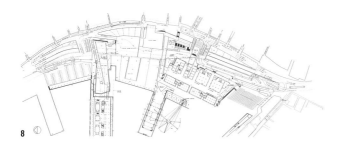

navigation. A central aim of the Building Workshop's master-plan was again to reconnect city and sea. As a reflection of the historic and nautical themes of the Exposition great emphasis was also placed on restoring some of the fine historic dockside buildings and exposing and conserving other traces of the sea-faring past.

Most significant among the restored buildings are a row of seventeenth-century bonded warehouses against the *sopraelevata* on the northern edge of the site, and a nineteenth-century cotton warehouse, the Magazzini del Cotone, which stretches 390 metres along a wharf in the south-western part of the site. Also retained, though not treated with similar respect, is an undistinguished warehouse building called the Millo, between the historic bonded warehouses and the water's edge. New structures include an aquarium on the northern edge of the site, a service spine behind the Magazzini del Cotone, the Harbour Master's office and Il Grande Bigo, a gigantic derrick that stands in front of the Millo.

In the early phases of master-planning the Exposition, the Building Workshop again proposed putting the *sopraelevata* in a long tunnel, which at one stage was even aligned to pass under the water. But such options were rejected as too expensive. Instead, it was decided to bury the ground-level road that runs beside the *sopraelevata*, for a short stretch in front of the Palazzo San Giorgio. This has allowed the Piazza Caricamento to be created around the palazzo. Once the railings around the Exposition site are removed, the piazza will extend from the porticoes of the Ripa right to the water's edge. Pedestrians will then be able to move freely between these two on their way to and from the new waterside facilities. The old city will thus, at last, be reconnected with the harbour which forms its ancient focus.

Excavations in the harbour area, and for the new submerged road and the metro station, which the Building Workshop is now building, revealed a wealth of archaeological remains. These include remnants of piers and quaysides from various periods between Roman times and the nineteenth century. The intention was that these would all be left exposed and that the Piazza Caricamento would become an archaeological park, a civic square in which traces of Genoa's history are revealed. Unfortunately, time and money ran out before the opening of the Exposition and most of these remains were quickly covered with earth and asphalt. This is to be removed later and work completed, but as yet no funds are available.

Columbus International Exposition

Historic relics.

1 Corner of docks as they were when freight was still handled.

2 Section through Piazza Caricamento as it is intended to be, an archaelogical park exposing historical remnants. In the background is an abandoned proposal for a footbridge to link piazza and aquarium.

3–7 Fragments from different ages exposed during excavations for construction.

8 Plan which charts the changes to the water's edge over the centuries.

9 Historic dry dock adjacent the site.

10, 11 Finely detailed edges of old wharves exposed during construction.

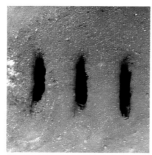
9

6

7

10

11

1

Columbus International Exposition

Looking back across the water.

1 View from the Via del Mare of, from the left, the end of the aquarium, the *sopraelevata* with the historic city and the *trompe l'oeil* decorated facade of the Palazzo San Giorgio behind it, and then the Bigo's spreading booms and tent with wind sculptures and Millo behind them.

2 Sectional elevation of harbour showing Bigo, tent and wind sculptures, with Palazzo San Giorgio and the Millo behind them.

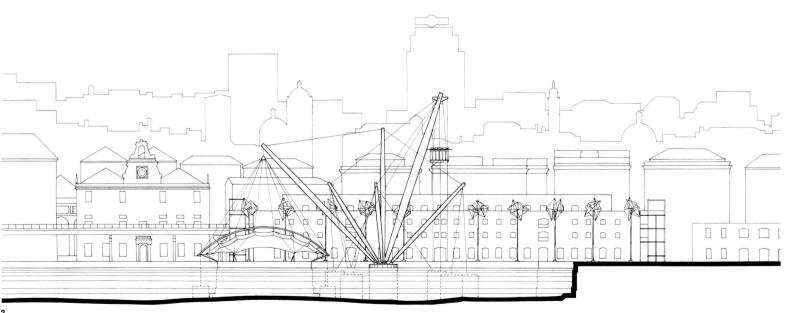

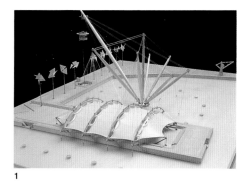

1

Columbus International Exposition

Erecting Bigo and tent.

1 Model.

2 Booms of Bigo being lifted into position.

3–6 Tent being raised and secured.

2

3

Most visually arresting of the new structures, both in location and exuberant design, is the Bigo, the symbol of the Exposition. This gigantic derrick is composed of huge hollow-steel booms, circular in section and tapered at each end. (These were made in sections in Parma and welded together on site.) These booms reach out in an expansive, welcoming gesture from a shared base set in the sea, seven of them leaning away from a vertical central member. The shorter booms prop the cables that stay the larger arms. The largest boom supports a panoramic lift that spins slowly as it rises on its central cable to offer fine views of the city and harbour. Two other booms hold aloft elements from which cables radiate to pick up the curving spars that support a Teflon-coated fabric roof. This roof covers a pier, the Piazza delle Feste, which is a festive multi-purpose performance area. It is daylit through its open sides and translucent roof and through clear glass rooflights that offer views of the supporting structure above. The first performance held here was devised and directed by Vittorio Gassman and based on the story of *Moby Dick*. Both set and 'whale' were designed by the Building Workshop and assembled from curved timber ribs.

Tented roofs, which were inspired originally perhaps by Frei Otto as well as by Archigram's carnivalesque projects, are recurrent features in Piano's work. This one (which together with the derrick structure was designed in collaboration with Peter Rice) is especially striking, however, in both form and detail. More than that, it is particularly apt in the associations it conjures. Just as the derrick recalls those of ships and wharfside, so it and the tent sound other nautical resonances with their rigging, curving spars and taut sail-like fabric forms. The Bigo lift cabin, which resembles a latter-day crow's-nest, reinforces these associations. Also attracting attention, and animating the front of the mundane Millo building, are the spinning, multi-sailed wind sculptures that sit atop a row of poles, which extend on either side of the Bigo. These sculptures, which call attention to the ambient power that drove Columbus' frail ships, were designed by the Japanese artist Susumu Shingu. (Shingu is collaborating with the Building Workshop on other projects, such as sculptures whose animation will make visible the air movement in Kansai airport's scoop-like open ducts.)

4

5

6

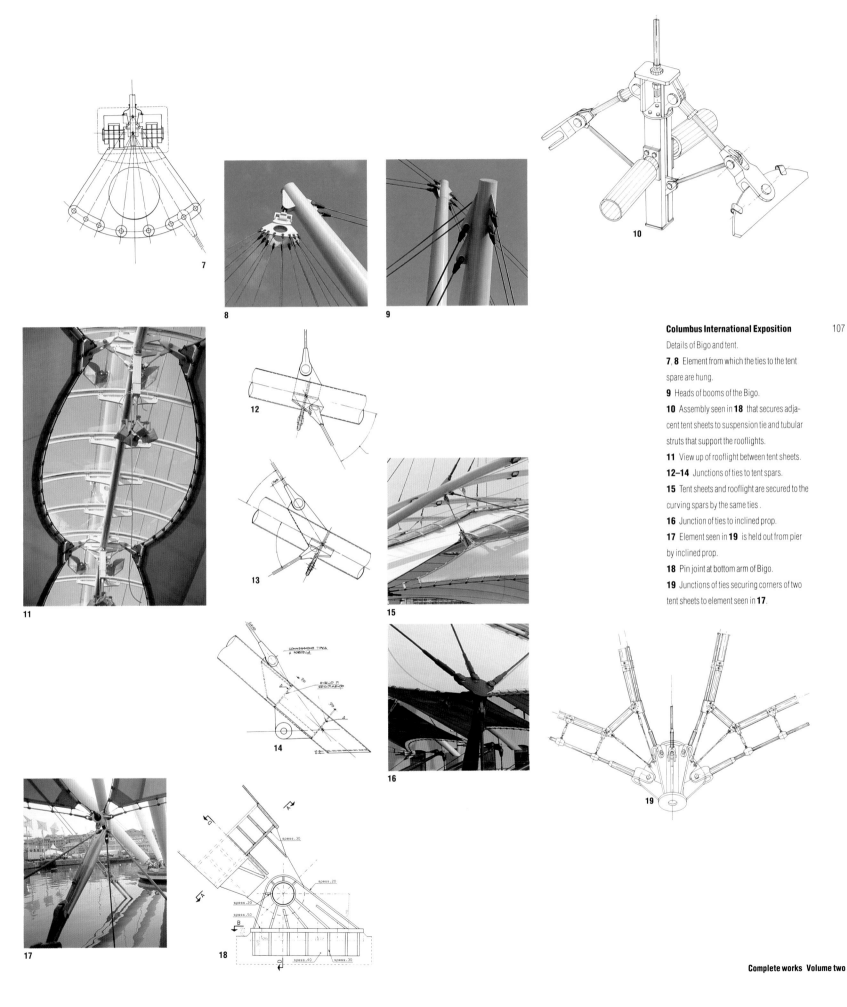

Details of Bigo and tent.

7, 8 Element from which the ties to the tent
spare are hung.

9 Heads of booms of the Bigo.

10 Assembly seen in **18** that secures adjacent tent sheets to suspension tie and tubular
struts that support the rooflights.

11 View up of rooflight between tent sheets.

12–14 Junctions of ties to tent spars.

15 Tent sheets and rooflight are secured to the
curving spars by the same ties .

16 Junction of ties to inclined prop.

17 Element seen in **19** is held out from pier
by inclined prop.

18 Pin joint at bottom arm of Bigo.

19 Junctions of ties securing corners of two
tent sheets to element seen in **17**.

108 **Columbus International Exposition**

Bigo and wind sculptures.

1 Elevation

2 Plan

3 Exposition seen from roof top terrace of the Millo. In the foreground are the spinning wind sculptures by Susumu Shingu. Behind these are the giant derrick-like arms of the Bigo, the tent that is suspended from it over a pier used for performances, and the panoramic lift cabin that spins slowly as it rises and descends. In the background is the aquarium, and then the city and the mountains that compress Genoa against the sea.

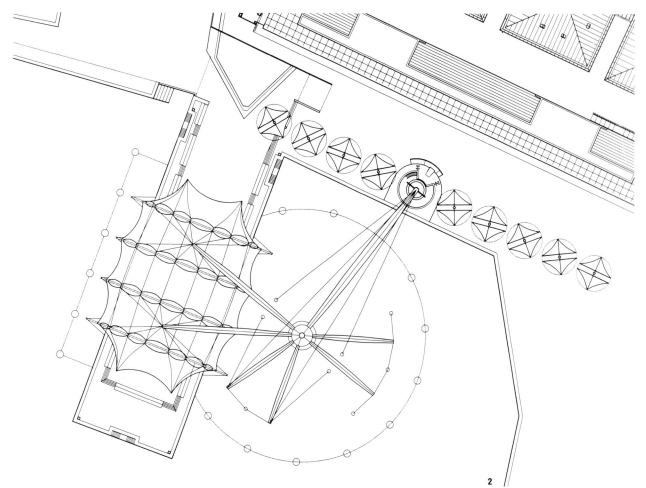

1

2

3

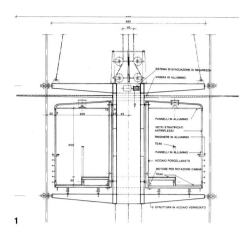

1

2

3

110 **Columbus International Exposition**

Lift cabin and wind sculptures.

1 Section of cabin that rotates within a separate structural chassis.

2, 3 Cabin with: **2** the arms of the Bigo and the cables that secure them and raise and lower the cabin, and **3** the sails of the wind sculptures.

4, 5 Close up views of sails that catch the wind and spin.

6 Details of head of arm of Bigo that supports lift cabin.

Installation under tent for performance of Moby Dick.

7 Set being constructed and lit.

8, 9 Stage and audience were installed on the deck of Captain Ahab's ship.

10 Longitudinal section.

11 Detail section through seating.

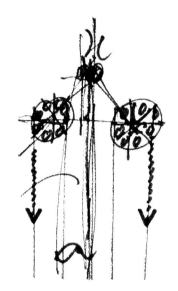

4

5

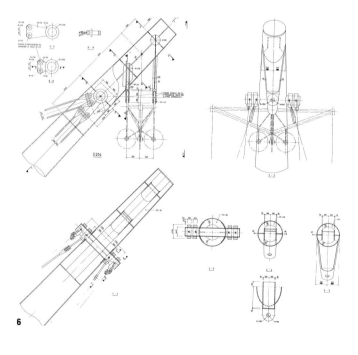

6

7

8

9

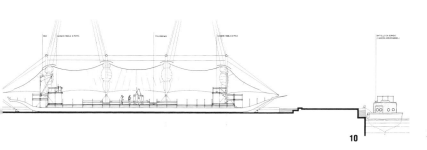

10

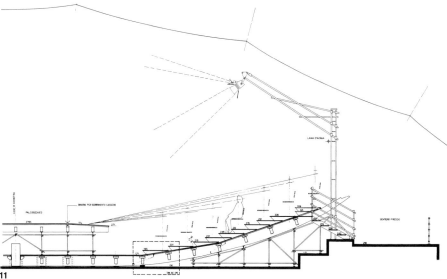

11

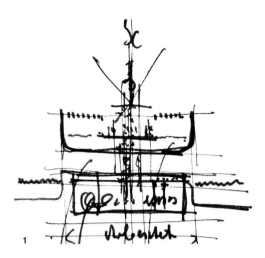

Columbus International Exposition

Aquarium

1 Piano's concept sketch of a water-filled hull raised above pier, below which is the mechanical plant.

2, **3** Construction views.

4 Elevation.

5 Longitudinal section.

6 The aquarium juts out into the harbour beyond the Bigo like a ship at berth.

After the central, spiky sculptural focus of the Bigo, the next most noticeable of the new structures are the raised and elongated aquarium and the ship-like Italian Pavilion. These project into the bay and together with a promenade, the Via del Mare, which extends past the pavilion yet further into the bay, they define the northern edge of the Exposition site. The aquarium and the pavilion both continue the nautical theme but reverse expectation as to where water tanks and grand gallery might be. Because the pavilion actually floats, its main exhibition floor is below water-level, while the aquarium holds its heavy tanks aloft inside the raised hull-like segments of its superstructure.

The American practice, Cambridge Seven Associates, which specializes in aquarium design, collaborated on the aquarium's interior design and exhibits. It is built over an old wharf, the Ponte Spinola. This was excavated behind its old sea walls, which were then tanked to create a large basement for all the mechanical plant upon which the aquarium depends. Beneath the two-storey aquarium, which is raised aloft on circular concrete columns, the reinstated quayside level has been left largely clear, except where enclosed as cafes, service and circulation cores. As well as carrying the internal structure, the concrete columns support exposed steel members, which in turn secure the pre-cast concrete cladding units that enclose the building's outermost longitudinal walls. At these points, the superstructure cantilevers out from the columns, and its soffit curves up to become the outer walls so that its raised form evokes the ships in the dry docks nearby. The aquarium is thus a curious inversion of Noah's ark, in that it is held up in the air, and holds fish and seals safely above a polluted sea.

Also very nautical, with its rather over-detailed teak treads and steel railings, is the external entrance stair at the eastern end of the building, which climbs upward to meet a deck that leads back to the entrance doors. This curious arrangement is the vestige of an earlier intention that this deck be merely the end of a pedestrian bridge which, as a sort of elongated gangplank, would have offered direct access from the north-east corner of Piazza Caricamento – thereby also extending one of the new buildings under the *sopraelevata* to emphasize the re-established link between the old city and its harbour.

In plan, the two levels of the aquarium are organized in five linear strips of differing width, length and function. The central strip handles all vertical movement of people and services and contains several staircases, including the external stairs at each end of the building, as well as many ducts, and both passenger and goods lifts. To one side of this is a broad circulation strip that extends right through the building from the entrance doors at one end to the exit at the other. But what might have been a straight promenade is blocked here and there so that the flow of visitors is guided throughout the building.

2

3

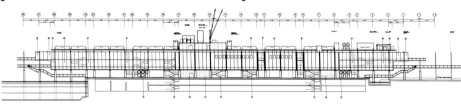

4

5

6

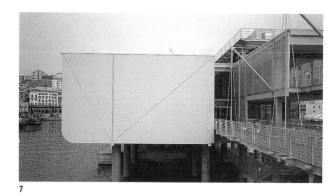
7

On the upper level, fish tanks set within it sometimes block this strip. On the western side of this circulation zone, the widest of the strips is taken up mostly by the main tanks, although it also includes an orientation room and an auditorium. The tanks are arranged to be viewed from both levels of the circulation strip, the lower level giving an underwater view and the upper level looking onto the surface which is brightly lit from a glass roof overhead. The intended route for visitors is from the orientation room to the bottom and front of the auditorium. Then, after an introductory audio-visual presentation, visitors will leave through the rear of the auditorium to view the tanks from the upper level.

On the other side of the central vertical circulation zone is a strip of long narrow light-wells and circulation bridges.

Columbus International Exposition

Aquarium

7 Western end of aquarium seen from Italian Pavilion.

8, **9** Displays in exhibition areas.

10 Cross section.

11 Walkway, for feeding and maintenance, above tanks and below skylight.

12 Shark tank.

And beyond this is a strip that will house offices and research laboratories, but during the Exposition served as exhibition space. The two levels of this space were at one time to have housed the Italian Pavilion. But when it became clear that, for various reasons, the aquarium was not going to be fully completed in time for the Exposition, it was decided to build quickly a separate structure for the national pavilion. Lack of suitable free land within the site, the presence of the adjacent shipyards and an earlier idea of converting a ship all led to the decision to build a floating pavilion. During the Exposition, only the lower of the aquarium's exhibition levels was used. It showed such relics of marine life as corals and whale skeletons.

The design of the aquarium includes other nautical gestures besides the detailing of the external stairs, the elongated form of the aquarium and the sweeping curve between the external concrete walls and the first-floor soffit that give it its ship-like shape. Among these gestures are the small round-cornered windows set in the concrete walls, the freestanding ventilators for the basement plant room and the orange-painted funnels rising above a

balcony, suggestive of the captain's bridge. Yet, for the most part, the exterior is a direct expression of the internal arrangements. Each strip of the plan is only as long as is required. That, combined with only the outer strips being encased in the cladding with hull-like curves (so that the building looks like a ship still in construction), gives the aquarium that air of incompleteness and indeterminacy which is still sometimes a hallmark of Piano's work. Like the Menil Collection in Houston (Volume One, p 140) which is another long building whose exterior merely manifests the interior, this is a rather awkward building externally. Emphasizing the sense of incompleteness and awkwardness, some of the detailing, particularly of the glazing, also seems rather poorly resolved, despite the long design period and its intentional 'roughness'.

A characteristic of Piano's architecture is that it is not fetishistically detailed throughout, as are many British High-Tech buildings, but often gets

113

8

9

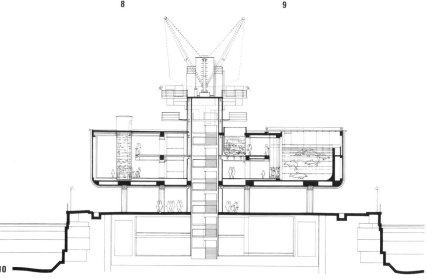
10

11

12

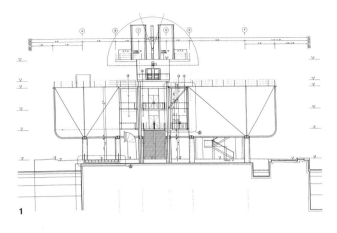

1

Columbus International Exposition

Aquarium.

1 Cross section through entrance landing.

2 Plan at first floor level: **a** entrance, **b** orientation, **c** tanks, **d** exhibition.

3 Plan at pier level.

4 Model of first proposal by James Carpenter for rooflight made of dichroic glass. It was to light the orientation room.

5 Aquarium is raised on cylindrical columns above pier and Via del Mare on left.

6 Entrance is reached by external stair that climbs away from the building.

7 Via del Mare extends out from under aquarium, past the ship-like Italian Pavilion and towards the centre of the harbour.

8 Exploded isometric view of the components with which the outer bays are assembled.

much of its more relaxed and humane quality through playing elegant and highly crafted detail against more matter-of-fact and sparingly detailed construction. The Menil Collection is a clear example of this. But at the aquarium, for instance, the fritted white horizontal stripes, which extend right across the large sheets of glass, are particularly disturbing on the interior. The stripes would probably have looked much better if they had stopped short of the mullions to leave a clear frame right around the fritted area. Certainly this would have been more consistent with the detailing of balustrades as independent elements set between supporting posts.

As they enter the aquarium, visitors are immediately deflected off the central circulation strip into the orientation room. Roof-lit and with dark walls (except for one which is

entirely taken up by a narrow tank displaying starfish against a stone wall) and jammed with tall bamboo, the effect is startlingly subaqueous. In navigating between the bamboo, visitors could easily imagine themselves as fish negotiating kelp. The impression of being underwater probably will be intensified if the proposal ever goes ahead to install a rooflight designed by James Carpenter, the New York-based master craftsman of new glass technologies. The rooflight's dichroic glass changes colour with the movement of sun and spectator, just as the light on the surface of rippling water changes when viewed from below. Particularly fine is the first of Carpenter's two proposals in which the glass is designed to flare from a circular top to a square bottom, grading imperceptibly from truncated cone to pyramid.

With Italy's present economic and political upheavals, the future of the rooflight and the programme for completing all parts of the aquarium

remain unsettled. As set up for the Exposition, only parts of the main entrance level were open to visitors who passed from the orientation room to the exhibition space on the other side of the circulation strips. Here, a cylindrical tank packed with a school of silvery sardines, which suddenly swirled this way and that, made a dramatic focus to the first room. Beyond the exhibition rooms, the route returned to the circulation spine, the dimly lit space of which widens against the floor-to-ceiling glass of the largest tanks. In the central third of each of these tanks, the 21cm-thick glass bulges inwards to form a viewing bay. Here visitors could feel almost as if surrounded by sharks or seals rather than merely looking at them.

The pair of freestanding columns in front of each of these tanks is about the only indication of either structure or primary construction on the interior. No matter how well the building serves its display functions, it is exceptional in Piano's *oeuvre* as it reveals internally almost nothing of its own structure and offers no characteristic 'piece' to view. Even with such buildings as the Rue de Meaux Housing in Paris (Volume One, p 214), the cladding panels make their presence apparent inside.

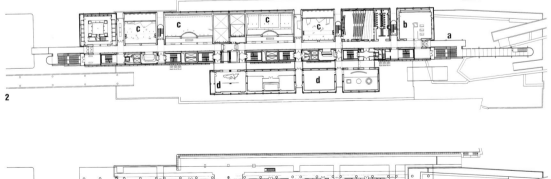

2

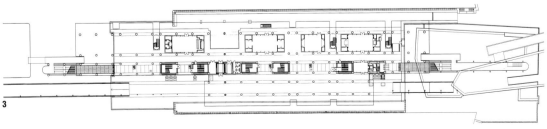

3

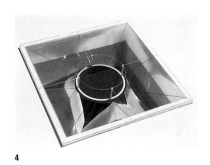

4

5

6

7

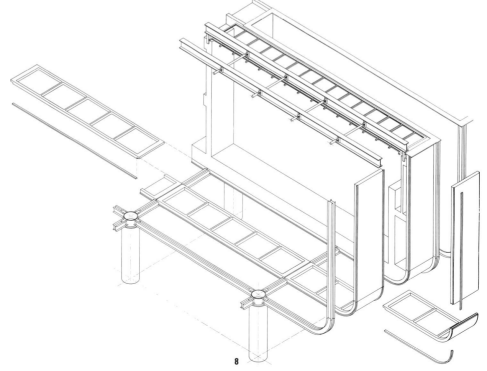

8

1

2

116   **Columbus International Exposition**

Italian Pavilion.

1 Looking east along Via del Mare to ship-like Italian Pavilion.

2 Deck of Italian pavilion looking towards the ship-like superstructure.

3 View from the superstructure deck of the Italian pavilion.

4, **5** Longitudinal section.

From the aquarium exit, the route proceeded to the bare deck of the floating Italian Pavilion. Built like a barge, which it basically is, and so again exhibiting no characteristic 'piece', this is a strange object with a broad, symmetrical, ship-like hull and asymmetrical superstructure. The ship-like form is in large part a hangover from an earlier idea, one eventually taken up at the exposition by Japan. This was to convert a ship to serve as the Italian Pavilion and to sail it to various ports to generate publicity prior to opening the Exposition. The asymmetry of the superstructure is then partly an acknowledgement that this is not a real ship – as well as an expression of Piano's aversion to gratuitous symmetry. Yet, as the exhibition inside showed, it can also be seen as reflecting a current trend in ship design:

many sorts of ship are now merely functional contraptions devoid of the grace that was once assumed to be the natural consequence of form following function.

More probably, the conflict between symmetry and asymmetry reflects Piano's ambivalence about simply carrying forward the earlier idea and following the literal dictates of contextual propriety (which might suggest that a dockside, floating vessel should be ship-like) and the absence of good reason for any new Italian Pavilion, whether floating or not, to resemble a ship at all. The result, however, might still be too literal, more so than any Post-Modernist would dare. And it lacks the knowing irony and humour with which Post-Modernists attempt to have their cake and eat it – that is by using overtly recognizable forms yet simultaneously distancing themselves from them by presenting them as parody. To contain an audio-visual show, the Building Workshop also designed a literal yacht modelled on its sponsor's posters for cigarettes. This heels in a sea of asphalt that swells past it as a bow wave and so, thanks to this surreally

3

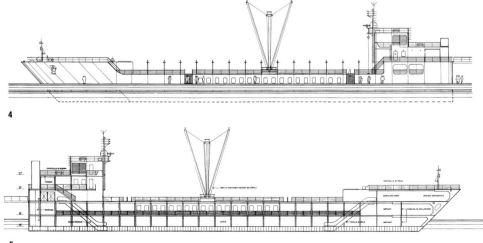

4

5

6

Columbus International Exposition

Italian Pavilion.

6 Floating pavilion seen across Via del Mare with aquarium beyond.

7, **8** Cross sections with Via del Mare: **7** looking west, **8** looking east.

9, **10** Views of the exhibition: **9** perspex globes and video monitors explain natural phenomena such as ocean currents and weather patterns, and **10** shows how other exhibits were displayed on plinths that looked as if they were the delivery crates for the exhibits.

11 Replica of one of Columbus' caravelles with the Bigo beyond.

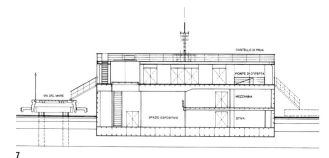

7

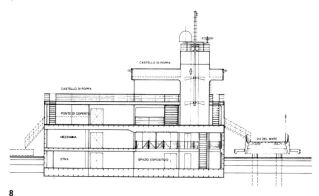

8

humorous touch, might leave some architects and critics less uneasy than would the Italian Pavilion.

An escalator took visitors down into the vessel's hull, which served as a large exhibition hall. This had its sides painted black so that it disappeared while the exhibits stood out in spot-lighting. The exhibition was curated by Giulio Macchi and included marvellous historic models of ships, real figureheads and hundreds of samples from an enormous contemporary collection of models, all to the same scale, of ships of every type throughout history. Some items sat on plinths that appeared to be the crates in which the exhibits had arrived – an idea originally and more logically proposed by Piano for travelling exhibitions.

In a didactic section, a number of Perspex globes and video monitors explained aspects of the earth's climate and ocean currents. For the design of the exhibition, the Building Workshop, with Giorgio Bianchi as well as Renzo Piano playing a large role, collaborated with architects, Marco and Matteo Lavarello, and with Franco Origoni. The latter was also responsible for the signage graphics used throughout the Exposition.

The Italian Pavilion, which like the rest of the structures that housed the Exposition, remains empty, unused and with an uncertain future, is moored against the Via del Mare. This promenade extends from the end of the Ponte Spinola, so that together they project some 350 metres into the middle of the harbour. Towards the end, a group of eighteenth-century barges were moored to form a sort of terminating piazza from where visitors could watch the ceremony that closed the Exposition each night. This consisted of a fanfare, composed by Luciano Berio, accompanied by fireworks set off from the base and tower of the Lanterna, Genoa's famous medieval lighthouse on the far side of the bay.

117

9

10

11

1

Columbus International Exposition

Magazzini del Cotone.

1 Eastern end of main quayside elevation.

2, **3** Views prior to restoration of: **2** exterior with staggered loading balconies, and

3 interior with cast iron columns and jack arches.

4 Portion of main (north) elevation as restored.

5 Portion of longitudinal section as restored.

6 Close up view of main elevation with new suspended balconies.

2

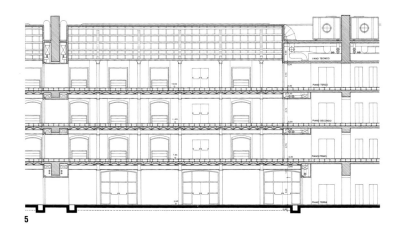

3

Across the water from the Via del Mare is the Magazzini del Cotone. The first nine bays of these cotton warehouses were built between 1895 and 1901 by British engineers who followed in their own country's fine Functionalist tradition of industrial and warehouse architecture. Cotton from ships was loaded directly into any of the four levels of the warehouses via balconies staggered on the facade. External walls are of rendered brickwork with exposed brick trim over, or right around, the larger openings. Inside is a frame of handsome cast iron columns and beams supporting jack-arch floors. In the 1920s another three similar, but inferior, bays were added, extending the building to 390 metres in length. Then repairs to bomb damage from World War II led to parts of the internal frame being replaced with concrete.

For the Exposition, the original bays were converted into spaces that served as showrooms for each of the participating countries. The intention was that at least some of these spaces would later be taken by the Department of Oceanography of the University of Genoa, while other parts might continue to be used as showrooms for specialist trade. These parts have been carefully restored and rehabilitated. Openings have been made through bulkhead walls that are now flanked by service cores containing lifts and stairs, ducts and lavatories. Inconsistently repaired parts of the structural frame were removed and replaced with new cast iron elements identical to the originals. And at the eastern end of the building, a well was cut through this frame to house the escalators, which rise from the main entrance hall.

The newer structural bays at the western end of the building were gutted completely so that only the external walls were left standing. The original window openings have been bricked up and a congress centre has been built within the space. Two identical 800-seat halls are arranged so that, when required, a wall separating their stages might be opened up to create a 1 600-seat hall. The resultant effect of looking from one hall to its mirror image is a considerable *coup de théâtre*. But with the seats disposed on either side of a central stage this is probably not the easiest of halls to use, even for concerts, with or without the aid of closed-circuit television projected onto large screens. Yet, given the space available, the solution adopted was the only way to get so many people close to the stage.

4

5

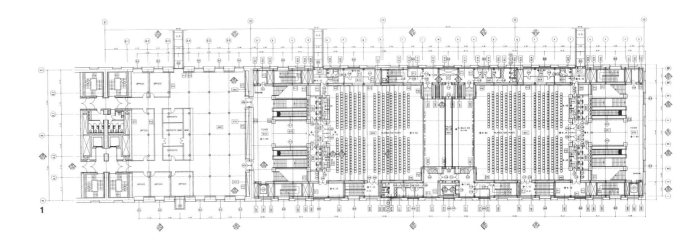

1

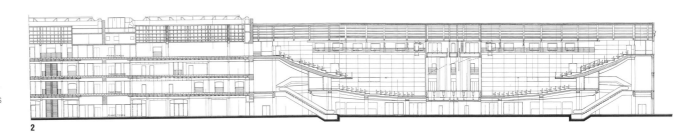

2

120 **Columbus International Exposition**

Magazzini del Cotone: congress centre

1 Plan.

2 Longitudinal section.

3 The two congress halls opened into one.
View from one hall across conjoined stages
and into the other hall.

Magazzini del Cotone: escalator hall and
typical modules

4 Plan of escalator hall and typical module.

5 Plan of pair of typical modules with services
and stairs against old bulkhead wall.

6 Entrance and escalator hall at eastern end.

7, **8** Interiors as renovated: **7** top floor, and
8 typical floor.

9 Cross section looking east through
escalator hall.

10 Cross section.

3

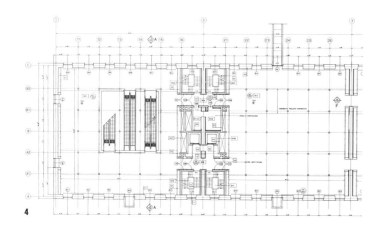

4

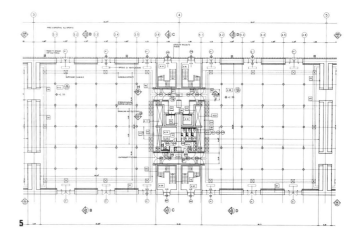

5

6

7

8

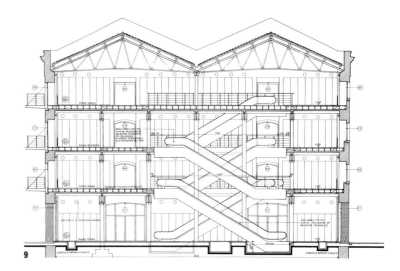

9

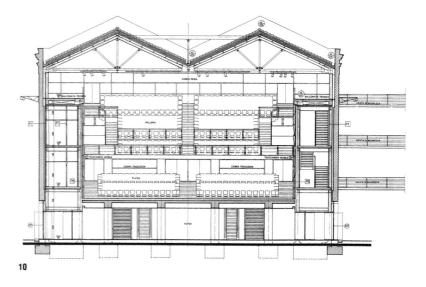

10

1

Columbus International Exposition

Service spine and Harbour Master's office.

1 Escape stair in western end of service spine.

2 Interior view of terracotta cladding to service spine.

3, **4** Comparative isometric views of assembly and details of: **3** structure and terracotta cladding of service spine, and **4** structure and glazing of Harbour Master's office.

5 Looking west with Harbour Master's office on left, Magazzini del Cotone on right, and service spine and bridges to it.

6, **7**, **8** Harbour Master's office: **6** north elevation, **7** east elevation, and **8** ground floor plan: **a** Harbour Master's office, **b** car park, **c** service spine, **d** Magazzini del Cotone.

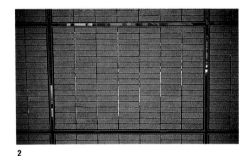

2

Behind the Magazzini del Cotone is a group of new buildings. Running parallel to, and almost the full length of, the cotton warehouse to which it is connected by bridges across a service lane, is the service spine. Besides housing new fire escapes additional to those in the old warehouse, this has space for storage and plant such as air conditioning. A multi-level parking garage is hidden behind the western part of the service spine, and projecting beyond the latter's eastern end are, at a slightly splayed angle to each other, the two wings of the Harbour Master's office. These wings range offices along both sides of a central corridor. But towards each end a single bank of offices extends alone, which expresses the strip-like composition of the plan and so suggests some slight familial similarity with the aquarium.

Both offices and service spine are clad (where not glazed or closed-in with panels of louvres, respectively) in aluminium-framed panels of terracotta units, which are very similar to those used on the tower of the IRCAM Extension in Paris (Volume One, p 202). Here, however, the terracotta is not as red and the units are smaller and not set so precisely in their panels as at IRCAM: the effect is a more subdued brown and slightly rougher. And where these walls meet sloping ground, the lowest modules are faced in stone, which is more readily trimmed to furnish the requisite angled bottom. Also, the cladding panels do not conceal the primary structure. Instead they are framed by the white-painted steelwork, which is expressed clearly to articulate what are much larger, if lower, buildings than the IRCAM tower.

In contrast to the sculpted components of the Bigo and its tent, which clearly express the structural stresses they are purpose-made to withstand, the structural elements of the service spine and office block are constructed from standard steel sections. The crisp composition and detail are abstractly graphic rather than sculptural, and express component assembly rather than structural forces. Yet, a comparison between the corners of office block and service spine shows that, in the precisely apt differences between the handling of the cladding and structure of these two buildings, there is also a concern with an expressive hierarchy that is true to the facts of construction.

On the service spine the terracotta cladding is merely a protective screen with no further weather protection or

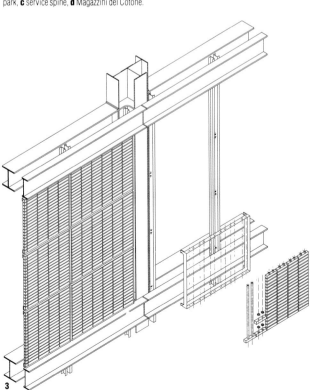

3

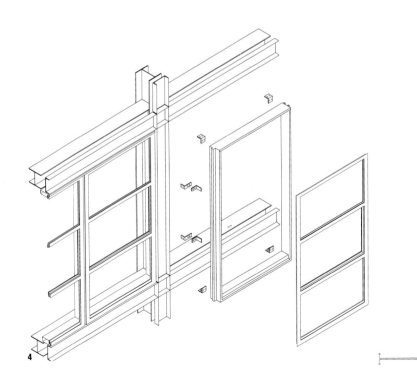

4

5

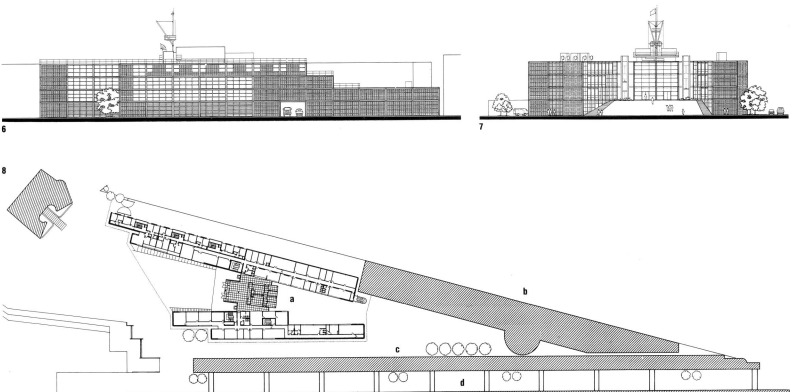

6

7

8

a

b

c

d

1

insulation behind it: light and air can pass through the chinks between the terracotta units. The panels are set just outside and stop short of the square columns to which the horizontal channel sections outside each floor are bolted. Projecting slightly forward of the terracotta and the columns, these horizontals dominate the facade. On the offices, however, the panels protect layers of weatherproofing and insulation. And they are set flush with a welded frame of steel channels in which horizontal and vertical members are equal in emphasis and face all but part of the outer corners of the fireproofed primary structure.

Also built in steel and detailed in the same manner as the bridges and stairs of the service spine, and to a lesser degree resembling the external stairs of the aquarium, are the new external escape stairs at each end of the Millo. Here, an obvious familial resemblance goes some way to suggesting a unity between the otherwise heterogeneous Exposition buildings. The Millo was not a building of much architectural value. Yet the Genoa municipality insisted on keeping it, partly because its large size and location made it inherently useful. But so that it would not overwhelm the outdoor spaces and other Exposition buildings, its top two floors were removed and the front of what is now the top floor set back to create a terrace. This terrace, which was part of a restaurant that filled this floor, commanded fine views of the Exposition and of the nightly closing ceremony. The three floors below served as showrooms for various commercial enterprises.

124 Columbus International Exposition

The Millo.

1 On the right, the warehouse as it was.

2 As converted with top floor terrace and steel escape stairs.

3, **4** Construction views.

5 Cross section of conversion.

6 Interwinding fire escape stairs.

7 Rear of Millo, with lift cabin of the Bigo peering over it, as glimpsed from between two of the bonded warehouses.

2

3

4

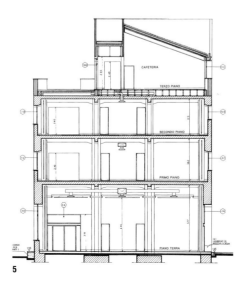

5

6

7

1   **2**   **3**

126   **Columbus International Exposition**

Restoration of bonded warehouses.

1, **2**, **3** Condition of seventeenth century
monuments prior to restoration: **1** the
sopraelevata is brutally juxtaposed to the rear
of the buildings, one of which was partially
demolished to accommodate it, **2** vaulted
interior, and **3** vestiges of *trompe l'oeil*
decoration.

4, **5** Restoration in process.

6 Front elevation of northernmost warehouse.

7 Section, and **8** ground floor plan of
southernmost warehouse with remnant of
promenade wall.

4

5

Behind the Millo and run-
ning parallel to it across a
stone-paved street, is the row
of four very fine seventeenth-
century bonded warehouses. At
right angles to the southern end
of this row, is a relic of an
enclosing wall from the same
period. Like all the old structures on site, these were in a
state of neglect. But the two
northernmost warehouses had
suffered also in being partially
demolished to make way for
the *sopraelevata*. Though these
parts could not be reinstated,
the buildings, with their
vaulted interiors, were otherwise carefully restored along
with the *trompe-l'oeil* frescoes
on their facades. During the
Exposition they served as independent pavilions, one of
which was taken by the USA.

Just as the excavations for
burying the road in front of the
Palazzo San Giorgio revealed a
wealth of archaeological
remains, so did those carried
out for construction and by
archaeologists in the dock area.
This led to the redesign of the
water's edge to show some of
its old alignments. Between the
Millo and the Magazzini del
Cotone, for instance, a channel
now extends in towards the old
town to show off the edge of
old wharves. The remnants of
the wharf edges and all sorts of
other relics were to have been
exposed on these quaysides,
just as they would have been in
the Piazza Caricamento directly
outside the docks. Again, however, all this was hurriedly filled
with earth and asphalted over
for the Exposition.

But the intended paving,
which would have articulated
paths between the exposed
relics, would also have helped
tie the various buildings
together. Now the buildings

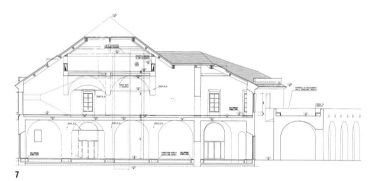

7

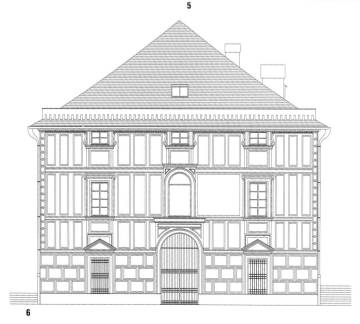

6

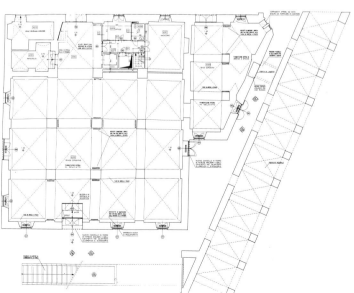

8

9

10

Columbus International Exposition

Bonded warehouses as restored.

9, **10** Details of the *trompe l'oeil* decoration.

11, **12** Restored interior: **11** attic, and **12** vaulted ground floor.

13 Pedestrian street between the bonded warehouses and the Millo.

14 Street elevation facing the Millo. Dotted line indicates *sopraelevata* behind.

Following pages Night view of the Exposition. On the right are the Bigo and the tent over the Piazza de Feste. On the left is the Palazzo San Giorgio in the old city with which the docks are again linked.

11

12

float somewhat disjointedly and forlornly in the sea of featureless black asphalt. It is little surprise, then, that the Exposition organizers felt compelled to enliven the asphalted areas with tasteless edifices such as snack-bar kiosks. Although the unexpected appearance of these enraged Piano, who was not even consulted on their design and location, the decision to permit them was probably in part prompted by the grey colour of all the new structures. But Piano's restrained use of colour reflects his intention that these structures serve not only the short-term event of Expo '92. They are primarily permanent additions to a city that is desperately lacking such facilities, which might be used for leisure and culture, education and trade, and so enhance the city for both its citizens and tourists.

Sadly, due to inadequate publicity and poor management of not just the event itself but also of the other things necessary to the success of such an enterprise, Expo '92 was not very well attended. When it closed, so too did its facilities and grounds. For the moment, the people of Genoa remain deprived of them as well as severed from their city's historic *raison d'être*. But these facilities are such a sorely needed resource for the city, and in such a central and significant location, that it is impossible not to imagine that they will be completed as planned and will once again bustle with activity. As an inevitable consequence, the once-noble porticoes and palazzi of the Ripa should in turn be restored one day and the Molo will take on a new lease of life.

127

13

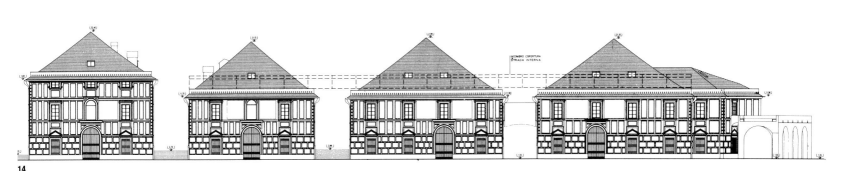

14

Columbus International Exposition

Client City of Genoa – Ente Colombo '92

Design team R Piano, S Ishida (associate in charge), E Baglietto (Italian pavilion), G G Bianchi (Magazzini del Cotone, Moby Dick set, Italian pavilion exhibits), P Bodega, M Carroll (aquarium, Italian pavilion), O de Nooyer (Bigo), G Grandi (bonded warehouses, service spine), D L Hart (congress centre), C Manfreddo (Mandraccio services, press centre, Molo Vecchio), V Tolu, R V Truffelli (bonded warehouses)

Assisted by A Arancio, M Cucinella, S D'Atri (CAD), S de Leo (CAD), G Fascioli, E L Hegerl, G Langasco (CAD), M Mallamaci, G McMahon, M Michelotti, P Persia (CAD), A Pierandrei, F Pierandrei, S Smith, R Venelli, L Vercelli

Structural engineers:

the Bigo: Ove Arup & Partners, London (P Rice)

Other structures: L Mascia, D Mascia, P Costa, L Lembo, V Nascinbene, B Ballerini, G Malcagni, Sidercad, M Testone, G F Visconti

Naval engineer Italian Pavilion Cetena

Services engineers Manens Intertecnica, Verona

Quantity surveyor STED, Genoa (S Baldelli, A Grasso)

Acoustics D Commings, Paris

Lighting design P Castiglioni

Collaborating architects F Doria, M Giacomelli, S Lanzon, B Merello, M Nouvion, G Robotti, A Savioli

Site supervision L Moni

Supervisor of historic areas and buildings M Semino

Collaborating architect for aquarium Cambridge Seven Associates (P Chermayeff)

Director of works for aquarium equipment E Piras, Genoa

Graphic design Origoni/Steiner

Curator Italian Pavilion exhibition G Macchi

Wind sculptures S Shingu

Stage equipment Scène, Paris

Contractor Italimpianti

130

'Galileo in Padua' exhibition Padua 1992

The Building Workshop has designed, and collaborated on the design of, numerous exhibitions. Two are particularly germane as precedents for the design of Amsterdam's National Centre for Science and Technology (p 132). These are 'Christopher Columbus: the ship and the sea', an exhibition which was installed in the aquarium and Italian Pavilion of Genoa's 1992 Columbus International Exposition (p 94), and the unrealized project for an exhibition on the work of Galileo Galilei.

Intended as a counterpoint to the Columbus celebrations the Galileo exhibition was also to have been held in 1992. It was devised to show that the discovery of new regions of this planet led on a century later to the scientific exploration of other celestial bodies and their respective relationships with our Earth. The exhibition was to have been sponsored by the City and University of Padua, where Galileo lived and taught from 1592 to 1610. Here, he had his famous laboratory, invented the telescope and did much of his best work including charting the surface of the moon in 1610. The science museum of Florence was also to have been involved and would have lent Galileo's original instruments.

The venue would have been the magnificent Palazzo della Ragione, a medieval hall of some 2 000 square metres. This is situated in the centre of the city, between two piazzas that are used as markets, and it is ringed by beautiful arcaded galleries. Except for the fact that its wooden roof culminates in a Gothic point, the hall is similar in size and shape to that of the Palladio Basilica in Vicenza, which the Building Workshop once planned to rehabilitate

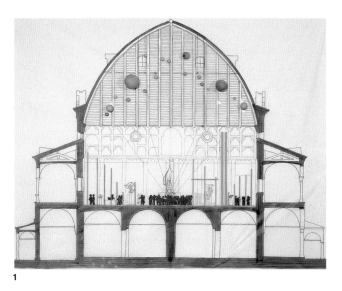

1

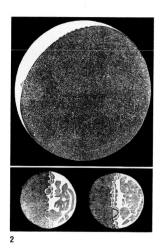

2

3

4

Galileo in Padua

1 (*Left*) Cross section of Palazzo della
Ragione with exhibition installed in hall.

2, 3, 4 Plates from publications by Galileo.

5, 6 Palazzo della Ragione: **5** gallery around
hall, and **6** as seen across piazza used as
market.

7 Longitudinal section of hall with exhibition
installed.

Client Padua City Council

Curator G Macchi

Design team R Piano, S Ishida
and N Okabe (associate architects),
P Ackermann, M Cattaneo

Documentation C Garbato

Model maker D Cavagna

Lighting P Castiglioni

Advisors on exhibits Comitato Scientifico
di Consulenza dell' Università di Padua
(E Bellone, M Bonsembiante, R Hipschman)

5

6

(Volume One p 177). The
Padua hall is richly decorated
in frescoes symbolizing various
astrological themes.

The design concept was that
the lower part of the volume of
the hall be treated as if it were
an enlargement of Galileo's
laboratory, while the space
within the huge vault of the
roof would represent the
cosmos. The laboratory was to
be suggested not only by the
display of instruments, both
historical and contemporary,
but by the liberal use of
wooden scaffolding to support
and frame the displays.

It is known from prints of
the time that similar scaffolding lined the walls and
filled parts of Galileo's laboratory, where he used it to support instruments while he conducted his experiments. Here,
the scaffolding would have
formed an appropriately elliptical shape within the hall. This

would have been punctuated by
ten 'stations', each dedicated to
an aspect of Galileo's work,
such as the telescope, gravity,
thermometer, pendulum and
so on.

Under the vault was to have
been a representation of the
cosmos as Galileo knew it.
Below a backdrop of the
brightest stars, were to hang
large models of the planets then
known, all in their correct relative proportions. The connection between the realms of the
laboratory below and of this
cosmos above would have been
made by an assortment of tele-
scopes standing in another
elliptical formation in the
centre of the hall.

Galileo worked in Padua for
18 years and 1992 marked the
four-hundredth anniversary of
only the first of these years. So
local academics hope that this
exhibition might still be realized at some future time.

131

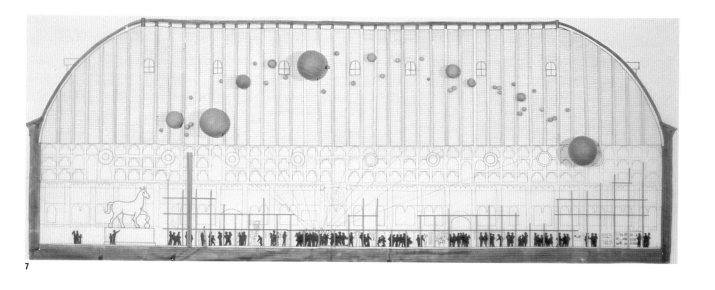

7

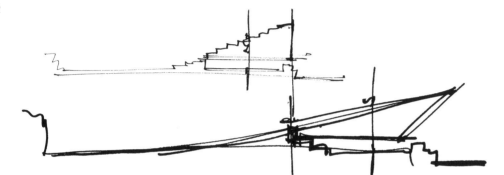

National Centre for Science and Technology Amsterdam, The Netherlands 1992–

When it is completed, the green shell of the National Centre for Science and Technology will seem to lunge out of Amsterdam harbour, sited as it will be over the entrance of a road tunnel, whose ramps project into the bay before disappearing beneath the waters. To best understand the project as it is now, it is as well to explain something of the initial design from which it evolved. This was a direct, almost diagrammatically gestural response to context. As the road dived deeper under the water, so a pair of pedestrian ramps flanking it swept up in counter movement. These ramps led onto the sloping roof of a striking structure with outward sloping metal-clad walls that terminated at its highest point in a curved end not unlike the bow of a ship.

That initial design, and the current one, represent yet another in the series of works in which the Building Workshop is exploring claddings of repetitive metal panels to cover complex curves, and in which the resultant shell is shaped as a response to context and suppresses any external expression of the multi-level interior. The defensive shield of the Bercy 2 Shopping Centre in Paris (p 16) was the first in the series, and

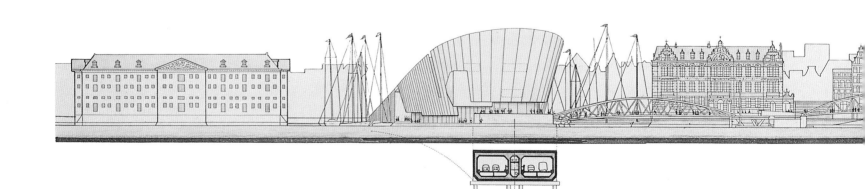

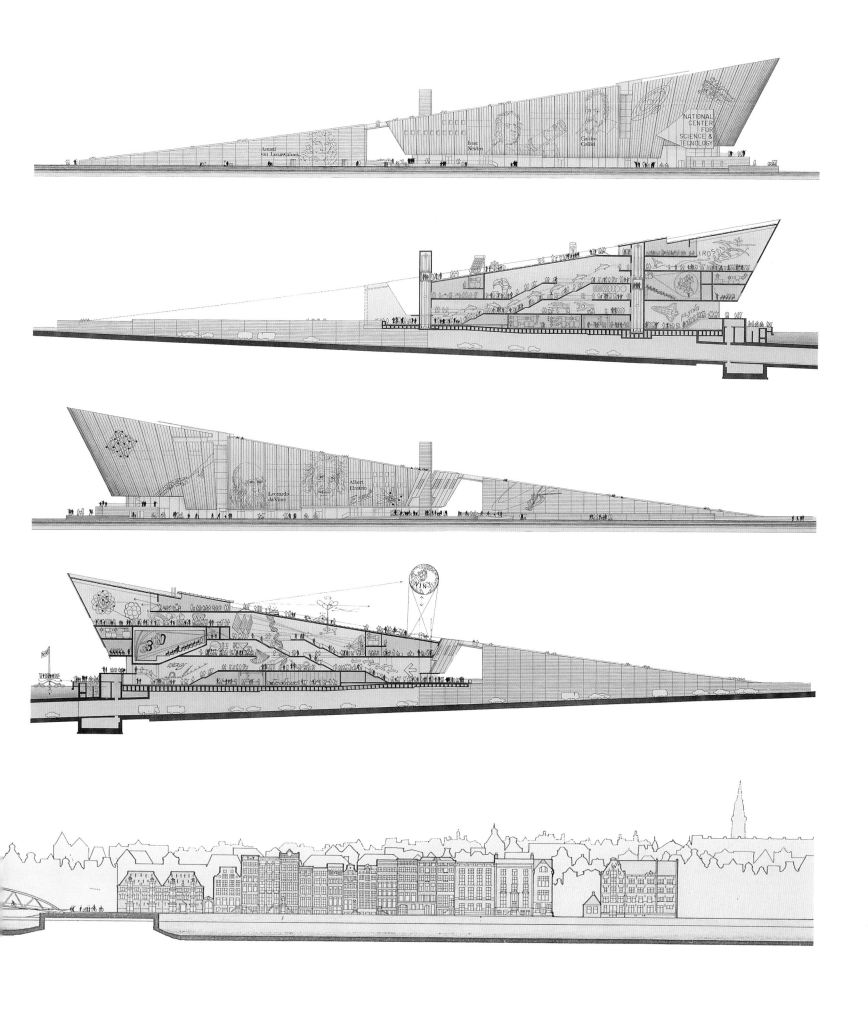

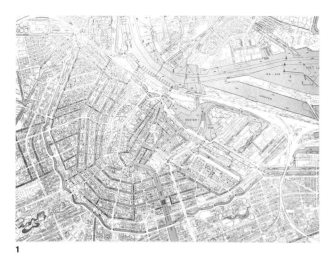

1

National Centre for Science and Technology

Context.

1 Map of central Amsterdam showing location of site projecting into the Ooster-Dok.

2 Computer image showing point from which conical form of the highest end of the building is generated.

3 Aerial view of site and its setting seen from the north.

4 Aerial view of site from south-east.

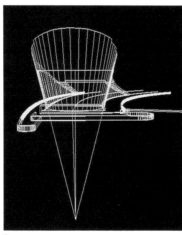

2

the glider-like form of the Kansai International Airport Terminal in Osaka (p 220) is much the most sophisticated. Compared to these, the geometrical intricacies to be resolved in cladding the walls of this museum are not at all forbidding. As if to make up for this, the cladding will take up the challenge of innovation in other ways, to create a skin that is robust enough to face the sometimes wild and always corrosive elements, yet which can also open up to breathe and even let in light and views. In the new scheme, the panels will be finished in copper and so will weather to a green colour.

Vaguely ship-like and decidedly dynamic in shape rather than conventionally architectural, the early design seemed aptly expressive of the building's associations with science and technology. Yet it was also sensitive to its extraordinary context. Towards the historic city it was low and understated, and it was only in the centre of the docks that it rose to its highest point. Here, it confronted across the water such very large structures as a postal sorting office and the twin vaults of Amsterdam's Central Station.

One approach to the new museum will be by means of a

footbridge that will cross the harbour from near the sorting office and the station. This bridge will land on the pavement around the base of the museum near a planned drop-off point for water taxis. The main entrance of the initial design was near the end of this bridge, its position signalled and sheltered by the angular bottom of a lecture hall/cinema, which projected through the curving shell just above its doors. For those approaching from the historic city to the south, it would have been possible to reach these doors via pavements on either side of the tunnel entrance; or, from these pavements, it would have been possible to climb the ramps to a roof-top entrance.

The interior of the early design (as with the current scheme) was taken up mostly by an 'exploratorium', which consisted of displays inviting visitors into degrees of interaction. It was arranged in several levels that stepped diagonally up the building, first from the entrance at the far end of the building, and then back in the opposite direction below the upwards slope of the roof. The exploratorium's various levels were connected by top-lit wells that also housed the stairs. Besides offering vertical

3

4

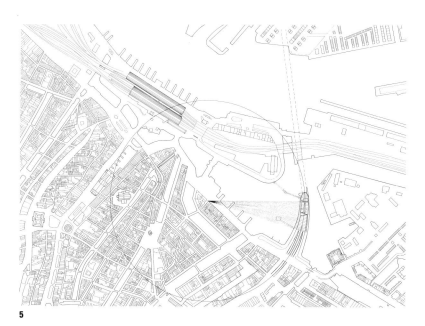

5

National Centre for Science and Technology

Geometrical responses to setting.

5 Centre line of ramped road is on a circle generated from a centre point on corner of dockfront buildings.

6,7 Computer studies of plans of upper levels of initial scheme with twin ramps.

8 Model of initial scheme and setting seen from south-west.

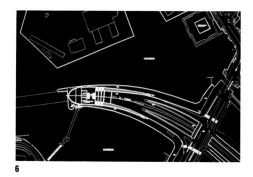

6

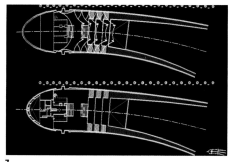

7

connections and short-cuts in the exhibition sequence, these wells would have facilitated orientation and given tantalizing views of things yet to be explored, thus drawing visitors on. As such, this promised to be the most sophisticated spatial sequence Piano had attempted to date.

From the earliest design stage, the external form clearly came first and the interior was then arranged within the available volume. Thus the design strategy continues as the antithesis of the Menil Collection in Houston (Volume one, p 140) also a museum, or the Genoa Exposition aquarium (p 114), another building which projects into its city's harbour. With these two earlier buildings, the external form is the product of the internal arrangements, which took precedence in the design process. Yet with both the earlier and current designs of the Amsterdam museum, what impresses is how convincingly the spaces work within the external envelope. They form a richly compelling sequence that will draw visitors up and onwards. This highly articulated processional route, punctuated by the stairwells that aid orientation, climbs towards its climax in the room at the top of the building, which is enclosed by the prow-like curve of the outward-leaning wall.

For all its considerable appeal and potential, the early design had some obvious redundancies. The current design is the product of a critical reappraisal of these, and of ideas that could be taken further. Formally seductive as the twin tails of the ramps were, one is sufficient. And because there is no habitable space below it, there is no need for its sides to be clad in metal sandwich panels. Some other form of cladding, such as the brick now being considered, is more consistent with functional realities. Removing the westerly ramp suggested moving the main entrance too, because it is then possible to make another front of what had been a rear aspect of the building.

In the current design the main entrance is now reached via a sunny forecourt that looks south and west towards the old city. Here it serves with equal convenience those arriving along the waterside pavement above the sunken road, and those who cross the pedestrian bridge. The entrance is also now visible from, and advertises its presence to, cars entering the tunnel. Most crucially of all, moving the main

135

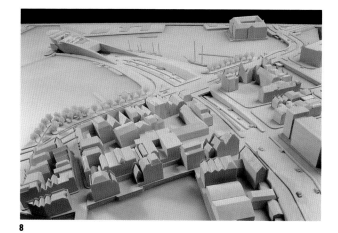

8

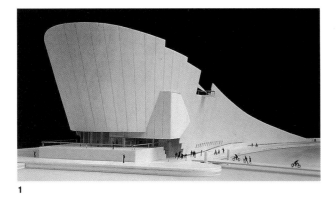

1

National Centre for Science and Technology

Initial scheme of May 1993.

1 Model.

2 North elevation.

3 South elevation.

4 Longitudinal section.

5 East elevation.

entrance has allowed the flow of space, which was developing as such an essential aspect of the former scheme, to be better realized. The spatial sequence is now more simply, clearly and intensely organized as a route and vista which, together, step straight up the length of the building.

From these changes, others inevitably followed. Piano felt that some vertical emphasis was needed near the lowest point of the roof to stabilize the truncated wedge-form of the museum. This is now provided by a lift shaft. He and the clients both thought the design would benefit from a more transparent ground floor, which there now is. Below the sloping metal cladding (which floats free of the ground rather than rising directly from it) the perimeter of the ground floor is almost entirely glazed. The

only exceptions are where the shafts of the four escape stairs descend, and where the curved end of the building buries itself in concrete walls, which extend from the housing for the emergency flood doors that can drop into the tunnel if required.

In the southern end of this floor is the entrance hall and, opening off it in the south-east corner, the museum shop. Beyond this on the eastern side, are the workshops where the public will glimpse exhibits being prepared. Putting important but normally hidden functions of a museum on show like this is something Piano had already done at the Menil. Filling the curved end of this floor, and so also on show to the outside, is a part of the exploratorium, a downwards extension reached from the floor above where the exploratorium is at its largest in floor

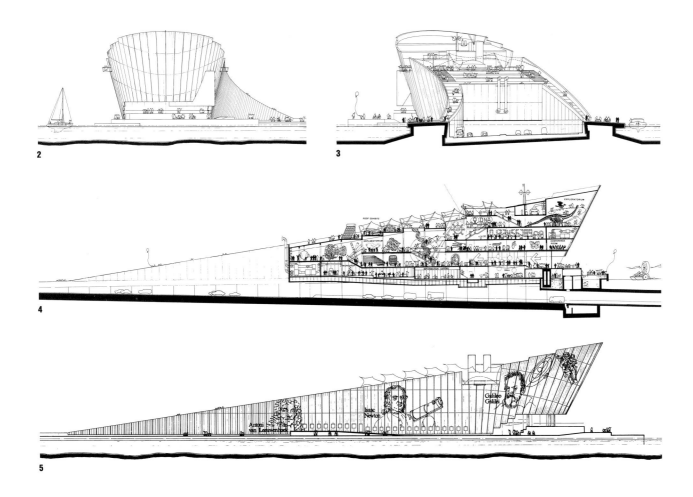

2

3

4

5

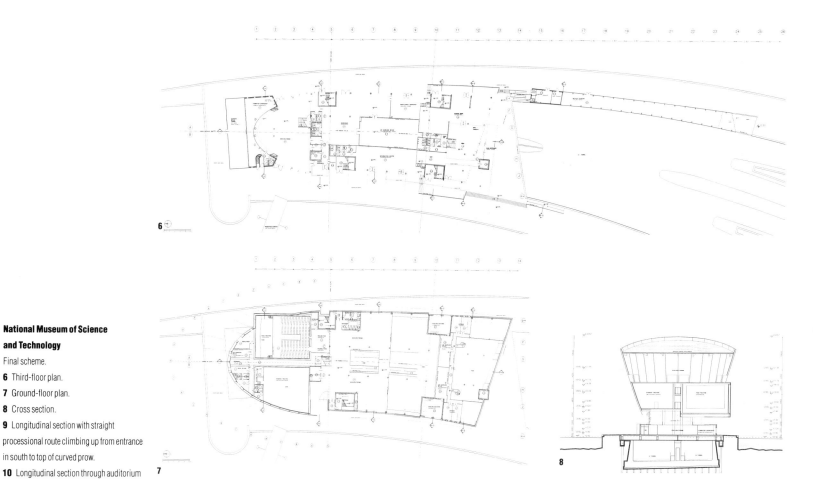

**National Museum of Science
and Technology**

Final scheme.

6 Third-floor plan.

7 Ground-floor plan.

8 Cross section.

9 Longitudinal section with straight
processional route climbing up from entrance
in south to top of curved prow.

10 Longitudinal section through auditorium
and top level cafeteria.

11 West elevation.

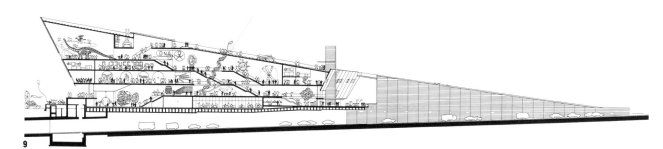

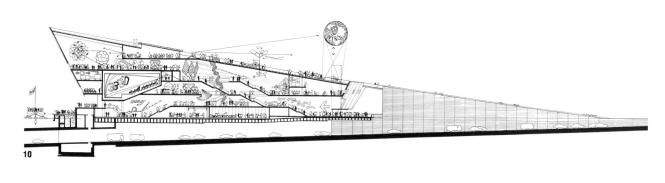

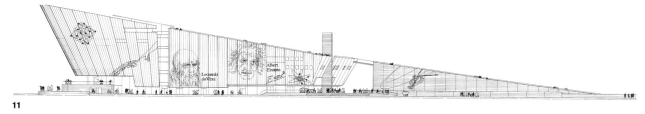

1

138 **National Centre for Science
and Technology**

Final scheme.

1 Model seen from south-west.

2 Roof plan.

3 East elevation.

4 Location plan.

5 North elevation.

6 South elevation.

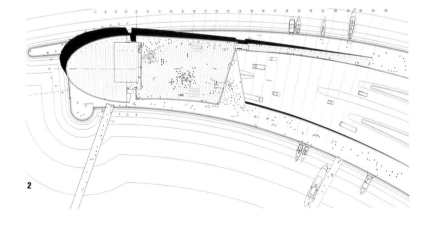

2

3

area. Beyond this, in the concrete-walled extension from the flood-door housing, is space for an independent group that designs much of the museum's graphics and displays. The roof of this element forms a terrace reached by stairs in the exploratorium. Also independent of the museum is the information centre on the west side of this floor. This will offer career guidance, particularly in science and technology.

The whole ground floor is designed to be tiled in a way that will suggest that the pavement outside continues through the minimal enclosure of the floor-to-ceiling glass. This emphasizes the hard and extrovert nature of this level, which is quite different to the museum above. Top-lit and enclosed by the sloping walls, the exhibition levels are introverted and, as glimpses of the proposed wood behind the copper-finished cladding and around windows and other openings will suggest, will be warmer and softer in treatment. Copper and wood will give a rather

Scandinavian feel, an apt response to the grey light and cold of northern Europe.

Even before passing through the doors, the vista across the entrance hall and up through the exploratorium will excite attention. Stairs straight ahead lead up to the exploratorium which fills virtually the entire first floor and the major part of the floors above, except for the topmost level. From the centre of this vaguely cruciform first-floor area, a rectangular well reaches up to a skylight in the roof. Besides bringing down light, allowing diagonal views up and aiding orientation, the well houses straight flights of stairs. On the floor above, the exploratorium occupies much the same area as on the first floor. But now its two ends do not overlook double-volumed spaces reaching up from the floor below. Instead the area over the entrance hall is occupied by offices, and that over the ground floor part of the exploratorium by a science theatre and an auditorium with a raked floor. The latter now projects through the sloped and curving cladding on the east, rather than on the west as in the initial design.

The next floor up, the third, extends southwards as far as the mid-point of the well and overlooks the rest of second floor as a balcony. From the far end of this third-floor area, stairs lead up to the final level of the exploratorium, the end of which again reaches as a

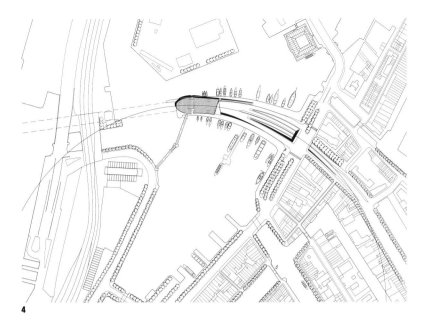

4

National Centre for Science and Technology

Client NIMT

Design team R Piano, S Ishida (associate in charge), O de Nooyer (architect in charge), H Yamaguchi, J Fujita

Assisted by I Corte (CAD), D Guerrisi (CAD), E Piazze, A Recagno, K Shannon, F Wenz, Y Yamaoka

Model makers M Bassignani, D Cavagna

Team coordinator A Giordano

Structural and services engineers for preliminary design Ove Arup & Partners (P Rice, T Barker, J Wernick)

Structural engineer D3BN (J Kraus)

Services engineer Huisman en Van Muijen bv (R Borrett)

Acoustics Peutz & Associés bv

Project management Brink Groep

Local support Bureau Bouwkunde (D Hoogstad)

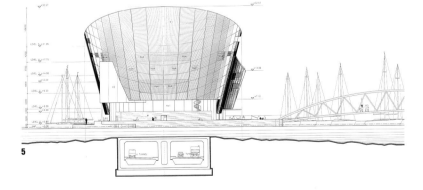

5

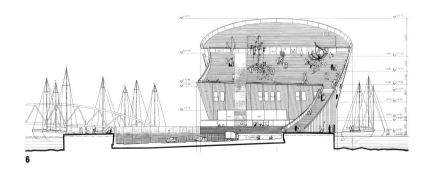

6

double-volume up and out along the curving sloped wall to the roof. The whole climb up to here is a carefully choreographed procession that passes alternatively through double-height and broad spaces, and then single-height and somewhat narrower areas. But though this room within the curved prow of the museum terminates the vista from the entrance hall, it does not end the processional route. This turns back up another stair to arrive at the fifth, top level. Here, a restaurant overlooks the end of the exploratorium as well as stealing a view of the old city across its small terrace and through a slit in the metal-clad skin. To see the best view of the old city, visitors will exit at roof level.

From here the roof steps gently downwards. The initial idea of making this a series of platforms (some of them shaded by awnings) to display further exhibits, was dropped as being excessive. Instead, some sort of low-key installation is intended, perhaps showing aspects of water flow. The roof will be made of stepping, pre-cast concrete beams with integral cast glass elements, so that the whole roof will admit light; although there will not be a great deal of light generally, certain areas will let in a lot more in a way that reinforces the spatial progression below. Although it has not yet been decided how, Piano intends to add warmth to the whole introverted upper area that constitutes the museum, through the liberal use of wood. This will form window surrounds, perhaps the floor, and may in places even line walls or form internal partitions.

When the Amsterdam museum is built, the attention of many will be drawn immediately to its dramatic shape, the cladding of green panels and the chance of walking up the ramp onto the roof. Closer to, what is visible through the transparent base will intrigue. But it is the choreographed flow of space inside that promises to be the building's most memorable aspect. In Piano's own development as an architect it is probable that his biggest breakthrough here is in the handling of a processional spatial sequence that could become as fluent, varied and precisely modulated as those some masters of modern architecture have strived for. Here, he might explore and assimilate an aspect of modern architecture of which there has so far not been much evidence for in his own work.

139

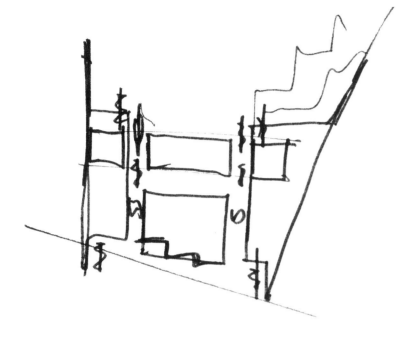

Credito Industriale Sardo Cagliari, Sardinia **1985–92**

Housing a regional division of the Bank of Italy, the Credito Industriale Sardo (CIS), this project represents an attempt to make a rather conventional corporate headquarters, built to a fairly standard budget, play a key role in a small city and its civic life. The city is Cagliari in southern Sardinia, and the commission was won in an open national architectural competition. In the brief, the client, Paolo Savona (Italy's Minister of Finance at the time of writing), stressed that, although these were intended to be high-security premises with which members of the public have no daily business, it was imperative that the building play some public role. The resulting familiarity with the building is meant to help the locals identify with the institution it houses. In the ways it tries to achieve this goal, the design represents one of Piano's earliest investigations of urban space. The design is also of interest for the way in which it extends the exploration of how to use natural materials, in this instance stone, in a manner consistent with contemporary construction.

The site lies towards the eastern edge of the town centre, between an old monastery and a cemetery. Along the site's northern edge is a major avenue, the Viale Bonaria, and along the southern edge a larger traffic route, the Via Armando Diaz. The original competition design filled only the southern half of the site with building. But along three entire sides of the site it presented an aspect as defensive as that of the nearby fortress, which in part inspired this proposal. The lower floors of the building extended up to blank walls that aligned the edges of the Via Armando Diaz and a proposed new street to the east, as well as the lane between this building and its neighbour to the west. Where the walls on the east and west extended northwards beyond the building, they retained planted banks of earth. These flanked the sides of a piazza that filled most of the northern half of the site and opened onto the Viale Bonaria. From this piazza, the public would have ventured under a raised east-west slab, which was the most prominent part of the building, and into a landscaped courtyard at the heart of the complex. Members of the public would also have penetrated beyond the courtyard and into the auditorium, which was always intended for use by both public and bank.

140

1

142   **Credito Industriale Sardo**

1 The building in context: it is in the centre of
the picture.
2 One of the two throughways under the
raised central block to link area sheltered by
glass roof over piazza on north, with covered
way alongside auditorium to south.

Competition scheme
3 Site and roof plan.
4 North-south section.
5 East-west section.

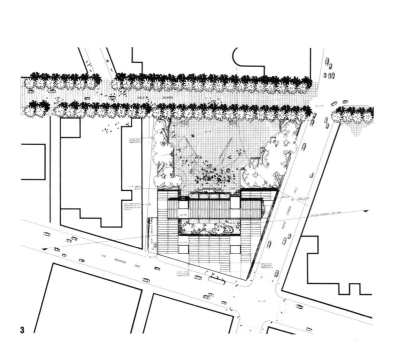

2

Many elements of this original design remain in the scheme that was eventually built. The building is placed on the southern half of the site and dominated by a taller east-west slab, and there is still the piazza to the north. Lower floors still line the eastern and western edges of the site, although no longer the southern edge. Instead, the planted courtyard has become a paved court that extends and opens on to the Via Armando Diaz, so that the building no longer turns its back on this major street but can be approached from it. Projecting into this court from the base of the taller slab is a glass box that now contains the auditorium. As a counterbalance to this, a glass roof identical to that of the auditorium now projects northwards from the other side of the slab and over part of the piazza. Lower banks of planting edge this piazza, which is less enclosed by walls and landscaping than it was in the original competition design. But the new road proposed in the competition scheme along the eastern edge of the site has not been built, so there is no need to shut out its noise from the piazza.

For all their similarities, there has been a marked change in character between the two designs, specifically in the relationship between building and open space. The architecture no longer enfolds a single piazza that progressively narrows and becomes more defined as it is funnelled (under what was to have been a tall portico formed by the raised block) into the serenely static space of the courtyard. Instead it thrusts into, and channels, a more restlessly dynamic sort of open space that sweeps through the transparent lobby between the piazza and the court, with a corresponding loss of intimacy in the relationship between architecture and public space. Without the building's side walls extending to embrace the whole piazza and its planting, as proposed originally, there is less of a sudden surprise and delight at discovering the piazza opening off the Viale Bonaria. Instead of interlocking architecture and open space by extending the building to the avenue, and vice versa, the piazza now merely separates the two. The glass roof that thrusts out over the piazza is intended to compensate by

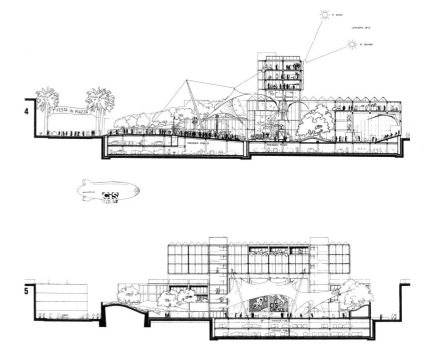

4

5

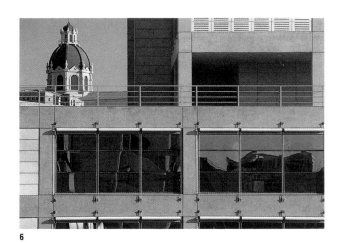

6

Credito Industriale Sardo

6 Close up view shows straightforward treatment of facade.

7 Escape stair is naturally lit through stone screen.

8 View through glass roof of canopy.

9 Night view looking under canopy to main entrance.

10 Looking east over auditorium roof with its adjustable external louvres.

11 Detail of facade of east-west slab with external blinds lowered.

8

7

10

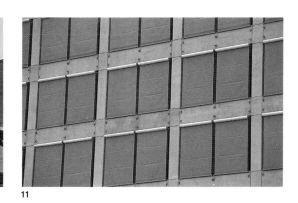

11

extending a welcome to the public so that they feel free to use the piazza.

The loss of the courtyard that the competition design enveloped at its centre, and into which the public were invited on their way to the auditorium, has eroded the clear hierarchy of public spaces. The court is now very similar to the piazza and, if internal blinds are not lowered, the glass walls of the auditorium make public the activities within. Hence there is some ambiguity as to which is the more important approach. The display of public functions in the auditorium and the southern court's direct relationship to Via Armando Diaz suggest this is the dominant side and that the piazza is somewhat redundant or merely a backyard. On this side the building seems disconnected and aloof from its context; while the neighbouring buildings that were planned at the same time remain unbuilt, it resembles too closely an out-of-town corporate headquarters.

Despite the liberal use of local stone to face the walls and pave the piazza, the building is rather plain and severe as constructed, with all components unadorned and bluntly expressed. The structure is an in-situ concrete frame. Set flush with the flat outer-face of this are blinds that shade the floor-to-ceiling glazing close behind them and the stone facing to the blank panels. At the ends of corridors and staircases is more stone, here used as screens with horizontal slots cut precisely in each slab. Although the use of stone for carved screens recalls Mughal architecture, the actual shapes used here might be those of the pressed metal or plastic panels of High-Tech buildings. Although deliberately mechanistic in form, the flickering rhythms of these screens considerably enliven the building's exterior and are among its more successful features.

Also playing a part in animating the building and the spaces around it, are the steel and glass elements that project beyond the main concrete frame. Above the uppermost concrete beams is the serrated profile of the compound-pitched roofs. These were adopted to give some of the scale of the older neighbouring buildings, and to give a more pleasant outlook from the offices in the tall slab than

143

1

144   **Credito Industriale Sardo**

1 View across piazza from Via Bonaria.

Plans of built scheme.

2 Second floor.

3 First floor.

4 Site and ground floor: **a** Viale Bonaria, **b** Via
Armando Diaz, **c** piazza, **d** auditorium.

5 View under glass canopy towards main
entrance doors.

6 View out under canopy of piazza on north.

7 Location plan.

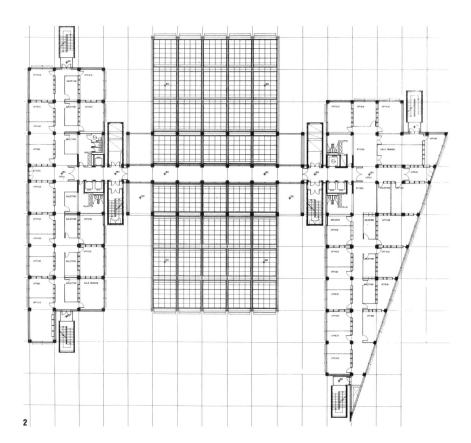

2

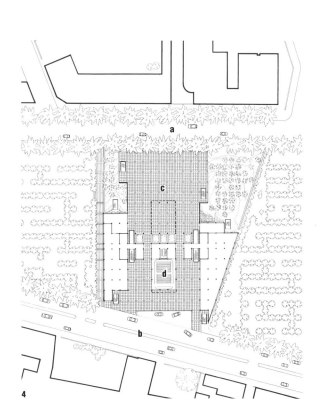

4

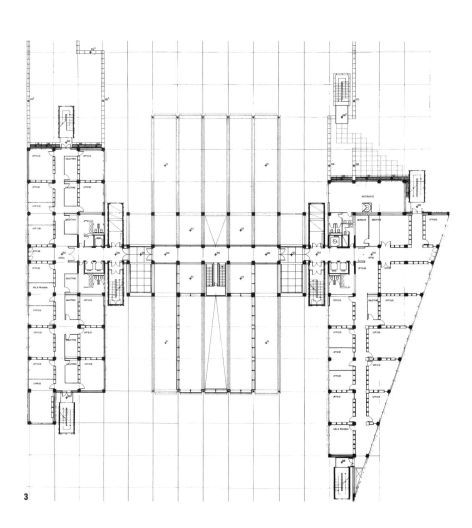

3

5

6

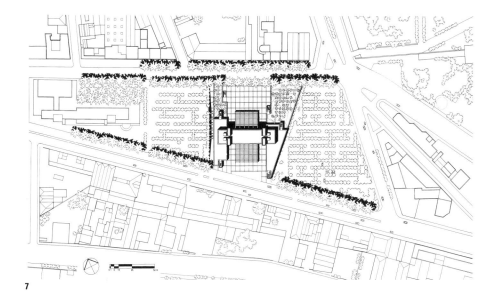

7

an ordinary flat roof would have done. Also, much of this pitched roofing is glazed to illuminate the spaces below. But the most prominent steel and glass elements are the roof that projects out over the piazza in the front, and the glass box of the auditorium that projects into the court at the back. The latter is a highly adjustable, multi-purpose room, which in this small city is a very valuable public resource. Each part of its floor can be raised or lowered allowing seating, stages and screens to be arranged in various ways. Blinds can be adjusted to block out light and obscure views in from all sides and the roof. For many functions, only the blinds on the street-side are lowered to give some privacy. Adjustable external louvres shade the glass roof, a device also used on the canopy over the piazza.

All in all, this remains an interesting building, if not one that fulfils all the promise of the original competition design. Since Mies van der Rohe's Seagram building in New York (1958), the piazza in front of a building set back from the street edge has become a cliché, usually destructive of urbanity because of its tendency to erode the spatial containment of the street. Here, however, this device was interpreted in the original scheme in a novel and vital way. Walls and planting reached out to mark the street-edge so that architecture and framed urban space were interlocked, and the building neither floated as an island in a sea of sloshing unshaped space, nor served as a channel to emphasize its restlessness.

A major reason for departing from the original scheme, besides that of giving more apt recognition to Via Armando Diaz, was Piano's worry that the relatively closed piazza and inconspicuous auditorium might have appeared too much the private domain of CIS. Perhaps a better solution would have been to make a broad opening and pedestrian path from the south-east corner of the piazza, across the north-east edge of the building, and through the earth bank and wall on the east. This would have invited the public to take a short-cut across the piazza encouraging them to become familiar with it and use it. A glass roof, such as eventually adopted, could have extended forward as a generous gesture of welcome to reassure the public of their rights to the piazza. But whatever the eventual limits of the quality and achievement of the final design, this remains a significant scheme for the Building Workshop. It is one of the first projects in which Piano began to grapple with urban space in a sophisticated manner, and it can be seen as the starting point for the sort of thinking that is now finding mature expression in the Potsdamer Platz scheme for Berlin (p 210).

145

1

3

2

4

146 **Credito Industriale Sardo**

The flexible auditorium.

1 View in from first floor bridge over entrance.

2 Looking south with seats arranged on both sides of central stage, roof louvres partly open and blinds across windows onto street.

3 Looking north across clear floor, with windows and roof unscreened.

4 With central stage, all windows screened by blinds and roof louvres closed.

5 West elevation.

6 North-south section through open passage way that links piazza on north and court on south.

7 Auditorium seen from end stage against southern wall with roof louvres closed but windows unscreened. Conditioned air is admitted through nozzles on the vertical ducts that rise along both sides.

8 North-south section through auditorium.

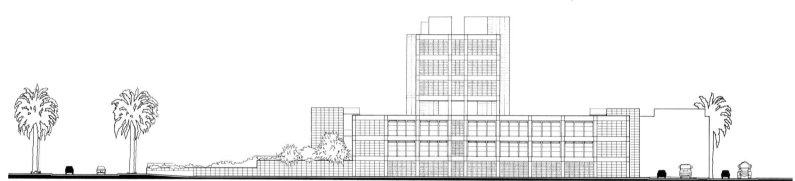

5

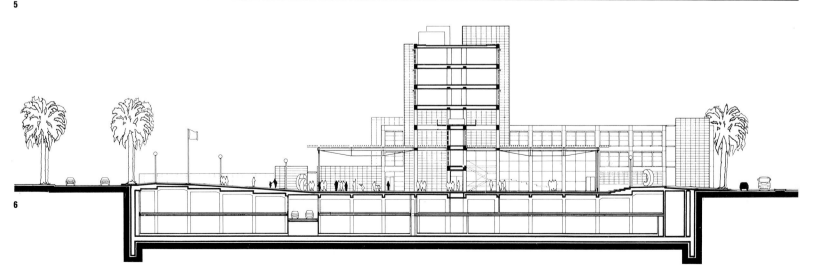

6

7

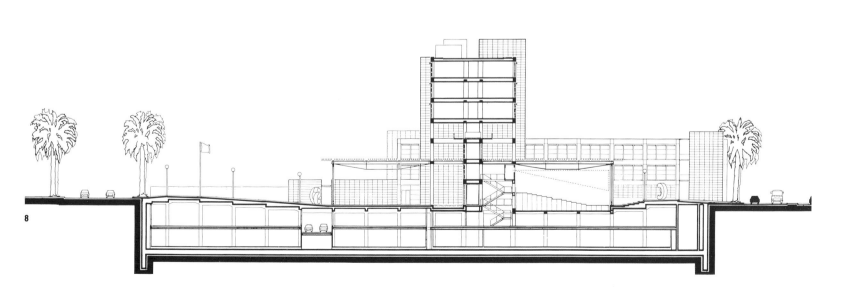

8

1

4

2

3

148 **Credito Industriale Sardo**

1–9 Details of stone cladding, screens,
paving and paving grilles.
10 Southern wall of glass box that encloses
auditorium.

Client Credito Industriale Sardo
Design team R Piano, E Baglietto,
R V Truffelli (architects in charge),
G G Bianchi, M Carroll, O Di Blasi, D L Hart,
S Ishida (associate architect), C Manfreddo,
F Marano (associate engineer), F Santolini,
M Varratta
Assisted by M Calosso, D Campo, R Costa,
M Cucinella
Model makers S Vignale, G Sacchi,
D Cavagna
Structural engineers Mageco (L Mascia,
D Mascia)
Services engineers Manens
Intertecnica Srl
Geological studies Pecorini, (Cagliari),
G Gatti, Milan
Contractors R Tireddu, I R C, So G Di Co,
Vibrocemento Sarda

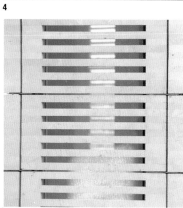

5

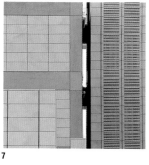

6

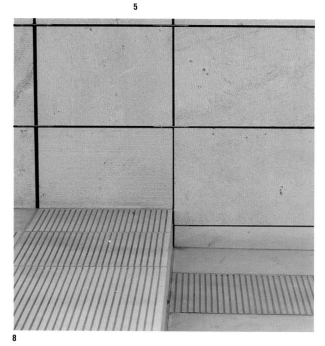

8

7

9

150

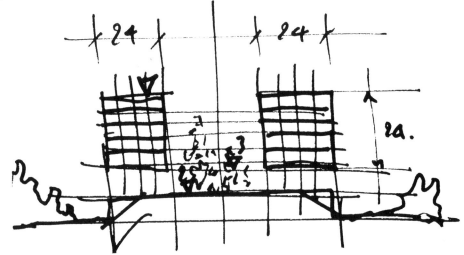

Lingotto Factory Renovation Turin, Italy **1983–**

Longer than an ocean liner, and with its banked roof-top test track and helicoidal ramps, which give both dynamism and finiteness of form to the repetitive rhythms of its concrete structure and steel windows, the Fiat Lingotto Factory was a prime icon of early Modern architecture. No fewer than three photographs of it grace the pages of Le Corbusier's *Vers une Architecture*. But after six decades of continuous use, automated production techniques have rendered it obsolete as a factory. It is now being converted into a multi-functional resource for Turin and for a large part of northern Italy. Here, trade and art exhibitions, conferences and concerts, educational and start-up facilities for new enterprises will co-exist and interact to mutual benefit.

As is typical of the Building Workshop, the phased conversion, which is now on site, shows ample respect for the legacy of the past while giving the building a new lease of life through the introduction of nature and the latest technology. Yet although this is a conversion of a historic monument, the result will also realize something of that most futuristic of visions: the megastructure. So the efficient production-line machine and icon of 1920s Modernism will become the multi-functional megastructure that was an icon of 1960s Modernism. But as well as having obvious roots in Piano's formative period as an architect, the scheme also looks further forward in promising to become a hub of creativity and innovation in the electronically-linked global system of the twenty-first century.

The Lingotto factory was built between 1915 and 1921 by the civil engineer, Giaccomo Matte-Trucco, after Fiat's founder, V G Agnelli, had visited the Ford plant in Detroit, USA in 1912 and seen applied there the Scientific Management principles of F W Taylor. When completed, the five floors of the 500-metre long Lingotto building housed the largest production line in Europe. By the time the advent of industrial robots had necessitated the relocation of these production lines, Fiat was not only Italy's premiere industrial enterprise but its prime corporate patron of arts and culture. Fiat sponsors all sorts of exhibitions and events, as well as funding the conversion and running of the Palazzo Grassi in Venice. It was inevitable, then, that the company would want to preserve a building as famous, and as

1

Lingotto Factory Renovation

The factory as it was.

1, 2 Aerial views show the length and nobility of the machine become monument.

3 Heavy equipment of the sort made obsolete by modern industrial processes.

4 Cars on the production line.

5 Fiat Topolino on the production line.

6 Helicoidal ramp under construction.

7 Cars speeding round corners of test track.

8 Office of clerks in the separate administration block known as the *palazzina*.

2

3

4

6

5

7

8

closely identified with both it and Turin, as is the Lingotto factory. However, no single function can be found today to fill such an immense structure, so Fiat's idea was to convert it into a multi-functional resource which, besides continuing to play a vital role in the economy of the city and its region, would contribute significantly to local and national cultural life.

Initially, a consultation exercise was organized in which proposals for the building were sought from an international range of selected architects.

This was not intended as a design competition, but was inevitably treated as such. Each architect submitted design proposals in addition to what was requested: ideas for the new functions the building might house and the broad strategy to be applied to its conversion. These were exhibited publicly and the people of Turin were encouraged to vote for the proposals they preferred. They overwhelmingly chose the scheme by the Building Workshop. This advocated using the building as a centre for technological innovation and entrepreneurial initiative, as well as for cultural events.

Predictably enough, almost as if by reflex, Piano's initial proposals for the conversion made liberal use of landscaping and tensile structures supporting tented roofs. The space liberated by the removal of the railway marshalling yards to the west of the main assembly building, and the demolition of later accretions around both it and the original administration block to the east, was given over largely to landscaping. This swept up to all sides of the

main building like giant waves around a liner. In so doing the landscaping concealed new ancillary structures, including a parking garage, alongside the old factory. And the tent-sheltered pedestrian routes over these landscaped roofs climbed towards the building so as to enter it directly at first-floor level. This became the main public circulation level, its routes overlooking internal courtyards which were also taken over by landscaping and tents.

The use of tents and landscaping concealing submerged structures together with a standard kit of parts with which to carry out and unify the conversion, draws on the Building Workshop's earlier experience of the Schlumberger Renovation in Paris (Volume One, p 90). Ultimately, however, as with the previous factory

9

Lingotto Factory Renovation

9 Model of complex in context of Turin.

10 Schlumberger renovation, Paris, 1981-1984: an earlier renovation of a large industrial premises and a key precedent.

11 Cross section through original consultation/competition scheme, with landscaping rolling over roofs of ancillary structures and copious use of tents.

12, 13 Original building prior to renovation:
12 view up vehicular ramp to roof, **13** the press shop where body panels were pressed from sheet steel.

14 Final landscaping plan.

10

conversion, Archigram is probably an inspiration for these elements: tents were a recurrent motif in Archigram's work, and spaces submerged by landscaping were a feature of its competition-winning entry for a leisure centre in Monte Carlo in the 1960s. But as the Lingotto design has evolved, the tents and rolling verdure have quite rightly been dropped in favour of a more restrained approach, better suited to the sobriety of the original factory.

With its huge scale and rich mix of activities, and as signalled by its helipads and globular conference rooms held aloft above the old stair towers, this respectful conversion of a historic monument may prove ironically to be the first real megastructure ever realized. For Piano, a major challenge of this project has been to retain the identity of the old building while inserting and expressing the presence and mix of its new accommodation. When completed in 1996, the complex will offer a microcosm of the city as an intense mechanism of interaction and innovation, its parts connected by the same electronic information systems that plug it into national and global networks.

Since starting on Lingotto, the Building Workshop has extended its involvement in the surrounding area and received commissions for further projects there. This will help in fulfilling the intention to improve Lingotto's connections with its immediate surroundings and the city beyond. Against the western side of the building where railway marshalling yards once stood, there will be a park and a train maintenance shed. Nearby will be a new railway station on the main railway line through to France. And linking Lingotto with the city market on the far side of the tracks will be an elevated public transit shuttle. The design of the park and the shuttle were awarded as later commissions from Lingotto's joint-venture client of Fiat and Turin City Council. The station and maintenance shed are yet later commissions from the Italian Railways.

153

11

12

13

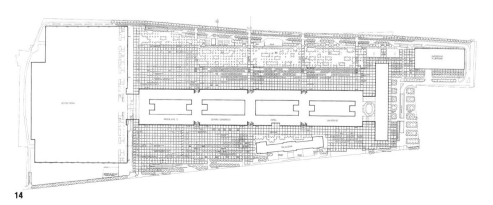

14

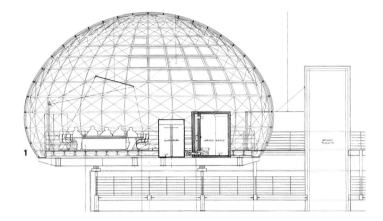

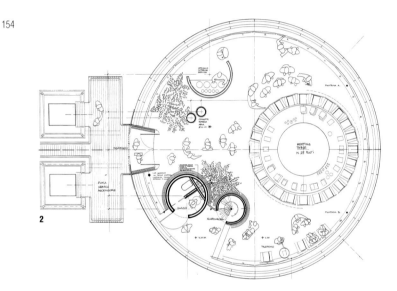

1

154

2

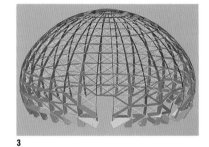

3

In the design being executed, all that remains of the original landscaping is the park on the west and the planting in the courtyards. The first floor is still to be the main level of public circulation, although the sloping landscaped paths leading up to it have been dropped from this proposal. Piano conceives of this level as being 'a piece of the city', a fragment of central Turin that has found its way into the old factory. Shops will occupy most of the first floor, organized along internal malls. Where these malls pass the paved roofs over the new halls, which fill the bottom of the two southernmost courtyards, they will open up to become arcades. These will recall those of Turin's Via Roma, which is exactly the same length as these malls. By such association, the arcades will tie these public promenades to the traditions of the city centre. They will also allow cafes to spill across the new roofs.

Below this level will be the activities that generate the heaviest public circulation and require regular vehicular access. Beyond the southern end of the main block, the old press shop (where steel body panels were once pressed) has been partially demolished and rebuilt as a large exhibition facility. This has been in use for trade fairs for some years. The ground floor of the southern end of the main block itself, and the roofed-over bottom of the southernmost of the courts, has been converted into a large gallery. This can be used either as an extension to the trade fair, or for independent art exhibitions.

The bottom of the court adjacent to the gallery has been excavated to accommodate a 2 000-seat concert and congress hall that is currently under construction. The volume and acoustics of this hall will be adjusted by raising or lowering the ceiling, which will be at its highest for symphonic concerts and at its lowest for conferences. Much of the rest of the ground floor will be refurbished as workshop spaces, suited to research

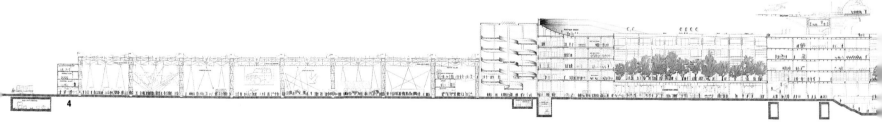

4

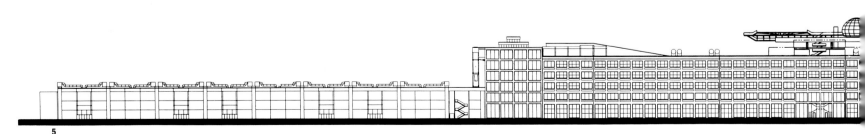

5

Lingotto Factory Renovation

Elements of the final scheme.

1, 2, 3 Roof-top conference suite: **1** section,
2 plan, **3** computer analysis of types and
magnitude of stresses in structure of dome.

4 Longitudinal section through, from left to
right: trade fair hall, gallery and concert hall
with business centre above, garden court with
hotel above and incubator units with Science
Faculty above.

5 East elevation.

6, 7, 8 Light fixture used throughout
building: **6** the most widely used variant, cantilevered on an arm to reflect off the ceiling,
7 floor-mounted variant used to light walls,
and **8** detail section of cast aluminium head.

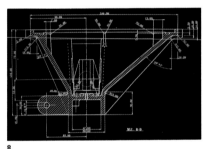

and light manufacturing, such as electronics and crafts. These 'incubator units' will be let to new businesses, which will enjoy suitable conditions in which to establish themselves before making way for other new ventures that will, in turn, benefit in their vulnerable early days from the support of the building's various resources.

The upper levels of the main building will house facilities that generate less intense public and vehicular traffic. Each occupying about a third of the building above first floor will be: a business centre offering rentable office space and back-up facilities (again suited to new businesses); a four-star hotel that will provide over-night accommodation for business people, visiting exhibitors and performers, and congress attendees; and four departments of the Faculty of Science

of the University of Turin. (The conversion of the business centre and hotel is currently underway.) Serving all these facilities, and projecting above the old service cores that separate the courtyards, will be the helipads and globular conference rooms. These will have independent structural supports standing in the corners of the courtyards.

To retain some consistency between the different kinds of spaces being created, as much of the conversion as possible is being executed using elements from a pre-designed kit of parts, a ploy the Building Workshop has adopted in several other schemes. This kit includes partitions and raised floors, windows and light fittings. To date, part of the ground floor has been enclosed in an elegant new glazing system with separate internal stiffening elements and external roll-down blinds. As usual with components designed by the Building Workshop, this is a system of exceptional delicacy and refinement, and one that uses cast aluminium elements to give a sensual tactility to some details. Also using cast-aluminium elements are the lights, designed by the Building Workshop, that project on arms from the ceilings.

Although usually used as uplighters reflecting off new suspended ceilings, these can also be angled downwards to light particular areas or exhibits.

The original building's 6 by 6 metre structural grid and generous floor-to-ceiling heights allow the various services and control installations to be deployed easily and efficiently. With these systems, Lingotto has the potential to set new standards for 'intelligent' buildings in Europe. Provision is being made for all services to be monitored by sensors connected to a computerized building-management system, which will make the continual adjustments required. A central computer system could also supervise security and safety systems, parking and entry, and access to all parts of the complex. And advanced telecommunications systems are being planned, which will allow immediate interaction between the building's different users and with those outside via video-conferencing and access to data-banks.

155

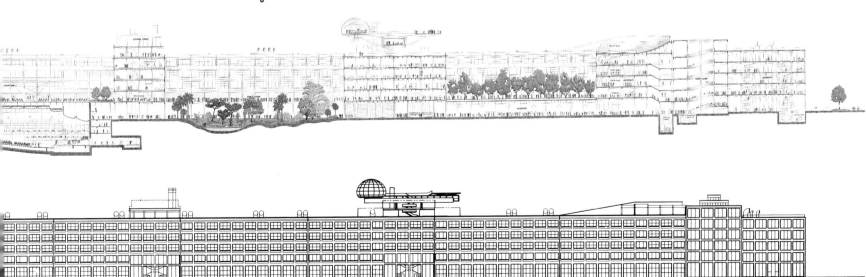

1

2   3   4

5

6

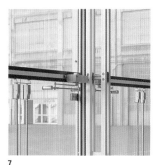

7

8

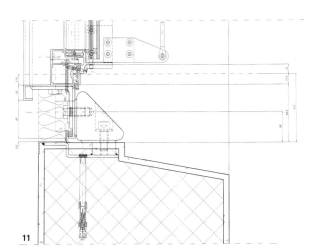

9

10

Lingotto Factory Renovation

157

Fenestration.

1 Close up of unrestored facade with the original windows that new ones match.

2, **3**, **4** Plan details of new windows: **2** side frame, **3** mullion used on upper floors, and **4** ground floor mullion.

5 Section detail of head of new window.

6, **7** Details of new ground floor windows: **6** head of windows and motorized external blinds, and **7** internal view of junction of mullion and transome.

8, **9** The colours finally chosen are terracotta blinds with vivid green casings, seen in **8** outside the new upper level windows, and **9** outside new ground floor glazing.

10 Close up of facade.

11 Section detail of bottom of window.

12, **13** The ground floor blinds move outwards with the bottom-pivoted windows.

11

12

13

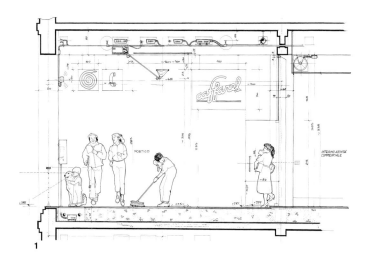

1

Lingotto Factory Renovation

1 Section of first floor public concourse.

2 Model viewed from east.

3 Roof plan.

4 Typical floor plan: **a** business centre,

b hotel, **c** Science Faculty.

5 First floor plan: public concourse and

shopping level.

6 Ground floor plan: **a** trade fair hall,

b gallery, **c** concert/congress hall,

d incubator units, **e** *palazzina*.

Very little of the Building Workshop's intervention could be said to be biomorphic in form: only the structure of the domed conference rooms will be pushed to limits that might be thought of as emulating the achievements of nature, and the presence of the landscaping will be more restrained than originally planned. Yet, like all Piano's work, this scheme is concerned with the organic. But it is dimensions of the organic, other than those listed above, that are to be explored further here, in a work conceived of as analogous to a living organism. The sophisticated electronics the building is intended to exploit will enable it to adapt spontaneously (as if endowed with primitive consciousness) to weather and other conditions outside, as well as to such internal conditions as differing patterns and

intensities of use. Besides allowing the building to regulate itself in this manner, this electronic central nervous system will enable it to reach out and interact instantaneously in a variety of ways with its region and the wide world beyond.

What might be thought of as another aspect of the organic will be realized by the catalytic conjunction of the various activities housed in the complex, their considerable scale, and their common concern with creativity and innovation. Lingotto is intended to play a leading role in ensuring the economic and cultural vitality of Turin and north-west Italy. This will not be the usual centre for innovation, corporate think-tank, or government department exhorting research and development, that is too often found ineffectually

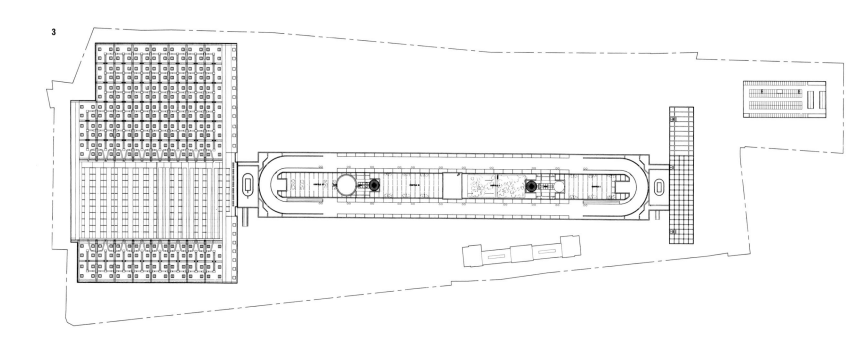

2

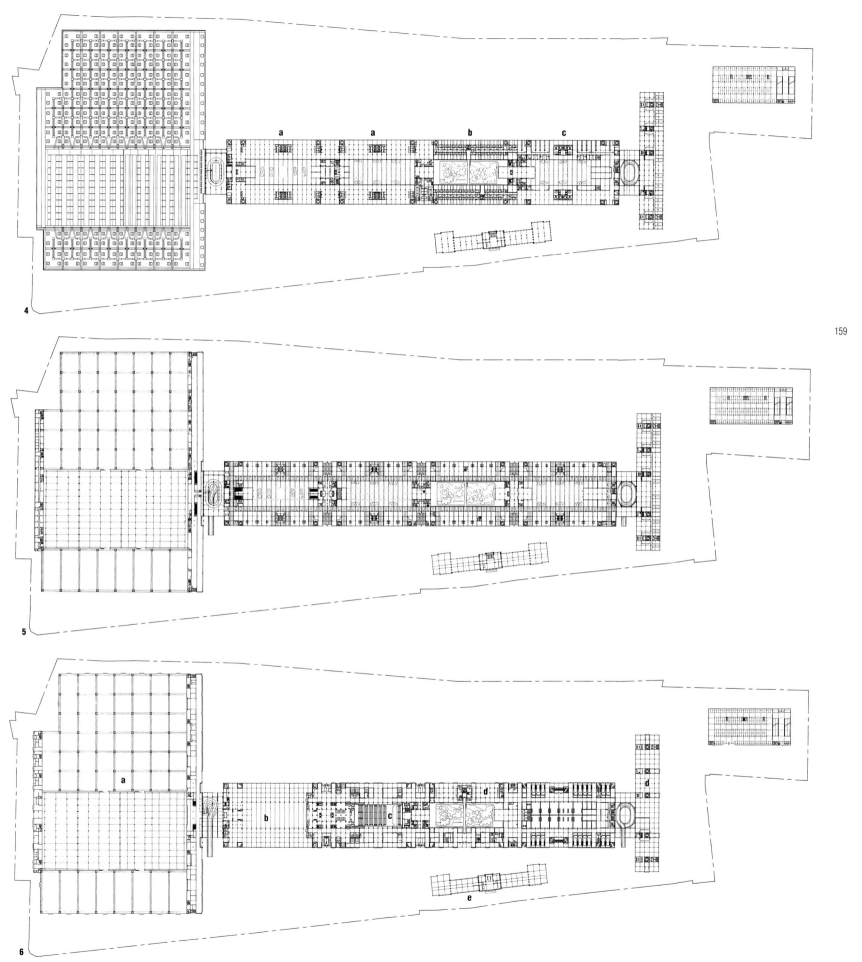

4

5

6

1

2

160 **Lingotto Factory Renovation**

Trade fair hall.

1 Escalator, and **2** head of escalator in east-west concourse that runs the length of the north side of the hall. The escalators give access to the first floor where there is a cafeteria and other ancillary facilities for the trade fairs as well as a connection to the public concourse level of the main building.

3, 5 Concourse thronged with people during a trade fair.

4 Lobby between concourse to left and exhibition hall on right.

6 Eastern end of concourse that extends behind entrance facade.

7 Detail of inside of entrance facade with stiffening elements behind each mullion.

8 Entirely glazed and flag festooned entrance elevation of trade fair hall that faces north towards the *palazzina*.

3

4

5

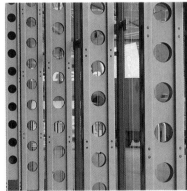

6

7

espousing such goals. Instead, its rich mix of activities together comprise a critical mass that is sufficient to support and interact combustively within itself, and with other ventures in the region. Lingotto will be big and diverse enough to have a fertile entrepeneurial ecology of its own, continuously spawning new ideas and enterprises. Not only can this dynamic be seen as inherently organic but, in the collaborative and participative ventures it encourages, it will realize at large scale, and across a broad front, the essential ideals that Piano pursues with the Building Workshop.

As well as being the architect for the ongoing conversion of the Fiat Lingotto Factory, the Renzo Piano Building Workshop has designed short-term installations for some of the events staged there. The first of these was to create a 3 000-seat congress hall in one of the now-demolished ancillary sheds, and to articulate clearly the path to it through the old press shop. An awning projecting from a building on the site's eastern edge marked the entrance to the broad route across the press shop. This passed between white screens and below the tracks of suspended spotlights, which together created a compelling perspective focused on the entrance to the congress hall. This entrance was right behind a raised dais, which was located in the middle of one of the hall's long side walls. There was space in the wide, shallow hall for only two blocks of seats to face the front of the dais. Most of the seats were, therefore, arranged symmetrically in banks on either side of these central blocks. The farthest banks were raked up to improve the view. So that all could see, the speakers' faces were projected by closed circuit television onto large screens above the dais.

1

2

162   **Lingotto Factory Renovation**

Concert/congress hall.

1, **2** Construction views: **1** casting sleeper foundation walls, **2** casting floor slab.

3, **4** Details of internal elevation: **3** panels of wooden louvres that are opened to increase acoustic absorbance **4** boxes fronted by curved wood acoustic reflector panels.

5 Longitudinal section: as arranged for concert.

6, **7** Views from back and front of stage as construction nears completion.

8 Portion of internal elevation with three tiers of boxes and, above them, louvres for adjusting acoustics.

9 Ground level plan: as arranged for congress.

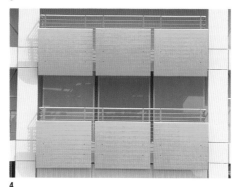

3

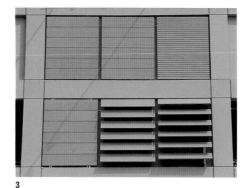

4

Other installations by the Building Workshop have been for art exhibitions. The two most important of these, 'Russian and Soviet Art 1890–1930' (June to October 1889) and 'American Art 1930–1970' (January to March 1992), were based in the gallery in the main block at the southern end of the ground floor. A smaller show of Andy Warhol's early illustrations as a commercial artist, entitled 'Success is a job in New York' (March to May 1990), was installed in the '*palazzina*'. This was formerly the factory's entrance and administration block and stands prominently in front of it, at a slight angle, on the street that marks the site's eastern boundary. The curator of the Russian and Soviet exhibition was Giovanni Carandente, who also curated the Alexander Calder retro-

spective installed by the Building Workshop in the nearby Palazzo a Vela (Volume One p 80). The curator of the American exhibition was Attilio Codognato.

The Russian exhibition did not use solid walls or partitions, but suspended the paintings on metal rods in front of sheets of fine white fabric. Weighted by aluminium bars in their bottom hem, these sheets hung tautly from a little below the suspended ceiling to a little above the floor. They were arranged in pairs on either side of the columns, whose presence they concealed. The sheets defined a series of rooms of similar width but differing depth on either side of a central aisle. Combined with the reflected uplighting and absence of visible structure they tended to dematerialize the space in a delicately ethereal and diaphanous manner.

A row of study tables with chairs on either side was placed down the middle of the aisle. On the tables were smaller works in glass cases, books for

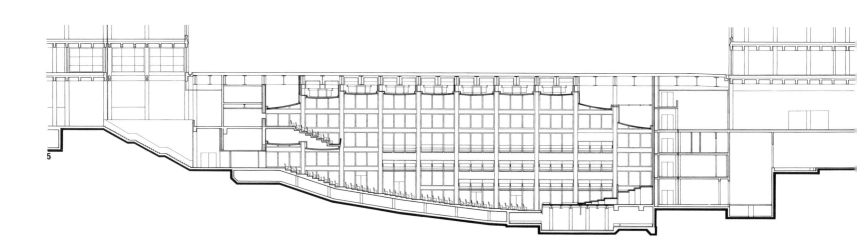

5

6

7

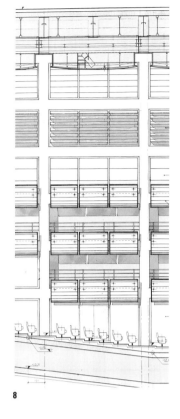

8

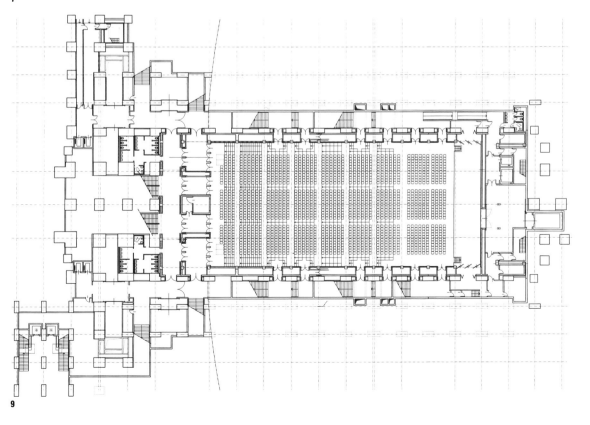

9

Lingotto Factory Renovation

Consultation 1983
Client Fiat SpA
Design team R Piano, S Ishida (associate
in charge), C Di Bartolo, O Di Blasi, M Carroll,
F Doria, G Fascioli, E Frigerio, R Gaggero,
D L Hart, P Terbuchte, R V Truffelli

Feasibility study 1985
Client City of Turin
Design team R Piano, S Ishida (associate
in charge), E Frigerio (architect in charge),
O Di Blasi, K Dreissigacker, M Mattei

Final scheme 1991–
Client Lingotto Srl
Design team R Piano, S Ishida (associate in
charge), P Ackermann, E Baglietto, A Calafati,
M Carroll (track, landscaping, south tower
1994), M Cattaneo (interiors 1994),
A Carisetto, G Cohen, F Colle, I Corte (CAD),
P Costa, M Cucinella (pavilion five 1987),
S De Leo, A De Luca, S Durr, K Fraser,
A Giovannoni, D Guerrisi (CAD), C Hays,
G Hernandez, C Herrin, W Kestel, G Langasco
(CAD), P Maggiora, D Magnano, M Mariani,
K A Naderi, T O'Sullivan, A Piancastelli,
D Piano (cinema 1994), G Robotti (CAD),
E Rossato, A Sacchi, S Scarabicchi (public
level, hotel, offices 1994), P Sanso, L Siracusa
(CAD), A Stadimayer, R V Truffelli, M Varratta
(Trade Fair Centre 1992, concert hall 1994),
N Van Oosten, H Yamaguchi
Structural and services engineers:
concept design Ove Arup & Partners
final design A I Engineering, Fiat
Engineering
Quantity surveyor Davis Langdon Everest
Acoustics Arup Acoustics, Muller Bbm
Lighting P Castiglioni
Graphics P L Cerri, ECO Spa
Fittings F Santolini
Theatre equipment Techplan
Site supervision:
trade fair centre Studio Vitone & Associati
(1992)
second phase F Levi, G Mottino (1994)
Building inspectors:
trade fair centre Studio Program
(I Castore) (1992)
second phase R Montauti, B Roventini,
G Vespignani, S Rum, E Bindi (1994)
Contractors:
pavilion five Fiat Engineering, Turin
trade fair centre Associazione temporanea d'imprese: Recchi, Pizzarotti, Guerrini,
Rosso, Borini & Prono
second phase Associazione temporanea
d'imprese: Del Favero, Maltauro, Aster

163

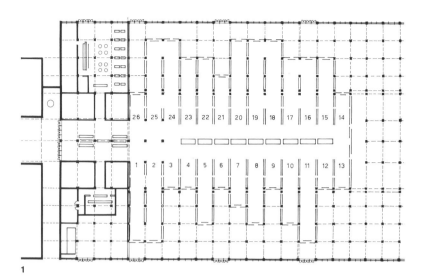

1

164 **Lingotto Factory Renovation**

'Russian and Soviet Art 1870-1930'.

1 Plan.

2 Billboard and banners outside the entrance to the show.

3 Entrance to the show exploited affinities between vehicular ramp and Tatlin's tower.

4 Detail section shows paintings suspended on rods in front of partitions made of double screens of fabric.

5 Section along central axis.

6 View across central axis with its study tables and posters sandwiched between suspended glass panes towards the individual rooms partitioned by suspended fabric sheets.

Client Fiat Lingotto

Curator G Carandente

Design team R Piano, M Varratta (architect in charge), S Ishida (associate architect), M Cattaneo, M Rossato

Lighting P Castiglioni

Graphics P Cerri

Installation Gruppo Bodino

2

3

study and TV monitors with headphones for video presentations. Perspex sheets protected photographs and documents filling in background information. Sandwiched in glass, and suspended above these tables were posters by the artists represented. A nice touch was the handling of the entrance. It was made via a broad corridor that passed one of the helicoidal ramps, the ribbed concrete underside of which had a remarkable affinity with a model of Vladimir Tatlin's famous tower, Monument to the Third International (1920) which terminated the vista.

Despite the dream-like, dematerialized ambience, the layout had a precise diagrammatic clarity. It also exploited the luxury of the generous space available. The rooms lining the central aisle were sized differently according to the number of paintings representing an artist or illustrating a particular theme. Each painting floated in abundant screen space and there was a considerable unused area around the exhibition.

Although space was equally abundant, a contrary design approach was used for the show of the much larger American works. Rather than concealing the structure and volume of the gallery, these were exploited to evoke the lofts in which most of these works were produced and first shown. And instead of illuminating the space with uplighters, which in the Russian exhibition made the ceiling with its pools of bright light as visible as the walls and floors, spotlights were focused on the artworks, so that the grey-painted ceiling receded from view.

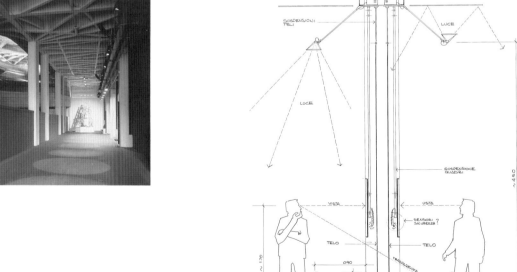

4

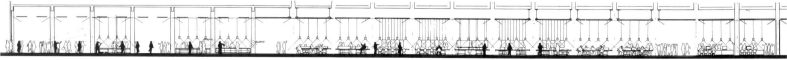

5

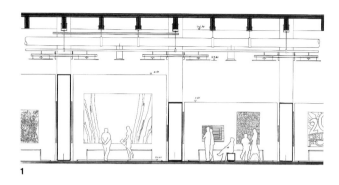

1

2

3

166 **Lingotto Factory Renovation**

'American Art 1930-1970'.

1 Partial section through gallery and installation.

2, 3 Light was focused on the exhibits alone so that sculptures sat in pools of light and paintings stood out on the white partitions.

4 Detail section and elevation.

5 Banners outside the entrance announcing the show.

6 One of the four study tables that formed the focus of the layout and from which all the partitioned rooms radiated.

7 Plan.

Client Lingotto Srl

Curators A Codognato, M Bevilacqua

Design team R Piano, M Cattaneo (architect in charge), S Ishida (associate architect), M Varratta

Lighting P Castiglioni

Graphics P Cerri

Installation Gruppo Bodino

5

6

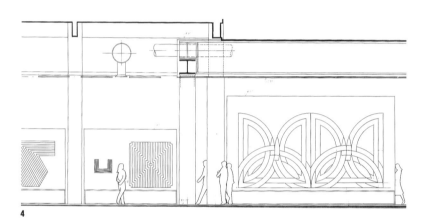

4

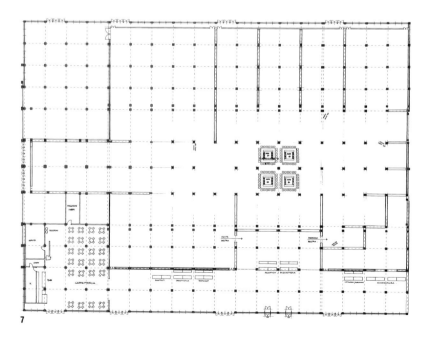

7

8

Lingotto Factory Renovation

'Andy Warhol: Success is a job in New York'.

8–10 Views of exhibition which was installed in the *palazzina* adjacent the main building.

Client Lingotto Srl
Curators A Codognato, D Desalvo
Design team R Piano, M Varratta (architect in charge), S Ishida (associate architect)
Lighting P Castiglioni
Graphics Grosz, ECO
Installation Gruppo Bodino

9

10

1

'Automobiles in Milan' exhibition Ansaldo, Milan **1990**

Like the Lingotto renovation scheme (p 150), this exhibition of cars manufactured in the region of Milan involved the conversion of old industrial premises, but as a much smaller and quicker exercise. The factory is in Milan's old industrial area of Ansaldo, and its conversion was planned as the first step towards establishing a permanent museum of Italian design. But, although the converted premises would be now perfect for such use, with some simple additions, no further progress has been made in founding the museum.

The factory chosen for conversion is dominated by a tall hall that runs the full length of the building. This main bay is flanked on one side by a narrower bay with a floor inserted above a high ground floor. For the exhibition, the old building was cleaned and repainted a pale grey inside. The lower parts of its walls were screened with white painted plasterboard; and some independent side rooms were similarly partitioned. Two rows of vintage cars were arranged on either side of the central axis of the long and brightly top-lit hall. Engineering drawings lined its walls and engines stood on low plinths before them. The rooms in the aisle contained further

exhibits. Over one end of the central axis of the nave, the Building Workshop suspended a new mezzanine. This offered an overview of the exhibition and served as a study centre.

In adapting the building for the exhibition, the Building Workshop kept in mind the design it had prepared for its intended future use as a museum. This would have entailed inserting an extra floor at what would then be first-floor level, and the construction of a narrow bay alongside the hall opposite the existing aisle. In this scheme the entrance doors open into a lobby/gallery for displaying items that give a foretaste of what is on show above. The rest of the ground floor is given over to the usual ancillary functions and a mock-up of a design studio. The main exhibition space is located above in the nave-like hall and double-level aisles that flank its long sides.

The space is now available for the fairly straightforward yet very suitable further conversion that was originally planned. Considering the importance of design to contemporary Italy, there must still be some chance of this project being undertaken, along with the formation of a permanent design museum.

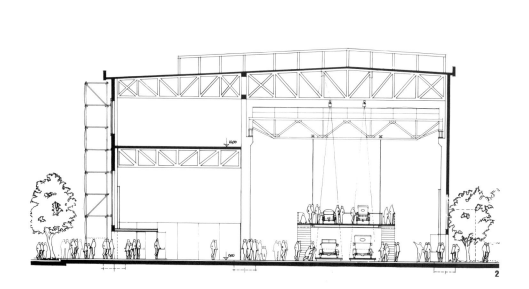

2

'Automobiles in Milan'

1 A huge billboard announcing the exhibition projected from the entrance facade.

2 Cross section.

3 One end of nave-like hall as arranged for the exhibition, with suspended mezzanine.

4 View along length of hall from suspended mezzanine.

5 View from ground level and opposite end from **4**.

6 Ground floor plan of conversion to museum.

7, **8** Two of the historic cars exhibited.

Client Milan City Council, Alfa Romeo
Design team R Piano, S Ishida (associate architect), F Marano (associate engineer), M Carroll, O Di Blasi, M Varratta
Assisted by M Nouvion, R Trapani
Structural engineer L Mascia
Lighting P Castiglioni
Graphics F Origoni & A Steiner
Installation Gruppo Bodino

3

4

5

7

8

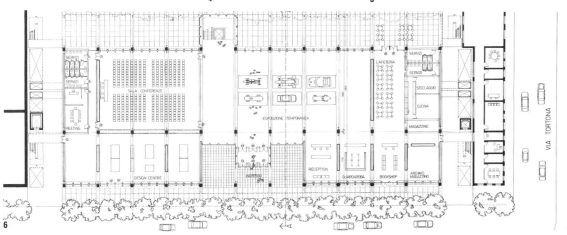

6

170

The Beyeler Foundation Museum is being constructed to put on public show the collector Ernst Beyeler's exceptional private collection of modern art. It will be built on publicly-owned land in Riehen, just outside Basle in Switzerland. Although very different, the design can be seen as an evolution from those for the Menil Collection in Houston, USA (Volume One p 140) and the Contemporary Art Museum at Newport Harbor in California, USA (Volume One p 164). It combines something of the room layout of the former with the parallel bearing wall layout of the latter. As with these earlier projects, the gallery will be capped by a roof canopy, which will admit and modulate natural light but will be otherwise independent in form and scale from the spaces below; and the roof canopy will oversail the building's external walls. In both earlier gallery designs, the elements that shade and diffuse the light are, or are part of, the structure that supports the glass roof. Here, in the Beyeler, the intention to make major elements serve more than one purpose, will be taken further in that the glass itself will be structural. Unlike these earlier schemes, the lightness of the roof will be in striking contrast to the earth-bound walls. Also, a ceiling of frosted glass or fabric will conceal the structural and light-diffusing elements above it so that these 'pieces' will not form an intrinsic part of the gallery interiors.

Although neither the plan of the museum, nor the concept for its roof, have changed much as the design has evolved, the character of the building has altered profoundly. The initial proposals differed from the designs for the American museums in that the building would not have engaged its setting in the obvious and intimate manner that they do: the Menil wrapping itself in the clapboarding of the surrounding bungalows and offering a colonnade for the public to promenade in; the Newport Harbor museum seamlessly interweaving galleries and gardens, and extending the adjacent park onto its roof. In marked contrast, the abstract and austere first design for the Beyeler Museum was somewhat aloof from its setting.

Although it was not contextual in the conventional sense of replicating or harmonizing with elements from the surroundings, the response of this first scheme to its context was in a way appropriate. Rational

Beyeler Foundation Museum Riehen, Basle, Switzerland 1992–

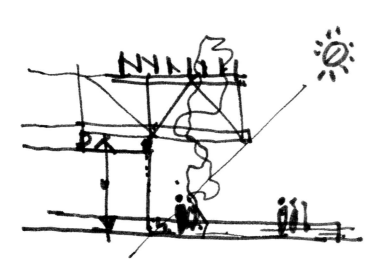

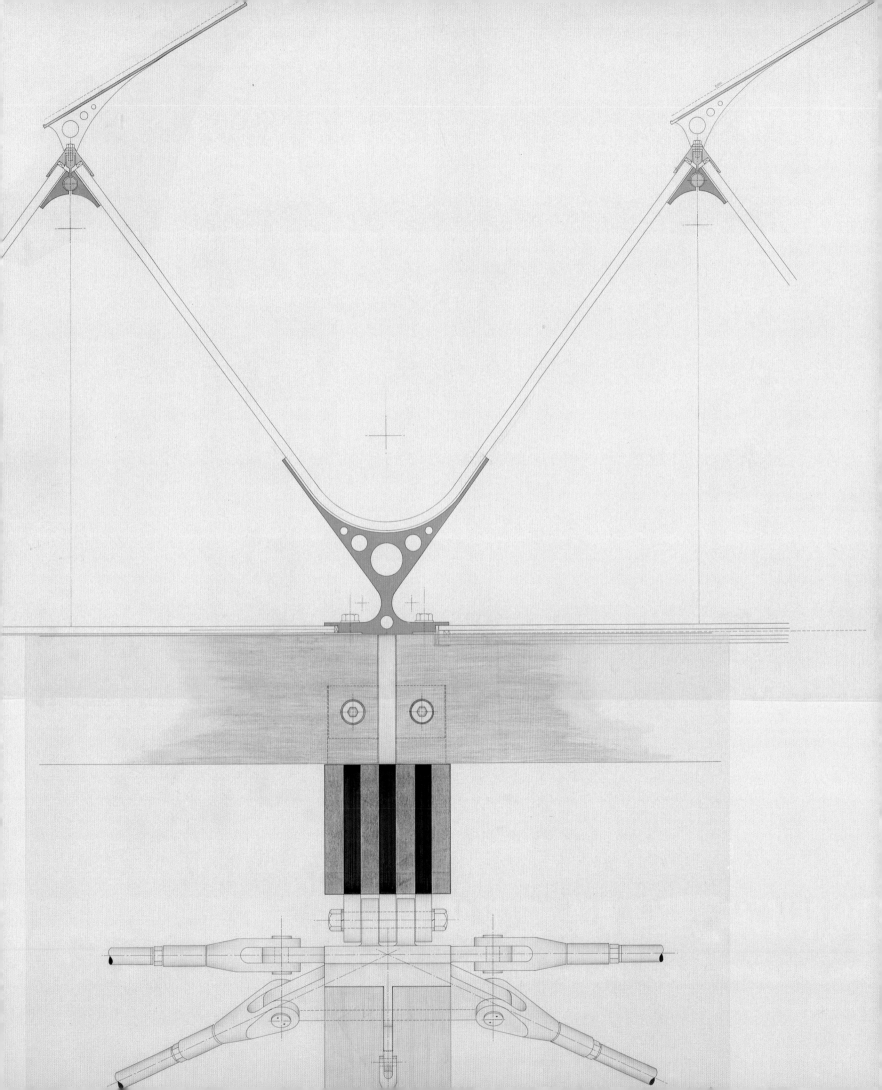

1

172 **Beyeler Foundation Museum**

Context and precedent.

1 Villa Berower and its park-like grounds
seen from where the museum is to be built.
2 The Menil Collection, Houston, USA, by
Piano & Fitzgerald, 1981-1986: its galleries
are top-lit through a glass roof.
3 Contemporary Art Museum, Newport
Harbor, USA, 1987: again lit through the roof,
it was to have merged into its park setting.

2

toughness and dry detachment
are the ultimate architectural
virtues for most Swiss architects today. Piano, with
Bernard Plattner (the associate
architect in charge of this project, and himself Swiss) thus
once again demonstrated a
capacity for divining the spirit
of a place. But however Swiss
this early design was, it was
incompatible in spirit with the
way Piano's work is developing, which is to be much
more intimate in its engagement with its surroundings and
nature, as well as with its users.
So the design has progressively
softened and become more
intrinsically embedded in its
site as it has become more complex in its elevations and
warmer in materials.

Yet the sense of clarity and
precision that persists in the
design, despite its much softened character, is apt in
another way: it reflects similar
qualities in the character of the
exacting client. And these in

turn are reflected in Beyeler's
approach to collecting Modern
and Contemporary art. The
collection, which has been carefully built up over a long
period, consists of about 180
exceptional paintings ranging
from Monet to recent East
German art. It includes fine
works by, among others,
Cézanne, Matisse, Picasso,
Braque, Klee, Kandinsky,
Rauschenberg and Lichtenstein.
There is also sculpture by
Giacometti, and from Oceania
and Easter Island.

The collection came to wide
international attention after
being shown to great effect in
Madrid's Centro Reina Sofia.
Something of the long, wide
and parallel vaulted galleries
of this converted seventeenth-
century hospital seems to have
re-emerged in the plan of the
proposed museum. But the section will be quite different, the
rooflights and translucent
ceiling being devised to fill the
galleries with a soft and even
natural light. Although only
a fraction as bright as that at
Menil, this light is also intended
to come alive as it reflects
changes in conditions outside.

The museum will be built in
what were once private gardens, of which very large trees
remain. These park-like
grounds extend northwards
along a major road from the
eighteenth-century Villa
Berower, a protected historic
monument. Sloping westwards
away from the road, the site
offers views down across
open farmland and towards
Germany. The museum will
fill more than a third of the
length of the site, and most
of its width. It lies between a

new wall to be built along the
street, and an existing stone
retaining wall that edges a
pedestrian path below the
park's eastern boundary.

Dominating the plan, four
straight walls will run roughly
north-south and parallel to a
straight stretch of the boundary
wall along the road. These
main walls will be of identical
length and rise from the middle
of the park to support the rectangular canopy of the oversailing roof. The three strips
of space between them will be
filled mostly with galleries; and
here and there openings in the
walls will create spaces two
strips wide.

Alongside the part of the
boundary wall that runs parallel to the main walls, and
beneath the flat roof it supports, will be various service
spaces opening off the entrance
lobby. This will extend between
these service spaces and the
easternmost of the four long
straight walls, and on through
a wide opening in the latter.
The resultant T-shaped lobby,
and a double-width gallery
immediately west of the bottom
of the T, will together imply a
cross-axis at right angles to the
parallel walls and somewhat
off-centre. Yet the entrance
doors will not be where one
would expect to find them in

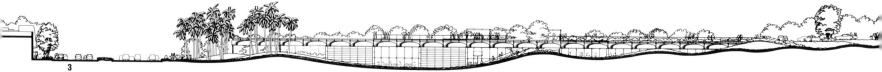

3

4

Beyeler Foundation Museum

Context and precedent.

4 Model superimposed on aerial photograph
of surroundings.

5 Basle Cathedral, built in the same red sandstone as that proposed for the walls of the
museum.

6 The Menil Collection: as with the Beyeler
Museum, its roof canopy also oversails its
external walls.

7 Location and roof plan showing the
museum and its grounds in relationship to the
open field that extends westwards down to a
stream.

5

6

such a configuration: on the cross axis and on the street. Instead, they will be behind the boundary wall and hidden from the street, at the end of each arm of the lobby.

In the earliest proposals, the four main walls rose as severe and identical rectangles to support a very light roof that cantilevered out on the ends of spindly steel trusses. It was a design of compelling clarity and frigid severity. Now, however, these walls will step up and down in rhythms that are syncopated in relation to each other and some of them will stretch out into the garden as low retaining walls. Like the boundary walls (which will be partly kept and partly rebuilt), these walls will all be built or faced in the same warm red sandstone that was used to construct Basle Cathedral. Also contributing to the changed character of the design, are the shapely props of laminated timber that will project to support the oversailing roof.

Approach to the museum will be from the south. Gates set opposite a tram terminus will open into the grounds just north of the Villa Berower. Once inside the gates, visitors will be faced with several choices: they may enter the villa, which will house the museum bookshop, cafeteria and administrative offices; or they may walk past it to see the landscaped garden and the view; or they may turn right to proceed directly to the museum. Those turning to the museum will be guided by a low stone retaining wall that eventually steps up to become the easternmost of the four long straight museum walls.

The approach path will continue between this wall and the angled boundary wall, which together funnel the path towards the entrance doors at the southern end of the T-shaped lobby. The angled boundary wall on the other (northern) side of the lobby will also funnel movement. Here will be both a secondary pedestrian route to another set of entrance doors and a vehicular ramp diving down into the basement, which will accommodate parking for staff cars, a loading dock, storerooms, plantrooms and workshops; there will also be a gallery for delicate works such as watercolours that can be lit only softly and artificially.

On the main floor above, the four long walls that modulate the galleries will project beyond the enclosed part of the building to support the end of the oversailing roof; the broad

173

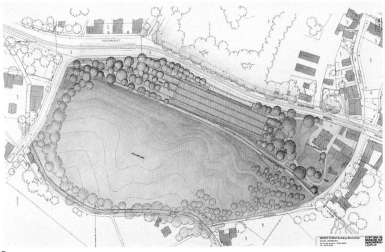

7

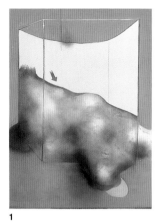

1

2

174 **Beyeler Foundation Museum**
The collection consists of paintings by such major modern artists as **1** Francis Bacon, **2** Joan Miro, **5** Piet Mondrian, **6** Mark Rothko, **7** Henri Matisse, **8** Henri Rousseau, and **9** Max Ernst. It also includes modern sculptures such as those by **4** Pablo Picasso, and Oceanic and African pieces such as **3** Melanesian Uli figure from New Ireland, and **10** Bakongo figure from Zaire.

3

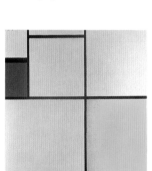

5

4

eaves will be supported in the cross-direction by the ends of the props that project from the outermost walls. The parallel walls, though forcefully expressed outside, will be discontinuous inside, interrupted by openings both large and small. And the galleries that fill the 7.5 metre strip between these 70 cm wide walls will stop short of the ends of the walls by differing amounts and terminated by fully-glazed screens. The effect will be to assert the dominance of the walls and suggest both a priority of enclosing frame over enclosed space (a rather Swiss trait), and a certain systematic, yet indeterminate, quality that is a hallmark of many Piano designs.

Stretched in front of the westernmost wall, directly below the outer edge of the roof overhang, will be a glazed wall with insistently close-spaced mullions. This will enclose a long and narrow winter garden which, in contrast to the introverted and softly north-lit galleries, will enjoy the view and direct afternoon sun. It will serve as a sculpture gallery and enclose a pair of stairs and a lift down to the basement gallery. The two ends of the winter garden will be used for watching videos.

Unlike Piano's earlier buildings, but in common with other projects in this second volume, much of the structure will be unexpressed. Elements of the roof structure will be visible around the building's perimeter, but none of it will be visible from the galleries; and the concrete frame will be concealed almost entirely. Although stone will line the external faces of all walls, it will be non-structural. The four main walls will enclose wide cavities, concealing the concrete columns and accommodating the extract ducts for air drawn from the galleries through the wall-heads.

8

6

7

9

10

11

Beyeler Foundation Museum

11–14 Views of study model of end of two north-south walls. The props that reach from the heads of these walls to support the rafters are also elements of triangular sectioned trusses that cantilever north and south and span internal openings.

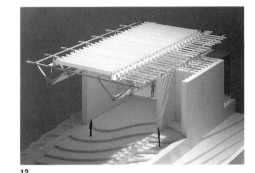

12

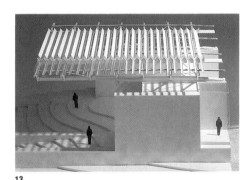

13

14

Conditioned air will enter the main gallery level through inlets in the timber floor, which will be raised 48 cm above the concrete slab.

Contrasting with the earth-bound understatement of the walls will be the roof hovering lightly above them, itself a mix-ture of understatement and considerable complexity. It is a design for which there is some precedent in Piano's work. Like the roof of the office/workshop he built in Genoa for his first practice, Studio Piano, in 1968–9 (Volume One, p 44) it will consist of a deep structure supporting compound roof-lights. In Basle, however, the primary structure was at first a series of trusses spaced three metres apart, rather than a space-frame. The north-lights will be small monitors, extend-ing like large corrugations across the roof canopy, except where interrupted by the gut-ters that will be located above each of the long walls.

The trusses and monitors are still undergoing design develop-ment, with various solutions being considered for both. At an intermediate stage, the favoured design for the truss consisted of upper and lower chords of tubular steel sup-porting steel joists that carried the longitudinal gutters and monitors; the splayed elements of the web between these chords were laminated timber. These looked, and in part func-tioned, like props which lean out from the heads of the walls and taper as they reach towards the upper chord. In the current scheme these props support flat rafters where the trusses once were, and are also components

of triangular sectioned trusses. These span openings in the wall below and cantilever beyond the ends of the projecting north-south walls.

Two very different versions of the monitors are being studied. Both use glass in long self-supporting sheets and are equally striking in their mini-malist approach to material and detail. In one version, the glass is used in vertical sheets which will span over the joists that connect the trusses. The glass will help support the rest of the small, but fairly conven-tionally shaped, monitor. As usual, this will exclude all direct sunlight and reflect downward a controlled amount of light. It is intended that these parts will be extruded in aluminium. But the size of this section is larger than is possible currently with a single extrusion, and the glass sheets are also too long for any tem-pering oven.

The second design being studied uses v-shaped glass channels to span between joists and carry water to the gutters. The north-facing side of the channel will admit light and be protected from direct sun by a shade cantilevered from the ele-ment connecting the top of two channels. An insulating panel against its inner face will

175

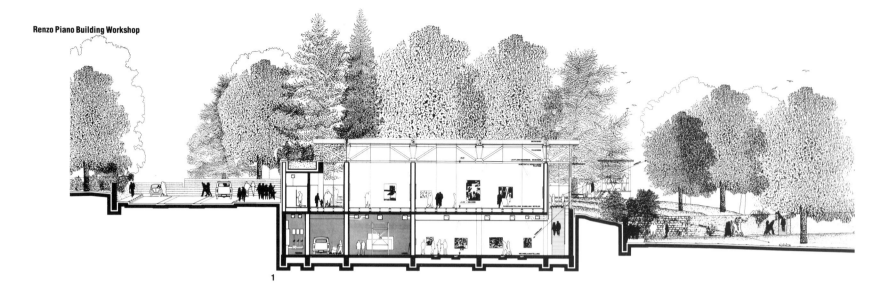

1

Beyeler Foundation Museum

Drawings.

1 Cross section looking south.

2 West elevation.

3 East elevation.

4 Longitudinal section looking east.

5 Ground floor plan. Scale 1:1 000.

2

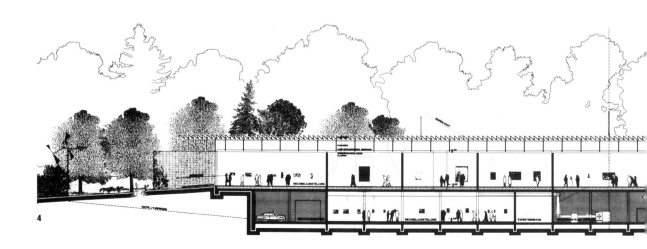

3

4

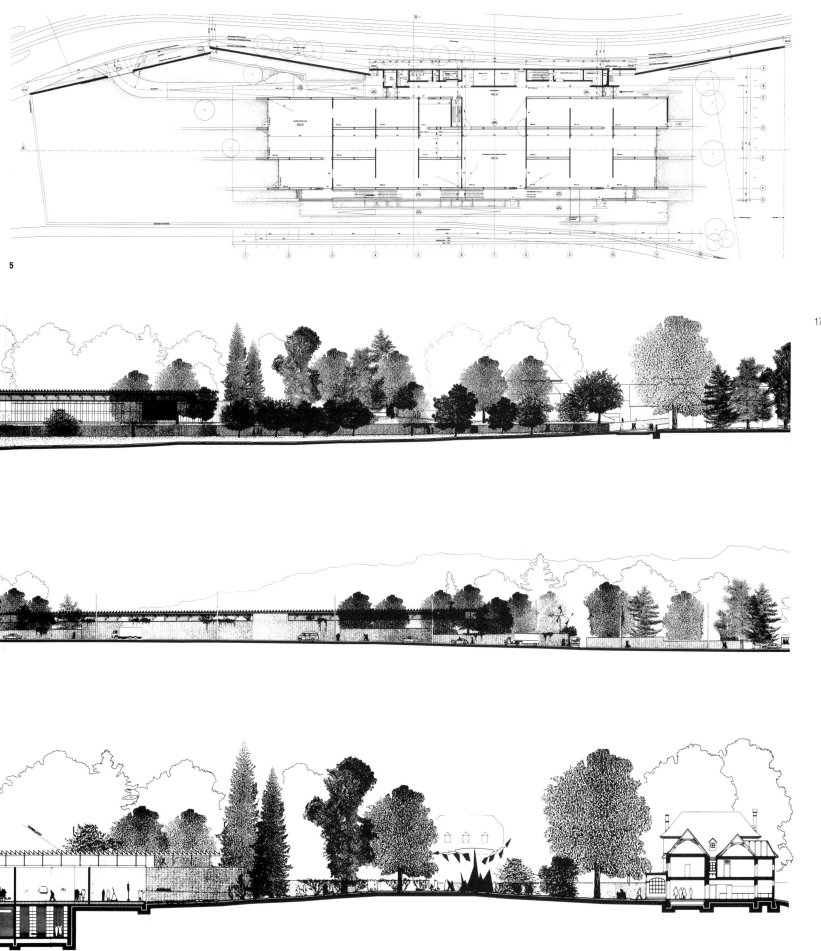

5

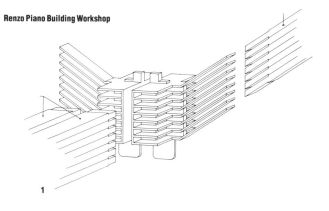

1

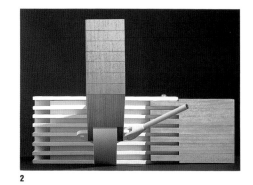

2

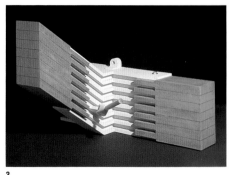

3

178 **Beyeler Foundation Museum**

Details

1 Exploded isometric view of steel finger-jointed element that connects the double beam/lower chord of truss, that sits on main walls, with props that support the rafters.

2, **3**, **7** Full size mock-up of joint shown in **1**, **5**, **6** & **9**.

4 Portion of west elevation with glazing of winter garden below and structure of roof and ends of glass monitors clearly revealed above.

5 Detail section of head of west wall.

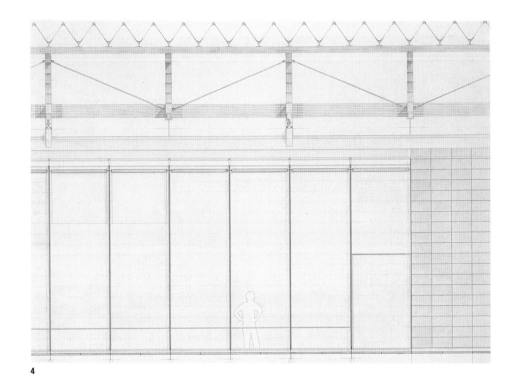

4

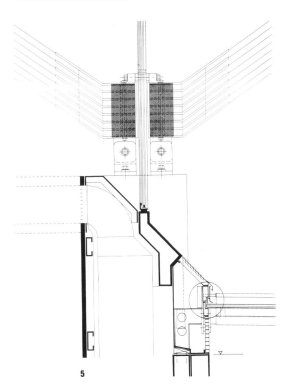

5

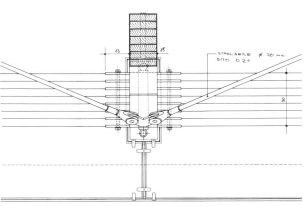

6

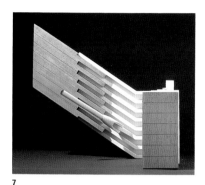

7

Beyeler Foundation Museum

7 Side elevation of variant of joint seen in all details on this page.

8 Aerial view of model.

9 Section through head of external wall and roof structure.

Client Beyeler Foundation

Architect Renzo Piano Building Workshop with J Burckhardt & Partner AG Basel (collaborating local architect)

Design team R Piano, B Plattner (associate in charge), L Couton

Assisted by E Belik, J Berger, P Hendier, L Epprecht, W Vassal

Model makers J P Allain, P Darmer, A Schultz

Structural and services engineers Ove Arup & Partners (T Barker, J Wernick, A Sedgwick)

Collaborating local engineers Cyrill Burger & Partner AG; Bogenschütz AG; Jakob Forrer AG; Eledtrizitäts AG, Basel

8

9

other side of the channel. Here again, the glass elements are too large for current technology. Both proposals for the monitors currently present unresolved technical problems. The final design will depend on resolving one of these proposals elegantly, in conceptual and visual terms, or, just as likely, on the research generating yet another solution.

To diffuse and further control the light admitted through the monitors, grilles of horizontal louvres will be suspended just below the trusses. This grillage will also provide a surface for maintainance workmen to walk upon. Further diffusing the light will be a translucent ceiling that will seal this

2.15 metre deep loft space from the gallery below. The architects would like the closure of the loft space above the head of the external walls to be achieved with clear glass. The transparency would emphasize the sense of the roof floating weightlessly in the air and in the light that it admits. But the mechanical engineers prefer an opaque material to exclude all low-level sunlight. And it has yet to be resolved whether a fine cloth velarium or some textured element might be stretched below the translucent ceiling. The problem is to avoid the frigidly clinical and lifeless feeling that may result from using glass alone in the very low light levels (250 lux) that conservation of the paintings necessitates.

In ecologically-aware Switzerland, air conditioning is forbidden on grounds of energy conservation unless a compelling case can be made for both its necessity and its

efficiency. Here, the conservation of fragile art works requires the stable temperature and humidity which can only be achieved by air conditioning; and mechanical engineers Tom Barker and Andy Sedgwick from Ove Arup & Partners have convinced the local authorities that their proposal will be exceptionally efficient.

With conditioned-air fed in through the floor and exhausted at the head of the gallery walls, the air in the museum will be stratified in layers of different temperature with the warmest of them under the high ceiling at 5.25 metres above floor level. People and paintings, however, will only occupy the lower two or three metres of the galleries where stable and comfortable conditions can be maintained efficiently despite fluctuations and higher temperatures nearer the ceiling. These high-level variations cannot be eliminated, since admitting natural light through the roof will limit the degree to which it can be insulated.

Nevertheless, the loft space within the roof will serve as an effective thermal buffer with temperature fluctuations restricted to between 32 degrees centigrade in summer and 20 degrees in winter (when it will have to be heated occasionally). The naturally ventilated and west-facing winter garden will also serve as a thermal buffer, with temperatures fluctuating through a smaller range of some 26 to 20 degrees centigrade. The exclusion of westerly sun from the basement gallery, and the problems of entering this relatively dark room, to which the eye will only adjust very slowly after the brightly-lit winter garden, have yet to be resolved as this design continues to develop.

179

In San Giovanni Rotondo in southern Italy, where the foothills of the Apeninnes start to rise from the Apulian plain, shallow arches made up from huge blocks of local stone will rise from a dished stone floor. These mighty arches will support the domed roof of a vast pilgrimage church set at the end of an enormous new triangular piazza, one edge of which will overlook the plain and the approaching pilgrims. With these arches Piano and his collaborators are not exploring the limits of some new material. Instead they are pushing to new limits one of the oldest and most natural of materials, the character of which and the skills available for working it, have influenced so much of architectural history.

This evolving design is the last to which the late Peter Rice contributed in its initial stages. He was largely responsible for the decision to use stone arches. Like Piano, he was as interested in exploring new potentials in old materials as he was those of new and as yet untried ones. With stone, it is the computer that promises to liberate new potential. The computer-guided precision cutting of stone which is now possible ensures an even distribution of stresses within it, and so a more predictable structural performance. These factors, combined with new theoretical understandings of arch action and the number-crunching capacities of the computer, which allows arches to be calculated as an infinite number of hinges rather than in terms of thrust action, might give new life to stone as a structural rather than mere cladding material. And because each block can be cut independently by computer-controlled saws, there is no economy to be gained by the repetition of identical blocks. These can just as easily be 'copies' of each other at different sizes. So each arch, as at San Giovanni Rotondo, can be slightly different in span.

Peter Rice had already explored the use of stone in the arched gateway to Seville's Expo '92, which he designed with the Barcelona architects, Martorell Bohigas Mackay. The arches of this gate are very tall and the granite colonettes so slender as to be the envy of any Gothic mason. But the structure at Seville is too virtuoso: the visual effect is so insubstantial that the arches have little presence and the viewer does not register and thrill to the fact that this precarious poise is achieved in

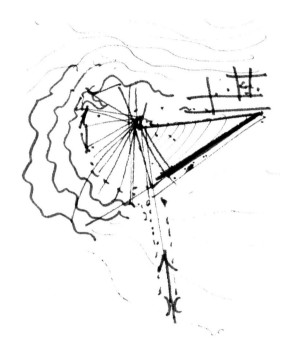

180

Padre Pio Pilgrimage Church San Giovanni Rotondo, Foggia, Italy **1991–**

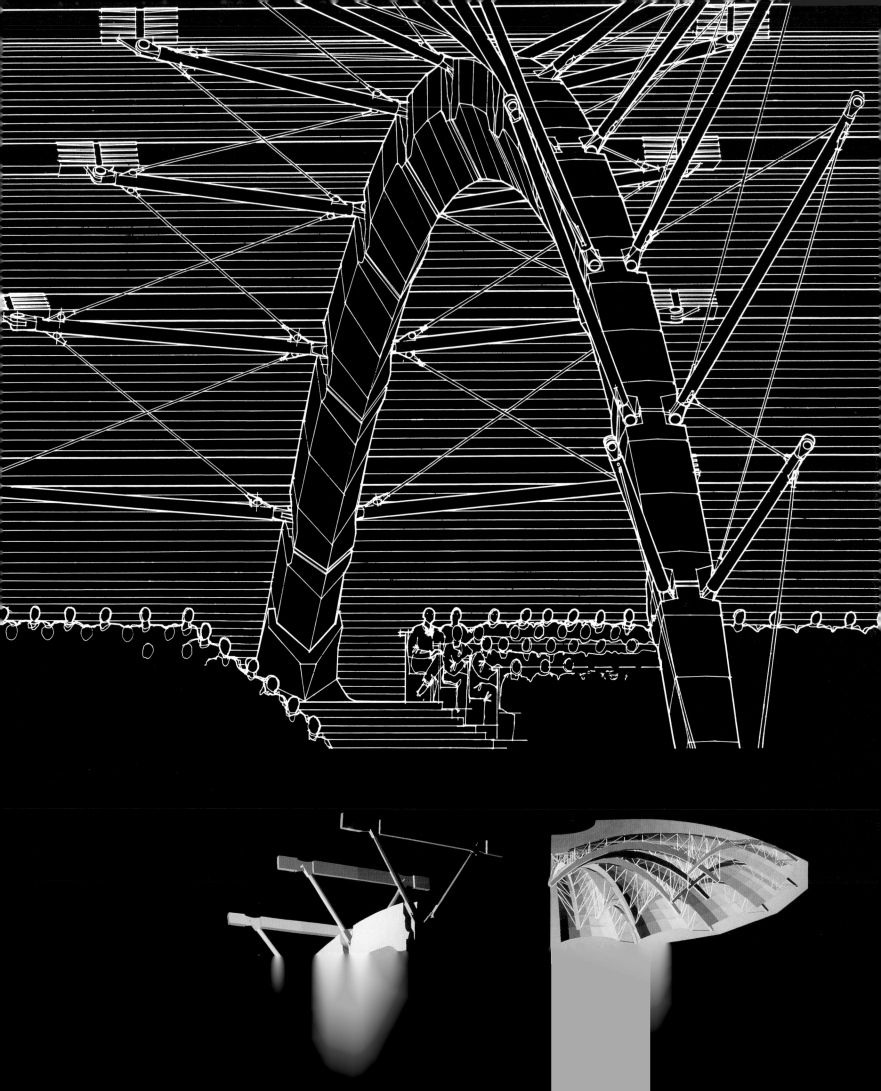

1

Padre Pio Pilgrimage Church

Precedent.

1 Martorell Bohigas Mackay: pavilion at Expo '92 in Seville. The slender columns and arches of granite are an earlier exercise in stone by engineer Peter Rice.

2 Pier Luigi Nervi: interior of the ribbed concrete dome of the Palazzo del Sport, Rome, an exemplar of Italian concrete engineering.

3 Elevation of the sports hall, Ravenna, 1986. The domed roof will be of ribbed concrete.

182

stone, not some light and ersatz material. The Padre Pio Pilgrimage Church will be quite different. Here the funicular arches, which will span up to 50 metres (a little more than the diameter of the drum of St Peter's in Rome), will be fairly shallow and built of huge and obviously heavy blocks. They are bound to have a powerfully commanding presence.

Until a few decades ago, San Giovanni Rotondo was a tiny town, with a Capuchin monastery close by. This monastery was the home of the charismatic and miracle-working monk, Padre Pio (1887–1968), the only cleric known to have been marked by stigmata, and the town is now a major pilgrimage centre visited by hundreds of thousands of pilgrims every year. They flock to see the original chapel where Padre Pio preached, and the

much larger church built in the 1950s to house the congregations he attracted. Several new hotels house the pilgrims, whose donations have funded a large hospital on the slopes above the monastery.

Now a much larger church is required, and with it proper facilities for parking cars and coaches, and for catering to the various needs of the throngs of pilgrims. The Building Workshop's original commission to build the church has expanded to cover the construction or masterplanning of many of these elements, all of which, like the church itself, are currently under design development. The scheme now includes the piazza and its retaining wall in front of the church, a hotel with its radiating rooms terraced into the slopes above the monastery, and a subterranean parking garage for coaches.

The new church will be sited to the south-east and down the slope from the old monastery. The main approach for the pilgrim throngs will no longer be from the town centre to the east but via a new road, which will climb the slope from the south. On both sides of this road will be new hotels and parking for coaches and cars. To those climbing the hill, the shallow dome of the church will be largely hidden by trees. Conspicuous instead, and serving as a surrogate facade

for the church, will be the piazza's huge retaining wall. This will be 25 metres high at its tallest end which marks a turn in the street and where its buttresses also serve as a belfry for a dozen enormous bells.

As with the similarly prominent wall of the famous pilgrimage church at Assisi, this one will beckon pilgrims and then guide them up alongside it or, where it is tall enough for these, within its arcades. Sheltering within this stretch of the wall will be cafes and souvenir shops of the type commonly found in pilgrimage centres. As the wall tapers in height up the slope it will lead pilgrims towards the monastery, its chapel and church. The wall will stop a little short of the monastery, at the apex of the new triangular piazza. Turning into this space, which will also accommodate overflow feast-day congregations of up to 30 000 people, the sloped paving will direct the pilgrims down towards the church. As one approaches, the church's interior will become increasingly visible through its glass entrance doors and screen. These will reach up to the roof, which extends beyond them as a shaded and welcoming porch.

2

3

4

Padre Pio Pilgrimage Church

Context.

4 Chapel and monastery as they were when Padre Pio first preached there.

5 Assisi: the church rises above a conspicuous retaining wall.

6,7 The area around the site retains a rural atmosphere.

8 The original chapel today, facing a piazza and flanked by the 1950s church.

5

6

7

The piazza's stone paving will continue uninterrupted under the glass screen and into the church. Here, it will curve to form the dished floor from which the huge radiating arches rise. The arches will be arranged in inner and outer rings, those in the inner ring coming together just behind the altar. From the vast spans of the arches near the entrance, the arches in both rings will shorten progressively in span so that the space will spiral somewhat tighter towards the sacristry which abuts the last of them. The 10 000 seats will be arranged in blocks defined by both radial and cross aisles set between the arches, which would otherwise obstruct the views of the altar. Also arranged radially will be the chapels and meeting rooms of a crypt that occupies some of the space below the dished floor.

Although the arches are bound to give a literal *gravitas* to this vast space, their heaviness seems to contradict Piano's persistent quest for lightness. Hints of this will come from the system of timber props and slender steel stays that will reach out to support the stone-clad timber roof. All these elements will seem to float in the chiaroscuro of light that will flood down from rooflights, the resulting impression of lightness emphasizing by contrast the grave massiveness of the masonry. The stainless steel post-tensioned cables that clamp the smaller blocks of stone into larger units, give a silvery metallic outline to the inside edges of these arches. Despite this the lower part of the church will project an archaic and earthy quality. This may seem appropriate to commemorate a simple monk and shelter the ancient rituals of the mass, but many might be surprised to find it coming from the hand of Piano.

The design is still far from fully developed. Particularly

183

8

1

Padre Pio Pilgrimage Church

Pilgrimage centre.

1 Aerial view of San Giovanni Rotondo which has mushroomed in recent decades. The field below the monastery is to be the site.

2 Pilgrim throngs in the piazza outside the existing church.

3,4 Pilgrim processions.

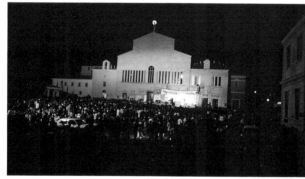

2

3

4

problematic is the question of how to place a conventional altar in this space. The wide-fanning arches are designed to swoop down to a single potent focus, with which it will be hard to compete. Yet a long and curving altar and/or altar rail from which several priests can dispense the sacrament would work well in a pilgrimage church attended by vast crowds. At least part of it would then certainly be seen from all seats, and might also have a presence strong enough to command the space. Another problem needing refinement is that, as currently designed, the propped roof shell floats too high above the arches and so threatens to dwarf them.

There have also been investigations into alleviating the jelly-mould or pudding-like character of the domed roof which will dominate the exterior, by leaving some segments between the outer ring of arches unroofed and unenclosed. This will allow planting to enter the apparent volume of the church, and so will interweave architecture with nature. It will also create pockets within the vast space, suited to smaller congregations such as weddings. These pockets can be opened up to the planted courts allowing them to be used in conjunction with any event inside. Opening the church out towards the landscape in this way also makes more sense and use of the trees, which will form a wood around it.

Another part of the design currently being studied is the glazed screen and entrance door between church and piazza. The intention is to emphasize the Capuchin notion of the church as an open house welcoming in the world, just as the simple materials and sparse detail inside are meant to be consistent with the spirit of Padre Pio and his Order. The idea at the moment is that the whole glass screen will rise very slowly as the bells summon the pilgrims to service. The result will be a drawn-out ritual that very visibly opens the church to the world, and emphasizes the notion of the church and piazza as a single sacred unit. In the latest study, the whole segment-shaped screen is designed to be raised to project above the roof by an almost neo-medieval contraption. This is certain not to be the final solution.

To isolate the piazza from the hubbub of arriving pilgrims below, and so intensify the sacred spirit of the piazza, the retaining wall will be capped by a broad, shallow-sloped, coping. Nothing in the immediate foreground will be seen, only the distant plain and horizon. This focus on the horizon, which will instil a sense of the sacred is, of course, a device often repeated by Le Corbusier. He had learnt how potent it could be from the monasteries of Mount Athos in Greece, as well as the Parthenon.

As with so many Building Workshop designs, this one might seem to be an anomaly, quite unlike anything it has done before. The huge domed roof of the proposed Ravenna sports hall might be seen as a precedent. But the Ravenna roof, like the domes of Pier Luigi Nervi, will be made of a single modern material, reinforced concrete. In the way it utilises traditional materials, wood and stone, the Padre Pio Pilgrimage Church is the antithesis of Ravenna and of what is thought of as almost a modern Italian tradition. However, in its proposed use of the stone arches to embrace

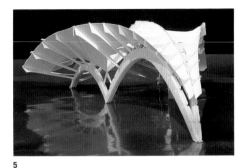

5

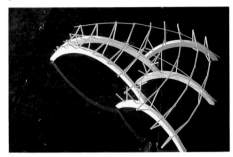

6

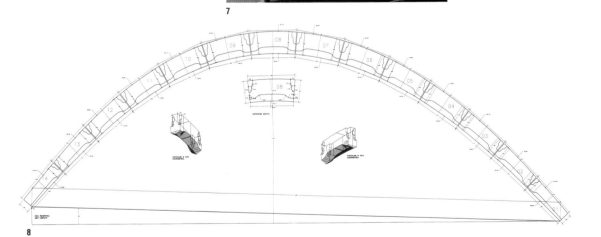

7

Padre Pio Pilgrimage Church

Structural studies.

5,6,7 Early study models explore different arrangements of secondary structure.

8 Elevation of a single funicular arch and views of a typical stone block from which it will be assembled.

9,10,11 Sequence shows induced collapse of a study model of an arch.

8

mother Earth as well as the congregation, and in shaping public space and architecture as an integral whole, it is indicative of some of the major directions in which Piano's architecture is moving.

Much of the inspiration to use stone and wood with steel at San Giovanni Rotondo came from Ravenna, not from the proposed sports hall, but from the famous church of S Apollinare in Classe. Piano had been pondering how to ensure that the vast space of the pilgrimage church would be quite different in character from a sports hall, which it is not unlike in scale and shape. At S Apollinare he was struck by how much of the sacred feeling came from two things: from the contrast of materials, brick and wood with some steel chains, and from the clearly expressed hierarchy of structural components, which together with the boarding make up the wooden roof. The Padre Pio Pilgrimage Church will exploit both these attributes to achieve its character, using stone instead of brick and steel cables rather than chains.

Also drawing on tradition, the Building Workshop has already set up a *fabbrica della chiesa*, or on-site workshop. This was inspired by the on-site workshops of the medieval masons who built the cathedrals (the subject of one of Piano's 'Open Site' television programmes, Volume One p 66). It also has a clear parallel in the model shop at Church of the Sagrada Família in Barcelona. In large part it is there to involve the local populace and visiting pilgrims, and enthuse them about the enterprise of building the church. At the moment it is being used to test the stone, and to build plaster and wooden models of the church and some of its details. Some of these models will be employed to test various solutions for the natural lighting. Associated with this venture is the establishment of a nursery for the trees that will one day surround and perhaps partially invade the church.

185

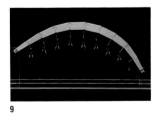

9

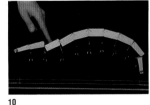

10

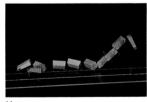

11

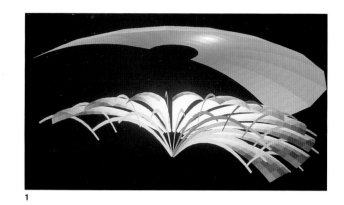

1

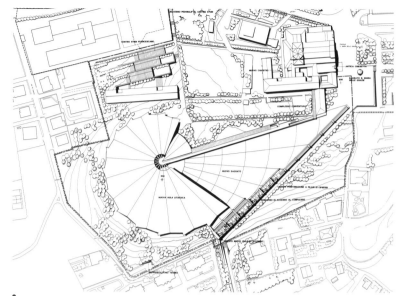

3

186

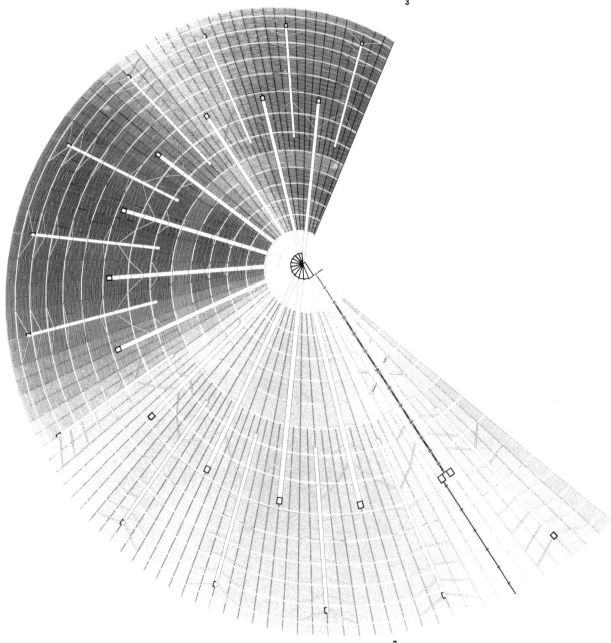

2

Padre Pio Pilgrimage Church

Church and piazza.

1 Computer rendering of arches with domed roof raised above them.

2 Reflected ceiling plan of church.

3,4,5 Plans of church, piazza and immediate context: **3** roof level, **4** main level (with parts within outer ring of arches left unroofed as planted courts), and **5** crypt level with chapels and meeting rooms/auditoria.

6,7 Views of study model.

8 Cross section through church and wall.

9 Long section of church and sloping piazza. Old monastery is seen in side elevation on right.

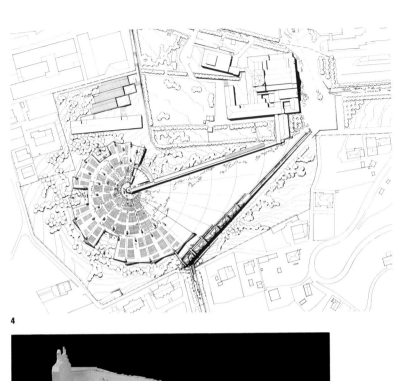

4

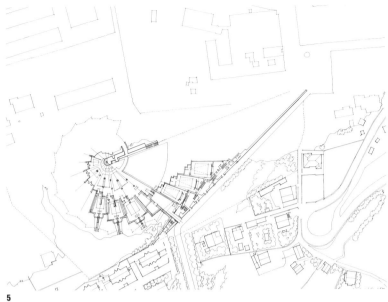

5

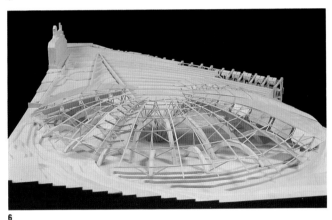

6

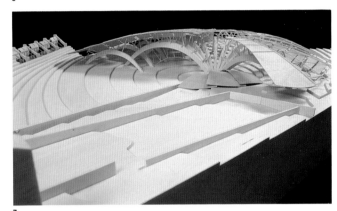

7

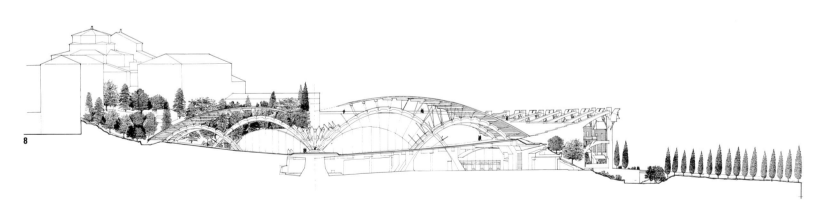

8

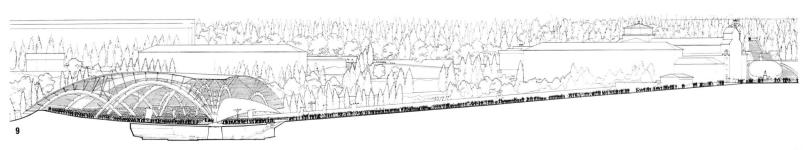

9

Padre Pio Pilgrimage Church

Detail studies.

1,2 Sectional elevations of wall that edges piazza: **1** early study of the tallest end with crypt below piazza and bridge from piazza to walkway behind top of wall, and **2** later study of similar portion now serving as belfry with curved wooden acoustic reflectors.

3 Sectional elevation of stone arch and secondary timber and steel structure supporting segment of roof.

4,5 Computer rendered perspectives of structural elements.

188

1

2

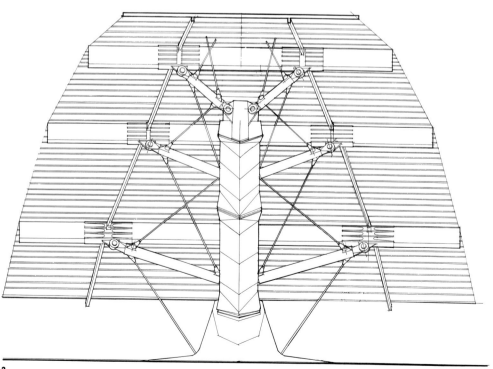

3

4

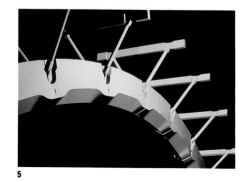

5

6

Padre Pio Pilgrimage Church

Client Frati Minori Cappuccini, Foggia

Design team R Piano, K Fraser and G
Grandi (architects in charge), P Bodega,
I Corte (CAD), S D'Atri (CAD), B Ditchburn,
V Di Turi, E Fitzgerald, S Ishida (associate
architect), L Lin, F Marano (associate engi-
neer), M Palmore, P Persia (CAD)

Assisted by H Hirsch

Model makers M Bassignani, D Cavagna

Team co-ordinator Alberto Giordano

Structural and services engineers
Ove Arup & Partners (P Rice, T Barker,
J Wernick), R Calzona, Rome

Acoustics Müller-Bbm

Cost estimations STED (A Grasso,
S Baldelli)

Site supervision and local support
G Muciaccia

Liturgical advisor G Grasso

Town planner G Amadeo

189

Padre Pio Pilgrimage Church

6 Study model of structure.

7 Plan detail of perimeter of church.

8 Detail section through perimeter of church.

9 Study of primary and secondary structure
where arches meet behind altar.

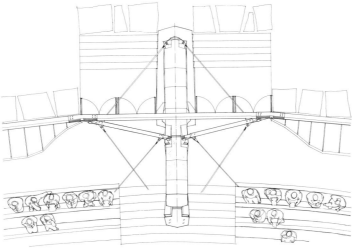
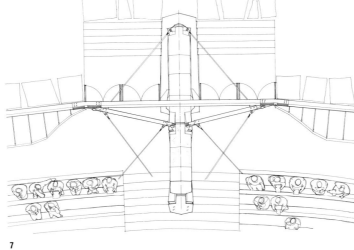

7

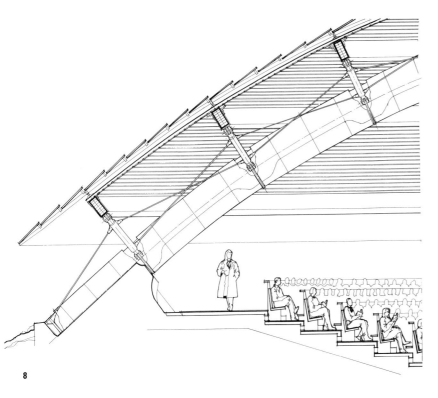

8

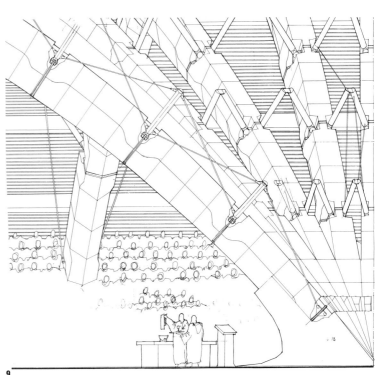

9

190

J M Tjibaou Cultural Centre Nouméa, New Caledonia **1991–**

A series of curving cage-like structures of wooden ribs and slats will soon rise from the central ridge of a promontory covered in palm and pine trees that separates the Bay of Magenta from a small lagoon. These striking structures, which will blend with, as much as emerge from, the dense indigenous vegetation, will crown and partially surround each of the major spaces of the Jean Marie Tjibaou Cultural Centre. The magnificent site for this project is on the eastern edge of Nouméa, capital of the Pacific island of New Caledonia; the building is to be a gift from the French Government to its overseas *département* and its indigenous people. The cultural centre will both commemorate the traditional society of the Kanaks and provide a focus in the inevitable evolution of its culture. Exhibitions and other forms of display, together with special events, music, dance and various day-to-day activities, are all intended to ensure that, no matter how much the Kanak culture changes, it need not be severed from a sense of contact with its historic roots. Aspects of this traditional culture inspired parts of the building's design and also the treatment of the surrounding landscaping.

The commission to build the cultural centre was won in competition with a small invited international group of architects. A few critics were unnerved by the Building Workshop scheme; it dared to flirt with the folkloric and yet was overly dependent on sophisticated technology. They also found its hugely romantic gestures at odds with the abstraction and austerity conventionally associated with Modernism. But the design struck a common and more sympathetic nerve with almost everybody else, thrilling architects and public alike, and was greeted with the most extraordinary enthusiasm. In part this was because it looked like nothing they had seen before, and yet also seemed a perfectly natural and highly evocative response to the programme and place. But much of the scheme's appeal stemmed from its suggestion of some South Sea island fantasy of achieving a harmonious relationship with both nature and with a culture that had always enjoyed such harmony, while still being blessed with all the benefits of contemporary technology.

For all the immense appeal of this competition design, the Building Workshop (in particular Piano and Paul Vincent, the

1

J M Tjibaou Cultural Centre

Significant precedent: earlier projects that
explored some of the same themes.
1 IBM Travelling Pavilion, 1982-1984: this
demountable exhibition pavilion also had a
structure of shapely laminated wood elements.
2 Il Rigo Housing, Corciano, Italy, by Piano &
Rice Associates, 1978: an early exercise in
community participation.
3 The late Jean-Marie Tjibaou, a Kanak leader.

3

associate in charge) was aware
that much of it was a largely
instinctual, and in some ways
excessive, response to the setting and local settlements. It
needed to be thoroughly
rethought, tested and refined.
The design has subsequently
evolved through several clearly
identifiable stages. These are all
illustrated here to show how a
'typically untypical' design by
the Building Workshop progressively evolves in interaction
with client and consultants, and
with the aid of design and test
models, computer analysis and
wind-testing, and even with
full-size prototyping of part of
the design.

2

In the original competition
scheme of April 1991, the centre nestled gently yet inextrica-
bly into the topography and
vegetation of the site, and
appeared to be similarly deep-
rooted in the local culture. It
achieved these two goals by
evoking vegetal analogies and
formal echoes with traditional
settlements. Along the crest of
the promontory, a covered
promenade curved like a stalk
connecting the fruit-like clus-
ters of the various departments,
the major spaces of which were
circular in plan. Around each
such kernel of fully enclosed
and technologically serviced
space was wrapped a tall husk-
like cage of curved laminated-
timber elements, braced by steel
rods and clad with thin timber
slats. The Building Workshop
came to call each of these elements a 'case'. They persist in
much-altered form in the design

that will be built. The cases
mediated between the building
and its setting in various ways.
Visually they were the dominant elements of the design, yet
they were akin to, and so would
blend with, the trees, particularly the indigenous columnar
pines. They also echoed the
forms of the traditional Kanak
huts so that the clustered cases
of each department in turn
recalled a traditional hamlet.

But the cases mediated also
between centre, community
and climate in ways other than
the visual. The idea at this stage
was that the cladding of slats of
local wood (bark strips and
woven palm fronds were for a
short time considered instead)
would be replaced periodically
by members of the community
in a participative ritual of
regeneration, in much the same
way as the villagers traditionally collaborated to rethatch
each of their huts. (For similar
reasons some of the landscaping was based on traditional
patterns of cultivation, so that
the community could participate in its upkeep and maintain
these customary social and
agricultural forms.) To mediate
in the building's relationship
with the climate, the cases were
designed to aid passive ventilation, either by scooping breezes
down into the building, or by
helping induce and guide convection currents up and out of
it, aided by the venturi effect. In
this original design the cases
were placed on both sides of the
spinal promenade, some opening up to the prevailing winds
and others turning their backs
to them; it was hoped these
might work in concert, inducing a through-flow of air in
parts of the building.

4

J M Tjibaou Cultural Centre

Significant precedent.

4 UNESCO Neighbourhood Workshop in Otranto, Italy, by Piano & Rice Associates, 1979: probably Piano's most seminal exercise in community participation.

5 Jules Vernes Leisure Park, Amiens, France, 1986: this competition also used natural materials (bamboo) to harmonize with surrounding vegetation.

6 UNESCO Travelling Workshop planned for Senegal.

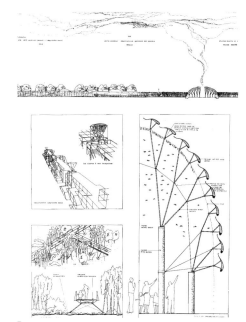

5

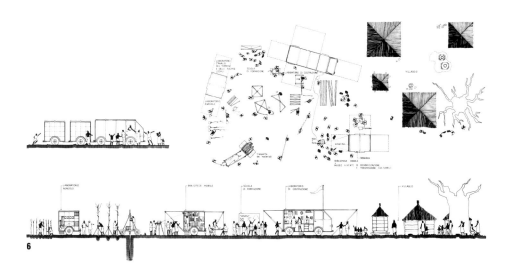

6

Access to the site is from the north. From here, in the competition scheme, the road passed a shaded car park, next to the lagoon, to reach the end of the covered promenade. It then swung eastwards to reach a residential compound with cottages and dining facilities for visiting artists. Between these cottages and the cultural centre, on lower land against the sea, was an arc of traditional huts with open space before them in which to show facets of Kanak life and to stage traditional ceremonies. This basic zoning has remained unchanged throughout all subsequent stages of the design.

Along the spinal covered promenade of the competition design, departments were arranged with those activities likely to be visited by the public in the largest numbers closest to the entrance. Those to which public access would be more restricted were located at the far end. Departments and activities needing relative quiet were placed on the lagoon-side of the promenade; those that would

be undisturbed by the sounds of the waves and the persistent monsoon wind coming off the ocean were on the opposite side. Near the entrance were reception and administration areas. Beyond these, on the lagoon-side of the spine, was an auditorium for live performance and film, which had a raked floor and a revolving stage set in the base of one of the largest of the cases. Between this and the lagoon was an outdoor amphitheatre, and then against the lagoon a *mediathèque*, which included a multi-media library. Further along the promenade, and again on the lagoon side, was a multi-purpose hall; and opposite this a bar/cafeteria and a lounge. Next came a cluster of exhibition spaces; and lastly a village of studios and workshops for various forms of work in progress, to which the public would have access only when invited.

If the cases were among the most striking features of the design, so too were their soaring scale and the rich mixture of materials used throughout the building. Standing as tall as the surrounding columnar pines, some of the cases were 30 metres high, giving these parts of the centre a scale comparable with that of a Gothic cathedral. And like the cases, the whole building was designed to be built of a mixture of specially adapted local materials and imported ones, resulting in a constructional palette much richer than those used previously by the Building Workshop. Just as the cases mixed laminated wooden ribs with thin slats (or even bark strip), stainless steel rods and

193

1

194 **J M Tjibaou Cultural Centre**

1,2,3 Kanaks marked the founding of a new settlement by planting a tree. Here, a columnar pine is selected, transported to and planted on the site to honour this ritual and to test the problems of moving more trees on completion of construction.

2   3

cast-aluminium footings, so the rest of the building mixed timber posts with infills of wood boarding, glass, and pressed metal panels of various sorts. The roof, which curved up inside each case, comprised panels of glass or metal, shaded by external louvres and supported on steel joists. The ceilings were suspended from the joists to conceal local air-conditioning units where necessary. In contrast, the base of the building was designed for local materials with floors of granite and retaining walls of concrete with a coral aggregate. In essence, the design could be said to consist of enclosed capsules of imported high-technology materials and equipment, set on a local mineral base and wrapped around with huge husks of local vegetal matter.

For all its rich and heady exoticism, the design had roots in earlier work by the Building Workshop. The vegetal cases which wrap the high-technology enclosures in a camouflaging contextual overcoat, have precedents in the clapboarding of the Menil Collection in Houston, and the terracotta elements of the IRCAM Extension in Paris, (Volume One, p 140 and p 202 respectively) although these lack what some may see as the excessive and rather redundant flourish of the cases. The intention of involving the local community in the periodic replacement of their cladding also recalls the participative exercises of the UNESCO Neighbourhood Workshop project and Il Rigo Housing at Corciano (Volume One, p 68 and p 18–19 respectively). And the rich mix of materials, in particular the sculpted, laminated-wood vertical members of the cases and their cast-aluminium footings, is reminiscent of the IBM Travelling Pavilion (Volume One, p 110).

All in all, this was an enchantingly evocative and seductive design. It encapsulated a vision of co-existing in close harmony with nature through an imaginative fusion of contemporary technology with a reinterpretation of traditional local forms. But parts of it were overly monumental in scale, and the actual enclosed areas of the departments tiny in relation to the overall built volume – which included the covered way as well as the external parts of the cases. There was too great a diversity of materials and components, too many of which would have been expensive imports, and too great a dependence on sophisticated

construction and technology. Also, it was not certain that the cases would work as assumed environmentally, or even serve well the functions they were designed to house; they were modelled too literally perhaps on the forms of traditional huts. The design verged uncomfortably close to the Club Med and the theme park, being almost analogous to modern man complete with Walkman, shades and sun-block, going native in a grass skirt.

Piano was well aware of the problems of this original design and very nervous about them, particularly those of the function and form of the cases. After the excesses of Post-Modernism, he was wary of the pitfalls of kitsch that might ensnare those who too literally evoke historic forms; nor did he want to caricaturize and patronize the local culture. Much of the design, such as the plan layout, was no doubt sound and very satisfactory. But, as is typical of Piano and the Building Workshop, much else, and especially the presence and form of the cases, arose not so much from rational analysis as from an intuitive and gestural response to the spectacular setting and the distinctive local settlements.

4

5

6

J M Tjibaou Cultural Centre

Site and vegetation.

4,5,6 Typical vegetation.

7 Aerial view of site with lagoon in foreground and Bay of Magenta beyond.

8,9 Typical conditions where land meets sea in areas close to the site.

10,11,12 Abundant local fruit.

7

8

9

10

11

12

1

2

3

4

5

J M Tjibaou Cultural Centre

Kanak arts, crafts and customs.

1,2,10 Characteristic sculptures.

3 Community collaborating on thatching a hut.

4,5,11,12 Natural materials woven to exploit the character of each.

6,8 Traditional dances.

7 Launching ceremonial outrigger.

9 Traditional hut.

6

7

10

9

8

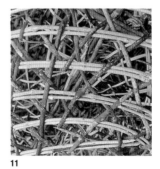

11

12

13

J M Tjibaou Cultural Centre

Traditional huts and ceremonies.

13 Interior detail of hut showing junction between central post and rafters.

14 Exterior detail of hut showing layered thatching.

15 Carved figure.

16 Spectators, and **17** dancers at a traditional ceremony.

14

16

17

However, much of the romantic appeal of the design and its whole generosity of spirit depended on the excesses of the cases (and the covered way), and once proposed they seemed almost to will themselves into being. Far from feeling patronized, the locals recognize the cases as both familiar and generous presences; they are adamant that the cases should remain and are very reluctant to let them diminish in size and number. So Piano has had to take courage and go with the irrational elements of this scheme, testing and refining them so that they work better and acquire a genuine rationale, while accepting also that they have their own very considerable value in the suggestive connections they make with local tradition, climate and the surrounding vegetable kingdom.

Nevertheless, Piano insisted that the cases should resemble the traditional huts less closely; so the vertical elements no longer meet at the top, nor are they all of the same length. In any case, wind tunnel testing soon proved that the cases, as placed and shaped in the original scheme, did not really work: they held little promise as wind scoops open to the prevailing winds. They could, however be developed to function as exhaust chimneys, using a combination of convection and venturi effects, if their backs were turned to the prevailing winds from the ocean and they were opened up to the sun from the north. Achieving these conditions also required a more open form for the cases, which although less closely associated with the traditional huts, is now even more beautiful and richly evocative.

All the cases, and the major spaces they enclose, have now been placed on the same side of the spine, projecting south towards the ocean. This has made it difficult to maintain the village imagery, especially in those stages of design development when the cases were too evenly spaced. Also, the notion of periodically replaced cladding of local wooden slats (like the bark strips and palm fronds) was soon abandoned as being poetic but impractical. Slats of iroko mahogany will now be used, which will last well with little maintenance and yet will still evoke some of the texture of traditional woven construction. Different slat widths and spacings will be used to generate areas of differing porosity and resistance to air movement. The differing optical vibrations so created will further enrich the building's visual appeal and affinities

197

15

1

2

J M Tjibaou Cultural Centre

Competition scheme, April 1991

1 North-east elevation.

2 Cross section through exhibition space.

3 South-east elevation.

4 Detail section of bottom of perimeter of

case .

5 Ground floor plan.

with surrounding foliage.

All these changes can be seen in the feasibility study of January 1992. (Interim investigations of the form of the case that led up to this are charted in the models of October, November and December 1991.) The cases were placed south of the promenade in this study, but were still massed to resemble three distinct villages; and although the tops of their vertical elements still swept in towards each other they no longer met, nor were they of the same height. They were also, at this stage, beautifully sculpted in form. In plan, these verticals defined a semi-circle; the soaring space they enclosed was similar in shape, and connected to the covered way by a transitional area formed like a

step-sided funnel. In section, the roof still curved up into the case, the glass suspended in fanning curves whose delicate grace would have been very problematic to realize. Elsewhere, the roof was a series of flat projections from the curving, covered way. In retrospect, another significant element of this design was the way in which the case began to separate from the curved back wall of the space it enclosed.

After reinvestigating a solution where all the verticals of the case were the same length but no longer met at the top (July 1992), and its antithesis where the ends defined a double curve in side elevation (September 1992), the case was extended in the design of October 1992 to define once again more than a semicircle in plan. And the outer wall of the space it embraced became an emphatically independent element. This was built of block work and supported a roof that stepped rather than curved up

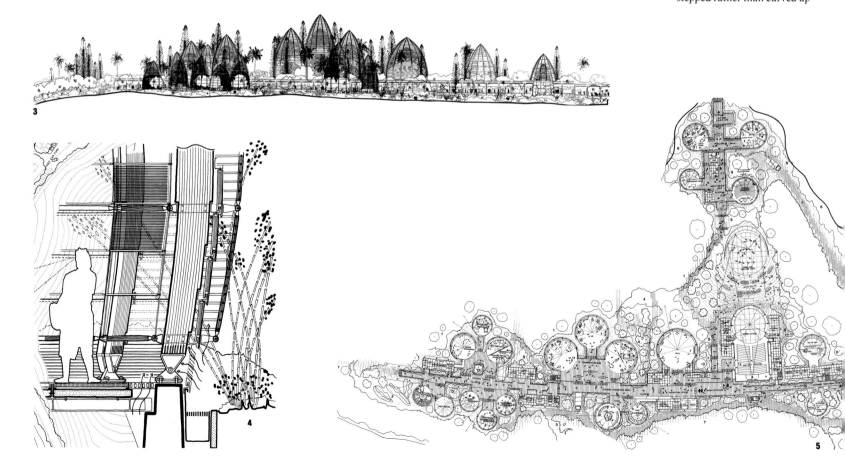

3

4

5

6

J M Tjibaou Cultural Centre

Competition scheme.

6 Cross section through theatre.

7 Aerial perspective.

8 Site plan

9 Typical section through case.

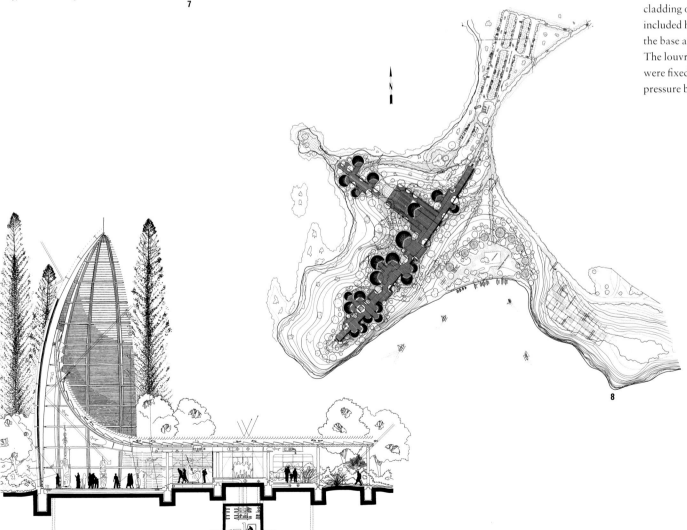

7

8

9

into the case, an altogether more pragmatic and cheaper solution than that of the feasibility study. The spacing of the big wide cases became so regular, however, as to rather diminish the impression of separate villages. The scheme of December 1992 was simply a refinement of the previous one.

By January 1993 the case had evolved considerably and was very close to the version successfully tested in the wind-tunnel in February of that year. At this stage, the case acquired a double layer of laminated-timber vertical elements. These were connected by a horseshoe-shaped steel beam oriented at the same level and slope as the glass roof. The vertical ribs of both layers projected far above this beam without curving

inwards to each other. The second and inner projecting corona may seem to compound the excessive nature of the case, but the case worked much better in inducing natural ventilation. Moreover, because the inner layer of verticals had become the outer wall of the major space, the case was once again utterly integral to the building instead of being an independent element wrapped around it, which it had become in some of the intermediate schemes.

To induce and control natural ventilation, the wooden slat cladding of the outer elements of the case became widely spaced towards the top and bottom but relatively closely spaced in the middle where they inhibited somewhat the flow of air. Similarly, the cladding of the inner elements included horizontal louvres at the base and below the roof. The louvres below the roof were fixed open to maintain a pressure balance between inside

199

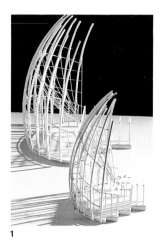

1

2

200 **J M Tjibaou Cultural Centre**

Evolution of the case.

1 November 1991.

2 December 1991.

3 Feasibility study, January 1992.

4 January 1992.

5 September 1992.

6 February 1993.

4

3

and outside and prevent wind-lift on the roof. By adjusting the lower louvres the case ventilated naturally and comfortably, regardless of the wind conditions outside. In soft breezes all the louvres were to be opened. As the wind strengthened, the lower louvres were to be progressively closed. In cyclones they were to be closed completely, as did the louvres on the promenade side of the case. The latter, though, were intended to remain open in all other conditions, especially if the wind came from the landside.

The cases as detailed in the design presented to the French Government in April 1993 are a refinement of these earlier ones, each now extended to define a little more than three-quarters of the circumference of a circle. Lovely objects though they are, the cases are now perhaps too evenly spaced so that the concept of forming a series of villages reads less clearly than in the competition scheme – which had nearly twice as many cases. But despite the diminished numbers, the cases still seem overly spectacular considering the more mundane uses some of them will house.

Each case now has a sloping roof, whose frame is stiffened by tension chords propped away from it. Depending on the functions they are designed to accommodate, the roofs of some cases are entirely glazed, others are opaque, and yet others a combination of the two. (Where glazed, the roofs are shaded by external louvres.) For similar reasons the amount of glass used to clad the sides of the cases varies. So, within the same basic form, there are spaces of very different character, which range from those that are blind-sided, top-lit and introverted to those that are

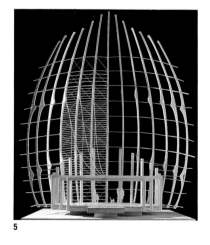

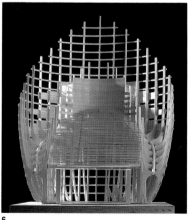

5

6

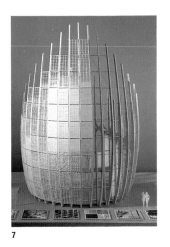

7

8

J M Tjibaou Cultural Centre

Evolution of the case.

7 April 1993.

8 Detail of 7

9,10 Cross sections of final design: **9** is through exhibition case, cafeteria and terraced gardens, and **10** is through artists' studio and teaching space.

11,12,13 Further views of case of April 1993.

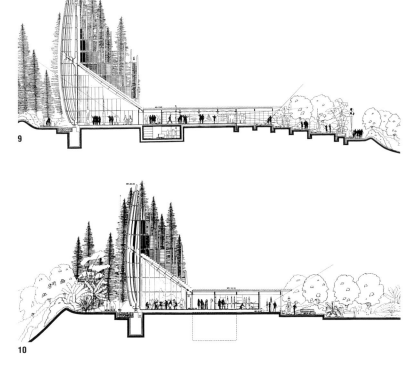

9

10

extroverted and entirely lit through big windows overlooking selected views. There is also a wide variety of cladding elements with different sorts of glazing, and with different sizes and spacing of wooden slats, to modulate such things as views in and out, sunshading and airflow. Cases designed for exhibition purposes are clad with panels with a white inner face; and those for teaching have storage elements projecting into the space between the inner and outer structural elements.

The overall design of the cultural centre and its grounds have evolved considerably too. The zoning of the major elements on the site remains unchanged, as does the presence of the curved promenade – although a much greater proportion of it is now fully enclosed. But the pedestrian route and point of entry to the promenade have altered, and another important pedestrian path has been added around the promontory and cultural centre. The spinal promenade is no longer entered at its north-eastern end by a route from the top of the parking area. Instead, a broad route now meanders a short distance along the shore from the bottom of the parking zone, then winds through dense indigenous vegetation and up a series of broad flights of stairs. These lead to an entrance court flanked by the projecting side of the main auditorium. The entrance lobby that opens onto this court is nearly a quarter of the way along the total length of the spine, at a point where this too has just climbed to the level of the top of the ridge.

The centre is now arranged in three villages linked by the two open sections of the promenade. The entrance lobby is in

201

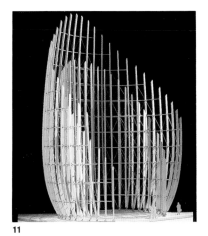

11

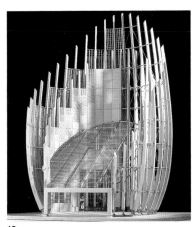

12

13

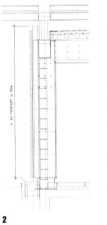

2

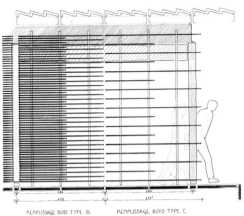

3

REMPLISSAGE BOIS TYPE B   REMPLISSAGE BOIS TYPE C

J M Tjibaou Cultural Centre

1 Case of April 1993, which is very close to the final design.

2 Study of external walls using differing densities of wood slat to achieve various degrees of privacy and openness, and also of sunshading.

3 Interior of case.

4 Study of relative opacity/porosity required to achieve best airflow.

the first village. Besides the reception area and the 400-seat auditorium, whose semi-sub-terranean volume flanks the court outside, this village is devoted to exhibitions. Permanent or long-term exhibitions occupy one each of the three sizes of case that line the promenade. Opposite the entrance doors and immediately encountered by those entering the building is the medium-sized case whose contents are intended to conjure the essence of Kanak culture. Down the slope, and to the north-east of this case, is one of the largest cases, devoted to the history of the Kanaks, and beyond that a small case showing the local environment and its natural history. Also at this lower level, opposite the largest case and overlooked from the entrance lobby, is a hall for temporary exhibitions. A medium-sized

case opposite the auditorium houses a cafeteria. Outside the end of the auditorium is an open-air amphitheatre, and beyond that an area for outdoor games.

The middle village contains offices for administrators, curators, researchers, designers, publishers and all the others whose role is to conceive, plan and realize exhibitions. These are on two levels. Those on the level below the promenade are tucked above the parking spaces that line the subterranean service road. This extends under the promenade for the length of the first and second villages. (There is only a service corridor below the third village). In front of the lower offices, and below the roof that extends to shade all these rooms from the fierce north-west sun, is a veranda which overlooks an amphitheatre of terraces densely planted with traditionally cultivated crops. The cases opposite the offices contain a conference room, a video library and, in the largest, a library.

203

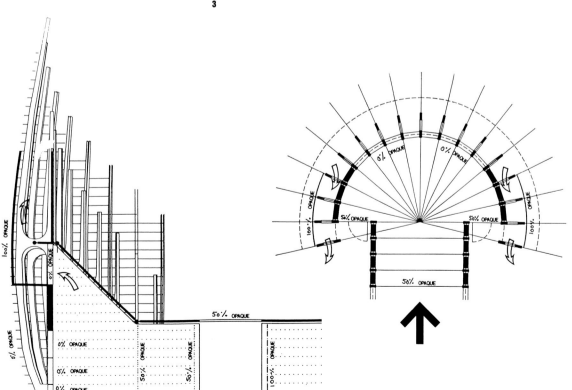

4

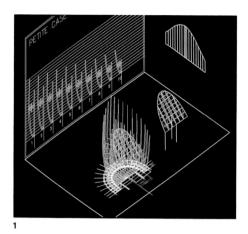

1

J M Tjibaou Cultural Centre

Computer and wind studies.

1 Projection of the components that make up a case .

2 Projection of competition case .

3 Study of intermediate scheme and its relationship to the site.

4 Setting up for wind testing.

5 Part plan of case structure.

6,7 Studies of structural loadings on case .
Colour indicates type of force and thickness its amount.

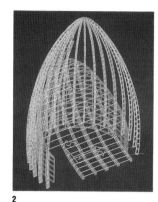

2

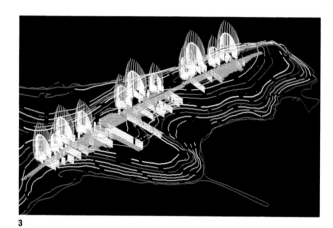

3

The third village is somewhat isolated at the end of the promenade. Here, its occupants will be able to concentrate on their creative pursuits relatively uninterrupted when not subject to specially arranged visits. The largest of its cases is a dance studio, with changing rooms in a basement below. Two of the smallest size of case are studios for graphics and music. A medium-sized case serves as a lecture hall to introduce school children to the traditional forms of these arts and the contemporary versions being explored here. Across the promenade are studios for sculpture and traditional crafts, a large photographic darkroom and a covered terrace, which forms an extension of the dance studio.

To keep some continuity with the cases, the structure of the rest of the building is also in laminated timber. As with the Bercy 2 Shopping Centre in Paris and the Kansai International Airport Terminal in Osaka, there is a double roof. The lower one is fairly conventional and drains to gutters 5.4 metres, 7.2 metres or 10.8 metres apart, corresponding with the three structural spans used here. The upper roof consists of stainless steel panels above a large ventilation space and acts as a sunscreen that also projects out to shade the external walls. These are made up of modular frames infilled in various ways. Some are merely screens of wooden slats, exactly like those that clad the cases, and are used mainly in the perpendicular direction to the promenade. Other panels are glazed and used both with and without *brise soleil* screens of wooden slats. Yet others are opaque sandwich panels.

4

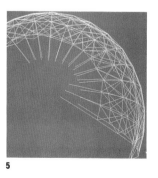

5

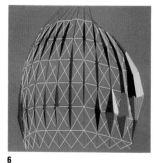

6

7

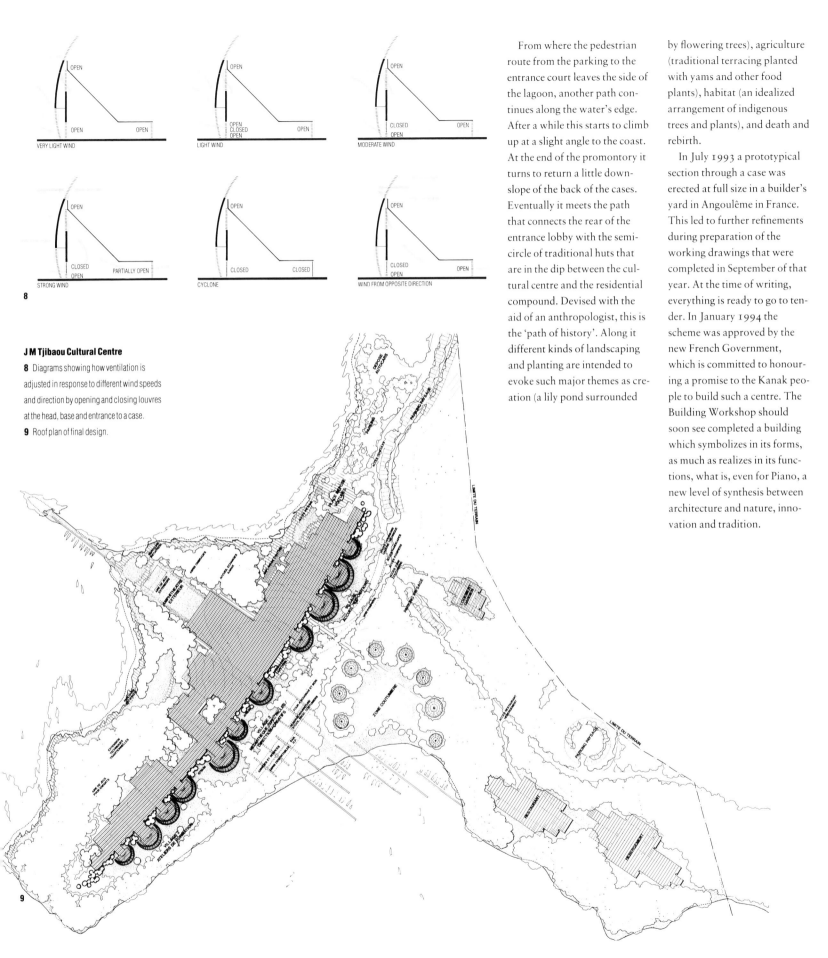

From where the pedestrian route from the parking to the entrance court leaves the side of the lagoon, another path continues along the water's edge. After a while this starts to climb up at a slight angle to the coast. At the end of the promontory it turns to return a little downslope of the back of the cases. Eventually it meets the path that connects the rear of the entrance lobby with the semicircle of traditional huts that are in the dip between the cultural centre and the residential compound. Devised with the aid of an anthropologist, this is the 'path of history'. Along it different kinds of landscaping and planting are intended to evoke such major themes as creation (a lily pond surrounded by flowering trees), agriculture (traditional terracing planted with yams and other food plants), habitat (an idealized arrangement of indigenous trees and plants), and death and rebirth.

In July 1993 a prototypical section through a case was erected at full size in a builder's yard in Angoulême in France. This led to further refinements during preparation of the working drawings that were completed in September of that year. At the time of writing, everything is ready to go to tender. In January 1994 the scheme was approved by the new French Government, which is committed to honouring a promise to the Kanak people to build such a centre. The Building Workshop should soon see completed a building which symbolizes in its forms, as much as realizes in its functions, what is, even for Piano, a new level of synthesis between architecture and nature, innovation and tradition.

J M Tjibaou Cultural Centre

8 Diagrams showing how ventilation is adjusted in response to different wind speeds and direction by opening and closing louvres at the head, base and entrance to a case.

9 Roof plan of final design.

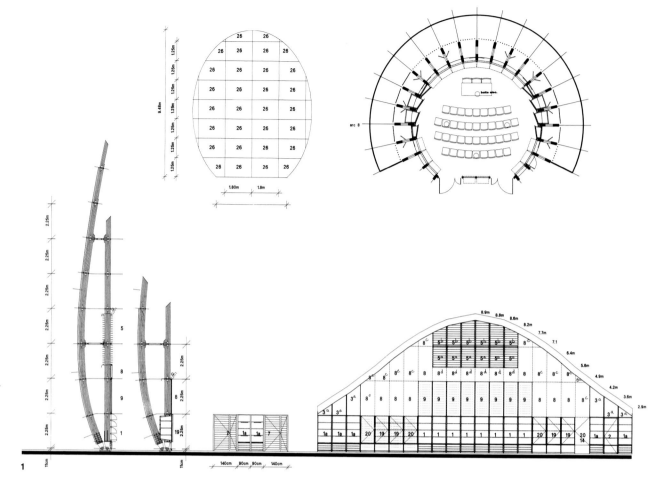

J M Tjibaou Cultural Centre

1,**2** Studies of small and medium-sized cases, the treatment of the walls (the smaller one has built-in cupboards projecting into the structure) and the distribution of different densities of slatting.

Details of structural footings of case.

3 End elevation and section.

4 Side elevation.

5,**6** Footings of structural elements around perimeter of case.

7 Footing of post along central promenade.

8 Anchor for ties.

9 Side elevation seen in **5**.

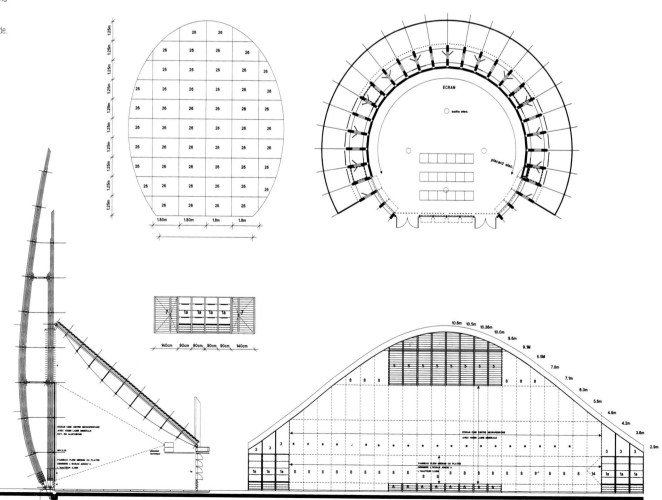

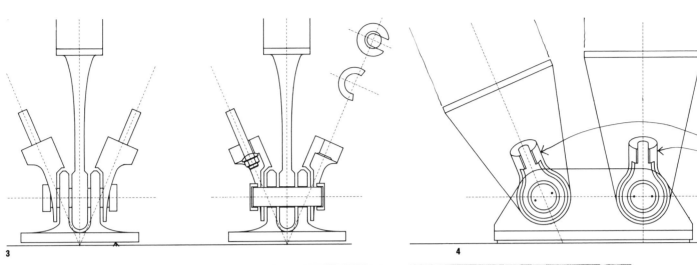

3

4

J M Tjibaou Cultural Centre

Client Agence pour le développement de la culture Kanak

Design team R Piano, P Vincent (associate in charge), A Chaaya, A el Jerari, A Gallissian, M Henry, D Mirallie, G Modolo, J B Mothes, F Pagliani, D Rat, A H Téménides, W Vassal

Assisted by R Baumgarten, C Catino, J Moolhuijzen, R Phelan

Model makers D Cavagna, O Doizy, P Darmer, A Schultz

Structural engineers and ventilation Ove Arup & Partners (P Rice, T Barker, J Wernick), CSTB (J Gandemer), Agibat (D Quost, J Gandemer)

Cost control GEC Ingénierie (F Petit, C Bache, T Plantagenest)

Acoustics Peutz & Associés (Y Dekeyrel, J M Marion)

Ethnologist A Bensa

Landscape architects M Desvigne & C Dalnoky, Vegetude (C Guinaudeau)

Stage equipment Scène (J H Manoury)

Study planning GEMO

Security Qualiconsult (J L Rolland)

5

6

7

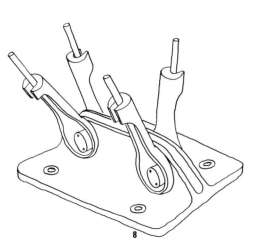

8

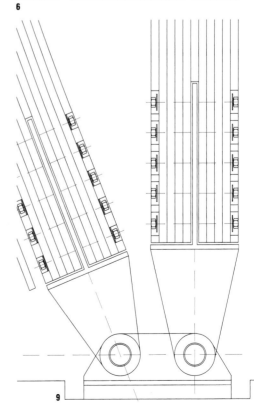

9

1

2

3

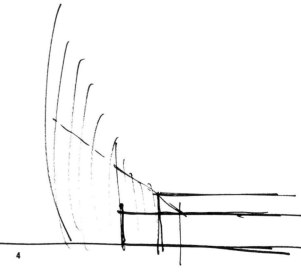

4

5

6

7

209

J M Tjibaou Cultural Centre

Full size prototype of part of case.

1 Spacing of slats is more open at top and bottom to allow air to move most freely between them here. In between these open areas, the gap between inner and outer layers of the case acts as a thermal chimney. Note how comfortably the mock-up relates to the nearby trees.

2 Roof showing options of clear glass, with and without adjustable louvres, and opaque panels.

3 Straight inner and curved outer structural elements.

4 Early sketch.

5 Sketch of junction of tension elements.

6–13 Further views of prototype.

14 Exploded sketch of junction.

8

9

10

11

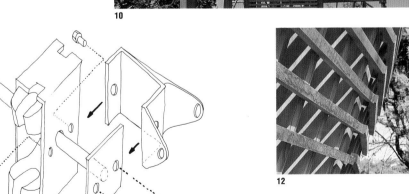

12

13

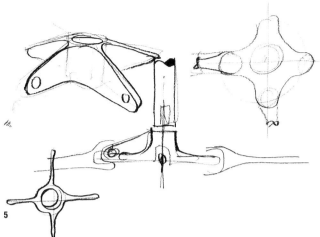

14

210

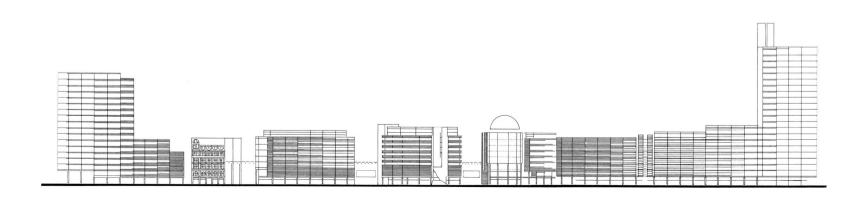

Potsdamer Platz Reconstruction Berlin, Germany **1992–**

Germany's reunification, and with it that of its old capital, has made Berlin a hot-bed of architectural and urban design activity. Developers and consultants from many parts of the world have planned many immense and ambitious projects for Berlin. Much the most interesting of these is a scheme by the Building Workshop: a masterplan for a large area that straddles parts of the former East and West Berlin and the design of more than half the buildings within this site. This area was heavily damaged by Allied bombs and was later razed by urban planners desperate to obliterate traces of, and so forget, the past. But, in the 1920s and 1930s, it was the centre of social and cultural life in Berlin, and so of Europe. Memories of what it once was have now been magnified to mythic dimensions, making this a particularly significant and sensitive area.

This developing design already marks a milestone in the development of Renzo Piano and the Building Workshop. Besides being the largest urban project Piano and his team have tackled, it demonstrates a much richer and more profound grasp of the purposes and potential of urban design than does any ear-lier scheme. For the first time, the network of public spaces, the streets and squares, is in no way residual but is designed as purposively as the architecture, and even takes precedence over it, as the permanent framework within which buildings will come and go. This framework needs, and is given, a coherence of its own that is both formal and functional. This 'structures' the area in a way that will invest it with a distinct order, liveliness and character, such as could endure even in the unlikely event of some of the buildings or their future replacements proving mediocre or disjointed from each other. More than that however, this scheme resurrects some of those key elements of the city's past that still live in the memory of its citizens. It also ties together what were East and West Berlin and, for the first time, integrates the cultural sector, the Kulturforum, into the larger city.

The Building Workshop's involvement in Berlin began yet again with it winning another international competition, this time for the reconstruction of a huge area between Potsdamer Platz, which is to be rebuilt in what was East Berlin, and the National Library by Hans Scharoun (1978), in what was

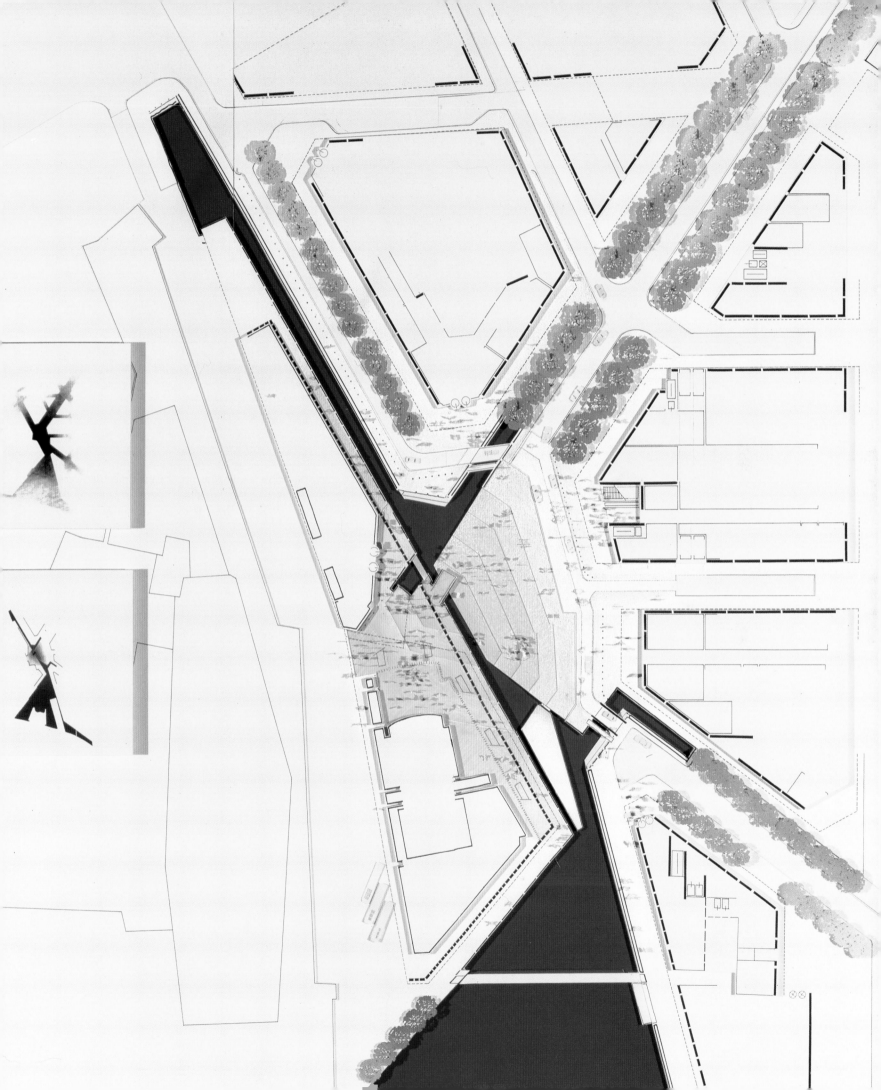

1

Potsdamer Platz Reconstruction

Historical context.

1 Aerial photograph, taken when part of the Wall and an elevated rail line still stood. It shows the site, with its rows of trees marking where the Alte Potsdamerstrasse was, in relation to the Kulturforum to the west (left) and the Tiergarten to the north.

2 Aerial view of the Potsdamer Platz in 1910.

3 Potsdamer Platz after the war with Kempinski Haus in background.

2

3

West Berlin. This site is the largest of a number that were put out to competition by corporate sponsors, in this instance Daimler Benz, in this bleak and bare area, where only the historic street pattern had been left visible. All these sites, and their masterplans, are themselves subject to a larger competition-winning masterplan by the locally based practice, Hilmer & Sattler, which reinstates and reinterprets Berlin's historic street and building patterns.

Unlike the schemes of some of the other entrants in the Potsdamer Platz competition, the winning submission by the Building Workshop's Paris office conforms to the layout of traditional Berlin blocks stipulated by the larger masterplan.

But while the Building Workshop's scheme obeys the rules within the site, it also flouts them outrageously by focusing its most trenchant proposals outside the boundary of the competition site. By giving an emphatic termination to the reinstated Alte Potsdamerstrasse (the position of which was commemorated in

West Berlin by two rows of lime trees that are now an historic monument), this is the only submission to restore some real importance to this street. The emphatic element at its end is a new piazza partially enclosed by buildings that also screen the mountain-like bulk of the National Library. Like the piazza, the proposed buildings adjacent to the library are not part of the brief and are outside the competition site. Yet together these buildings, and the piazza, also tied the presently rather isolated Library in the south-east corner of the Kulturforum (which includes Scharoun's Philharmonie and the concert halls completed by Scharoun's partner Edgar Wisniewski) into the competition scheme, and so reintegrated Berlin at the point where it was once severed by the Wall. No other competition entry attempted this linkage, yet when achieved as convincingly as it is here, its virtues are blindingly obvious.

The competition scheme goes further still. It extends a lake from the Landwehrkanal, which lies to the south, past the entrance to a road tunnel and between the competition site and the unrequested elements. And it also proposes that landscaping and trees should sweep up from near the canal, through the Kulturforum and on to link with the Tiergarten in the north. The combined impact of these connects the

Kulturforum with the Tiergarten so that the whole of the Kulturforum effectively becomes an extension of the old park. This is one of the very rare instances in which the contemporary, almost automatic response of introducing landscaping to fill residual spaces – as if landscaping were some balm that can heal the wounds of the fragmented city – actually contributes something more than the cosmetic concealment of scars.

Here, the proposed intrusion of the water and landscaping was neither meaninglessly cosmetic nor dissipated any real cohesion and urbanity. The extension of the Tiergarten into the Kulturforum gave added meaning to (and was facilitated by) the unconventional forms of its buildings, which all appeared like rocky outcrops rising from the park. By giving to the south-east corner of the Kulturforum an emphatic edge, which isolated it from its surroundings in this direction, the water reinforced the sense of orientation towards, and connection with, the Tiergarten. Along its opposite bank, the water confined the street and pavement that marked the boundary of the original competition site, so that this edge retained a certain definition

4

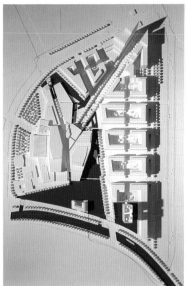

5

Potsdamer Platz Reconstruction

Competition scheme.

4 Section along Alte Potsdamerstrasse from the Potsdamer Platz, on the left, to the National Library, on the right.

5 Model of the proposals for the site and for the area adjacent to the National Library on the left.

6 Model of the proposals in the larger context of Berlin.

7 Study of the piazza that was to terminate the Alte Potsdamerstrasse as the largest of a group of ice floe-like islands.

8 Plan with site and Kulturforum tinted red.

9 Diagrams showing the proposals in the context of Berlin.

6

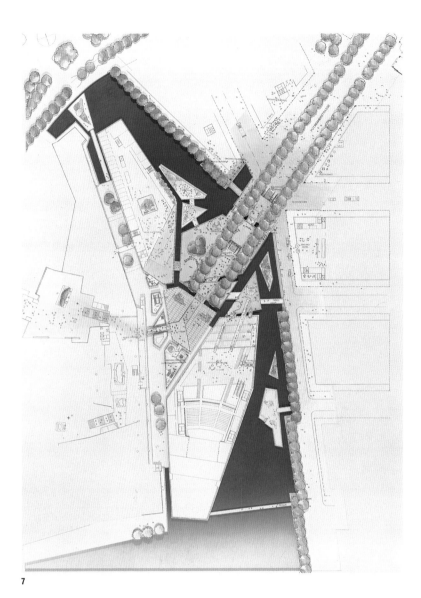

213

7

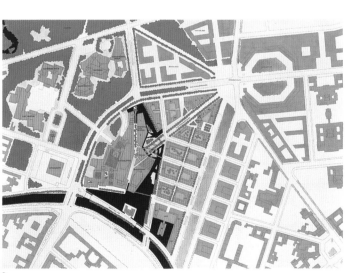

8

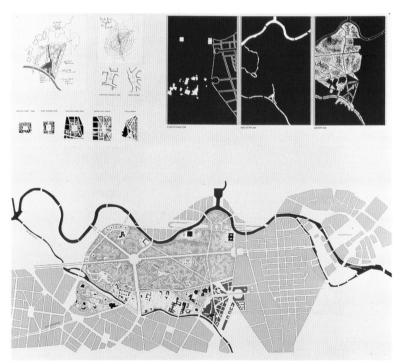

9

1

214 **Potsdamer Platz Reconstruction**

Current scheme.

1 Model of proposals in context.

2 Detailed street plan with ground floor plans of all buildings: **a** Alte Potsdamerstrasse, **b** new piazza, **c** Landwehrkanal, **d** new lake, **e** entrance to road tunnel, **f** National Library, **g** music theatre, **h** casino, **i** Daimler Benz tower, **j** shops and offices, **k** shops and housing, **l** galleria, **m** existing building, **n** hotel by Rafael Moneo, **o** old peoples' housing by Hans Kollof, **p** office tower by Hans Kollof, **q** shops and offices by Richard Rogers Partnership, **r** shops and offices by Arata Isozaki.

3 Plan with buildings in new masterplan area tinted yellow.

4 Plan study of roadways and pavements.

5,6 Plans of galleria and adjacent shops:

5 basement level, **6** first floor.

7 Section of galleria and adjacent shops. Above these are offices on left of galleria and housing on right.

8 Longitudinal section of galleria.

2

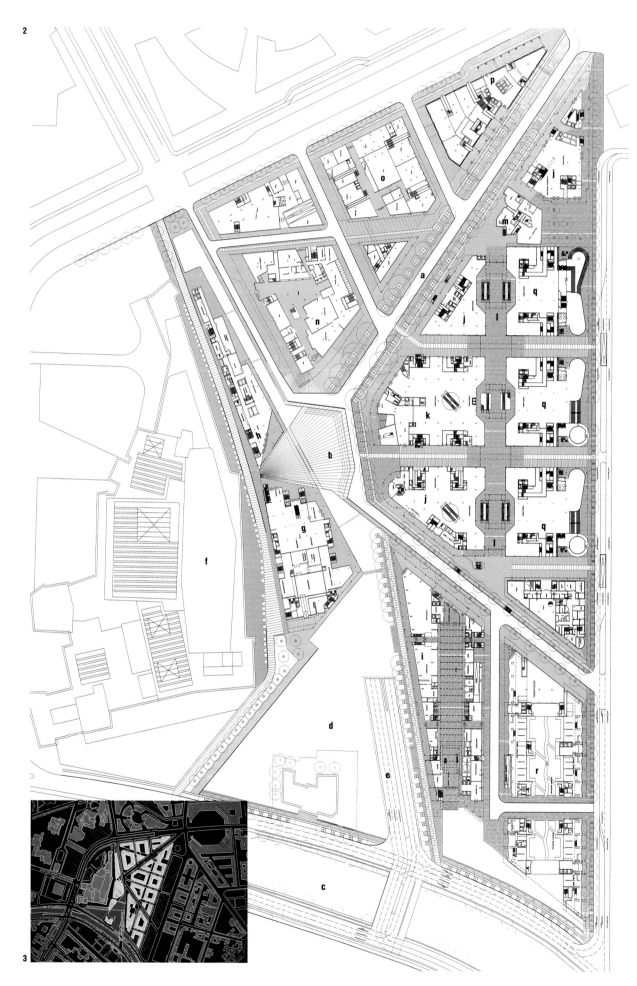

3

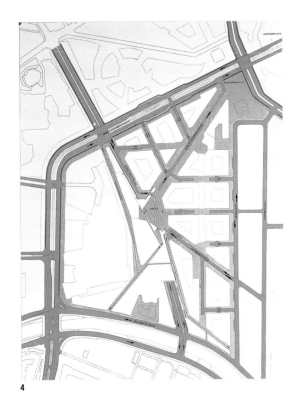

4

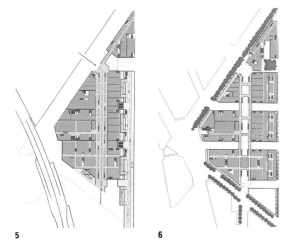

5
6

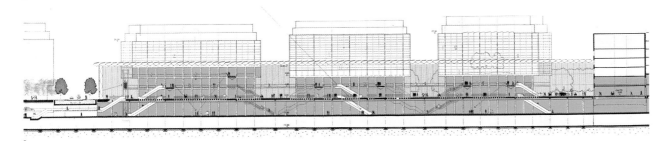

7

8

and intensity. From this bank, the water also set off the large structures that would flank the back of the National Library.

In the competition-winning scheme, the new buildings adjacent to the National Library would take their formal cues from Scharoun's building, their shapes also suggesting gigantic boulders. These would shelter a multi-level grotto that terminated Alte Potsdamerstrasse, through the back of which was to be a new entrance to the National Library. But the glass skins being considered for these buildings would also have given them a glacial aspect, further emphasized by the piazza with its adjacent triangular islands suggestive of iceflows breaking up. Hence the metaphors conjured by the buildings and the piazza are natural rather than conventionally architectural. This seems

exactly apt when in the shadow of Scharoun, the prime exponent of the German school of Organic architecture. Once again, Piano proved his sensitivity to place and tradition, and not just an expertise with technology, and the desire that this harmonize with, and emulate, nature.

Despite Piano's flagrant transgression of the conditions, the virtues of this scheme were so compelling that it won the competition. The Building Workshop was commissioned to advance the masterplan and design in detail the urban spaces and their street furniture. It was also commissioned not only to build the Daimler Benz tower and six other buildings, but to work up the unasked-for buildings adjacent to the library. However, the opinion was voiced by architectural critics and local planners that these latter buildings should not embody a formal vocabulary similar to that of the Scharoun buildings lest they be mistaken for part of the original complex, which is extensive enough as it is. Although of debatable wisdom on all scores, the Building Workshop is complying with this edict. The evolving design retains all the key ideas of the competition-winning scheme,

particularly those that were outside its site and brief.

Initially, as the design was developed, the buildings adjacent to the library lost their angularity. As another of the Building Workshop's current explorations of complex curves clad in metal panels, these buildings sheltered together under the same curved and tapering stainless-steel skin. Like the Bercy 2 Shopping Centre in Paris (p 16), but unlike the Kansai International Airport Terminal (p 220) and the first proposals for the National Centre of Science and Technology in Amsterdam (p 132), the enclosing shells of which have an organic completeness of form, this carapace seemed to be a fragment from a larger form. Its shiny curves, which only partially enclosed the volumes below it, were only on the side facing away from the library. Yet, despite being in a very different material and formal vocabulary to the Scharoun buildings, the incompleteness of form related the new buildings back to the library, completing it and giving it a suitable edge with which to face the buildings in the competition site and the new stretches of water.

The shell is now much simplified in design. But it is useful to describe this earlier scheme further as it was a crucial intermediate step towards the design currently being developed, which in turn is probably still far from being the final one. All the internal

215

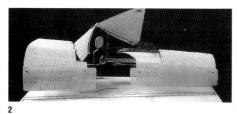

216 **Potsdamer Platz Reconstruction**

Operetta theatre and casino block:
intermediate design.

1,2 Model studies of curved shell roof that
opens up over foyer.

3 Diagrams showing how curved shell fits
over internal elements and opens up to
summer sun.

4 Longitudinal section.

9 Section through (from left to right): courtyard of housing block, new piazza, foyer of
intermediate design and National Library.

Operetta theatre and casino block: current
design.

5 East elevation facing new piazza.

6,7,8 Operetta theatre: **6** plan at top of
auditorium, **7** longitudinal section, **8** cross
section of stage and fly tower.

3

uses and ideas of this earlier design persist in the latest scheme, though they too, like the shape of the shell, have continued to evolve. From the curving shell's southern end, its highest and widest part, projects the blocky fly tower of a large theatre for operettas that fills this end of the building. Projecting from the opposite end and occupying the lower part of the shell, is a casino. Between the multi-level foyers of the theatre and the casino, that overhang it as bustling balconies, is an indoor piazza. This is the apex of the piazza outside which terminates Alte Potsdamerstrasse. Besides giving access to the leisure uses in the new building, it also provides access from the new piazza to a new entrance into what had been the rear of the library.

Overhead, it is intended that some large stretches of the glass and steel skin that encloses this winter garden will sometimes move. In spring they will tilt slightly and open up slowly. As summer comes they will tilt

progressively more and swing aside to open up the internal piazza and foyers to the skies. In autumn the process will slowly reverse itself. Through opening up the roof to sun and weather in harmony with the cycle of the seasons, as if the building were a living thing, this earlier design explored yet another dimension of the organic beyond those of extending works of Scharoun's Organic architecture and using non-Euclidian geometries inspired by new studies of nature. Now, for the moment at least, the roof has been greatly simplified. Although still clad in metal panels, these form huge angular planes at different pitches.

Since the competition, the main piazza beyond this indoor one has changed in location and shape as the urban spaces are continuously being refined. The piazza no longer projects from the original site as an island away from the buildings and the confluence of streets. Instead, it is now somewhat folded back into the site and much of it is edged by traffic rather than water. To keep it lively throughout the day and to make it the focus of the scheme in more than just a formal sense, the piazza is now fronted by all three of the major functions accommodated by the masterplan: offices and commerce, the latter in the form of shops leading through to a multi-level shopping galleria; residential in the form of

a housing block and a hotel; and culture and leisure in the forms of the operetta theatre and casino, and cafes in most of the buildings around the piazza.

The Building Workshop is designing all the buildings around this piazza, with the exception of the hotel. As well as the theatre and casino block, there is a continuous row of buildings that lines the length of Alte Potsdamerstrasse (where it is interrupted by the one old building remaining on the site), then wraps around the eastern edge of the proposed piazza, and angles back along the water's edge to terminate in the Daimler Benz tower. The tallest buildings are those at each end of this row: one which meets the Potsdamer Platz at an acute angle, and the Daimler Benz tower.

The current intention is that these tallest buildings will be the most transparent, or at least glassy, particularly at their acute-angled extremities. These are intended to evoke Mies van der Rohe's famous perspective of his unrealized office tower for the nearby Friedrichstrasse. From each of these ends the buildings are designed to become progressively less glassy as a greater proportion of their facades are faced in ter-

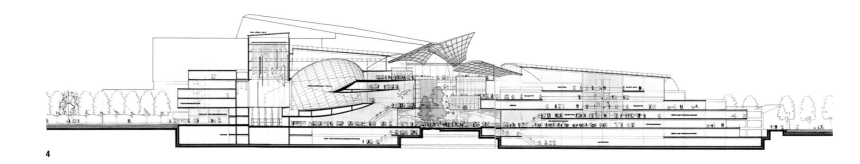

4

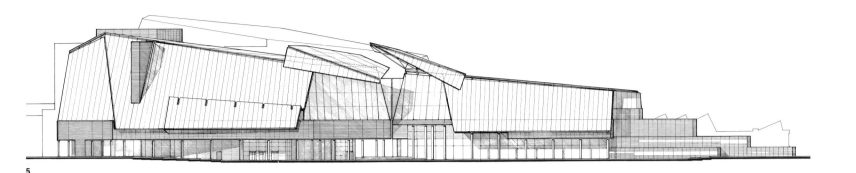

5

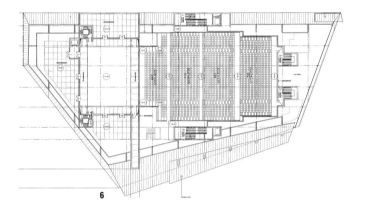

6

Potsdamer Platz Reconstruction

Client Daimler Benz AG, debis
Immobilienmanagement GmbH

Project manager Drees & Sommer,
Stuttgart

Architect Renzo Piano Building Workshop
with Christoph Kohlbecker

Design team R Piano, B Plattner (associate
in charge), S Baggs, E Baglietto,
R Baumgarten, G Bianchi, P Charles, C Hight,
S Ishida (associate architect), M Kramer,
N Mecattaf, J Moolhuijzen, F Pagliani,
L I Penisson, D Putz, M Rossato Piano, J
Ruoff, C Sapper, S Schäfer, R V Truffelli, L Viti

Model makers J P Allain, D Cavagna,
P Darmer, M Goudin

Structural and services engineers
Ove Arup & Partners

Acoustics Müller Bbm

Planning and organization
Quickborner team

Traffic engineers Studiengesellschaft
Verkehr mbH

*A full credit list for this project will appear
in the relevant future volume*

217

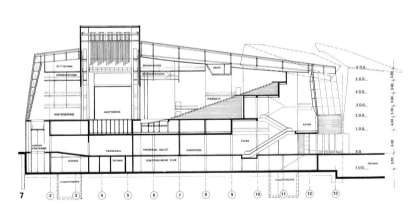

7

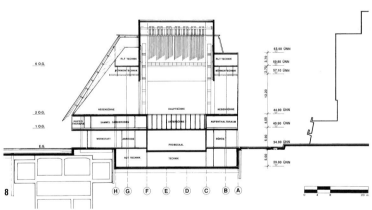

8

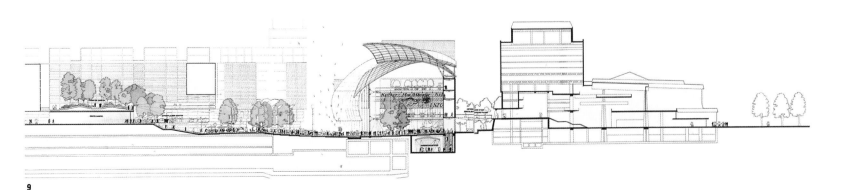

9

1

2

218 **Potsdamer Platz Reconstruction**

1 Mies van der Rohe: Friedrichstrasse project.

2 Perspective study of office tower that presents to Potsdamer Platz an angular, crystaline quality inspired by Mies.

3 Elevation of block modelled to recall the Kempinski Haus.

4 Kempinski Haus (now destroyed).

5 Elevational study of buildings from tower on Potsdamer Platz (*on left*) to the Daimler Benz tower (*on right*).

racotta. The way this material is used draws on the experience gained with it on the IRCAM Extension and Rue de Meaux Housing in Paris (Volume One, p 202 and p 214). Towards the centre of the site, the façades will have some of the texture and proportion of solidity found on those of traditional buildings, and like them will weather gracefully with age. Of the buildings in this row that edge the piazza, one is a housing block arranged around a raised garden that connects with the piazza. The corner of the other forms a rotunda modelled on that of the Kempinski Haus which stood nearby and is fondly remembered by older Berliners.

The other buildings will be designed by different architects, but subject to design guidelines drawn up by the Building Workshop as part of the masterplan. These stipulate that in

those blocks that align with the galleria, as with those by the Building Workshop, shopping is deployed over three levels: ground, first floor and basement. The courtyard layout of the blocks is also mandatory wherever the site allows it, and so is the use of terracotta as a facing material. This material will ensure some unity to the overall scheme despite the very different design idioms of the architects.

Except for mention of the basement shops, what has been described is only what the masterplan proposes above ground. Below it, the Building Workshop is planning another complex realm. Inherited from traffic-engineering plans for the whole city, is a large underground road that runs under the western boundary of the competition site. From this tunnel, lorries will descend further to a large parking and

unloading area directly below the piazza. From here, goods will be taken via a network of passages to the basement storage provided for each shop. Above this deepest level, those basement areas that are not designated for shops will be used for car-parking. A comprehensive system of car access ramps is integrated with the ground-level traffic flow.

With most large-scale urban interventions today, the problem is how to modernize without compromising the character and identity of that particular city. At Potsdamer Platz, the problem is how to rebuild and reinstate in all-new construction some of that lost identity and character while also dealing with the new elements on, or near, the site. As masterplanners and architects, Piano and the Building Workshop have reconciled the virtues of the traditional city (its contained urban spaces and densely mixed uses) with those of modern technology (its construction methods and materials, its servicing and transport systems). But this synthesis of old and new has also been shaped by the need to reconcile three other prime pressures: the memory of the historic city of Berlin as it was until 1945; the potent yet isolated buildings of the Kultur-forum; and the reunification of the former East and West Berlin. The scheme is remarkable for the balance it promises to achieve between all of these factors.

3

4

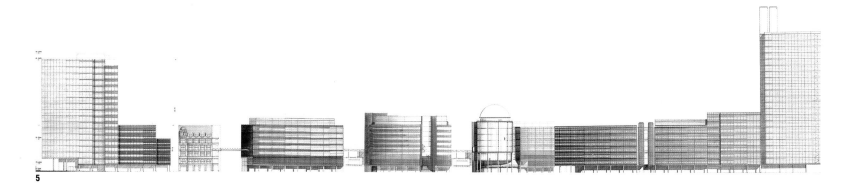

5

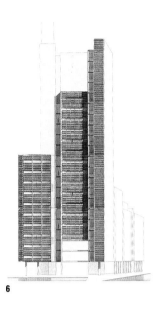

6

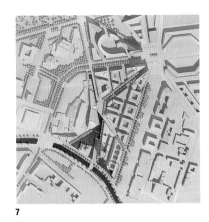

7

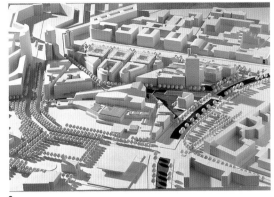

8

Potsdamer Platz Reconstruction

6 Elevational study of Daimler Benz tower.

7,8 Model views of current proposals.

9,10 Sectional studies of external walls

11,12 Sectional studies of offices exploring different solutions to lighting, ventilation, thermal inertia etc.

13 Perspective of galleria.

14,15 Plans of housing block: **14** courtyard level, **15** top floor of penthouses.

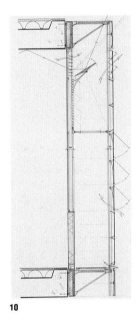

9

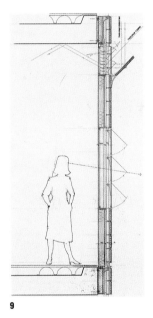

10

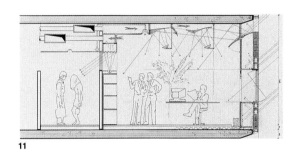

11

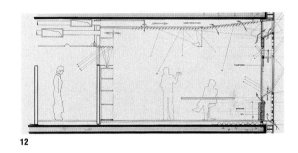

12

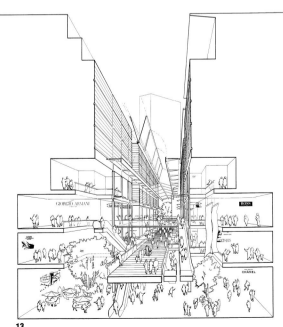

13

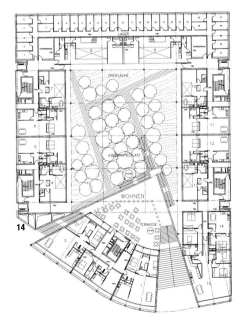

14

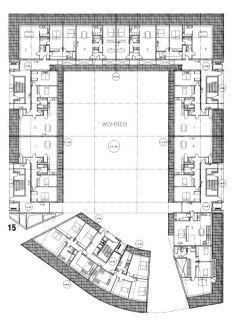

15

220

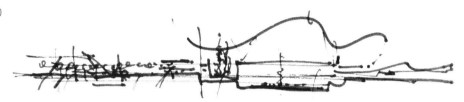

Kansai International Airport terminal Osaka, Japan **1988–94**

The Kansai International Airport passenger terminal, located on a purpose-built island offshore of Osaka, is currently the largest project under construction by the Building Workshop. Indeed it will probably be the longest single building yet constructed. As a herald of the future, and because it exemplifies in a most advanced manner many of the evolving ideals of Renzo Piano and the Building Workshop, it is shown as a project in the first volume of the complete works (Volume One, p 24). At the time of preparing this volume, the terminal is nearing the end of its remarkably rapid construction. Although it is proposed that a major portion of Volume Three will be devoted to Kansai, a selection of construction photographs is shown here. This is to highlight the whole process of making the artificial island and erecting the building which has been so exciting in itself, and to emphasize the fact that this huge venture has been going on as a backdrop during the design, development and construction of most of the other works shown in this volume.

Constructing the island was itself a formidable undertaking. Then came the coordination and assembly of components, which arrived from many parts of the world, into this highly disciplined structure; it is so vast that it physically dwarfed the labour force of some 4 000 workers, a number of whom lived on the island. Although still being completed internally, the building is now entirely enclosed in its shiny, curving, carapace of stainless-steel panels, which glint brightly in the sun or lie pale below dark skies. The long tapering arms of the boarding wings seem both to zoom across the island in subtly exaggerated perspective and gently embrace the flat surface of the island. It is already possible to appreciate a most extraordinary sequence of spaces inside the building. These move with the heaving and tapering curves of the roof and are modulated by the regular rhythms of the exposed structural elements. The long vistas and lofty spaces, the indissoluble unity of space and structure, the emulation of natural forms by advanced technology, and the collaborative effort required to build the terminal all evoke a rather surprising precedent: the Gothic cathedral, the construction of which was the subject of some of Piano's 'Open Site' television programmes in the late 1970s (Volume One, p 66).

1

2

3

4

5

6

Kansai International Airport terminal

1–3, 5 Interiors of boarding wing.

4 'Canyon' between entrances and check-in facilities.

6 International departures hall with scoops to entrain air suspended between main beams.

7, 8 Arches that are the primary structural element of the boarding wing.

9 End wall of international departures hall.'

10 Main beam and airscoops over international departures hall.

11 Wind sculpture suspended in airscoop to make visible the air movement.

12 Delivery of air-conditioning ducts.

13 Air inlet that jets air along ceiling.

14, 15 Securing sections of main beams in position.

7

8

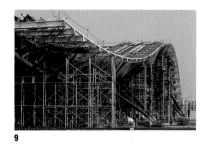

9

10

11

14

12

13

15

1

2

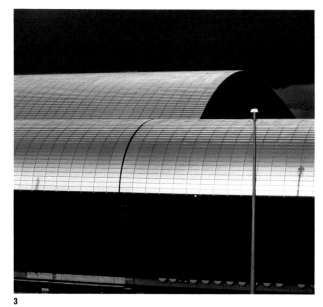

3

224 **Kansai International Airport terminal**

1, **2** Laying the inner weather-excluding layer of roof.

3 Roof with its protective outer layer of stainless steel panels in place.

4 View from the airside shows differing structural rhythms of boarding wing and departures hall behind it.

5, **7**, **8** Glazing the boarding wing.

6, **9** Glazing of the end wall of international departures hall.

10 Structural junction on boarding wing.

11, **13** Structure and glazing along end wall of international departures hall.

12 Telescopic gangways from boarding wing.

Following page The curvature of the boarding wing and several phases of construction can be seen clearly.

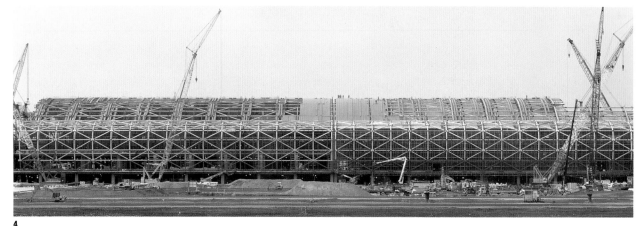

4

5

6

9

7

8

10

11

12

13

Kansai International Airport 227

Client Kansai International Airport

Competition-winning design
Architect Renzo Piano Building Workshop
R Piano, N Okabe (associate in charge)
Engineer Ove Arup & Partners International
Ltd (structure, P Rice), (services, T Barker)

Basic design and detail consortium for terminal building
Design leader and coordination
Renzo Piano Building Workshop, Japan KK
Design architects and engineers
Renzo Piano Building Workshop, Japan KK
R Piano, N Okabe (associate in charge) in
collaboration with Ove Arup & Partners
International Ltd (P Rice),
Nikken Sekkei Ltd (K Minai)
Basic concept, analysis of function and circulation
Aéroports de Paris (P Andreu)
Negotiation with government departments and civil aviation authorities, and airside planning Japan Airport
Consultants, Inc (M Matsumoto)

A full credit list for this project will appear in Volume Three

Acknowledgements

The development of the Building Workshop since its birth nearly 30 years ago is due to the efforts of those listed below; a list that includes those who have either worked with us or with whom we have had a close association. The list does not include the many more people who have contributed in some other way to our efforts over the years. We take this opportunity to express our gratitude to all.
Renzo Piano

228

Camilla Aasgaard
Laurie Abbot
Maria Accardi
PeterAckermann
Naderi Kamran Afshar
Emilia Agazzi
Alessandra Alborghetti
Jean Philippe Allain
Michele Allevi
Michel Alluyn
Arianna Andidero
Sally Appleby
Andrea Arancio
Catherine Ardilley
Magda Arduino
P Audran
Véronique Auger
Frank August
Alexandre Autin
Carmela Avagliano
Patrizio Avellino
Rita Avvenente

Carlo Bachschmidt
Alessandro Badi
Susan Baggs
Emanuela Baglietto
Antonello Balassone
Nicolo Baldassini
François Barat
Henry Bardsley
Giulia Barone
Sonia Barone
Fabrizio Bartolomeo
Christopher Bartz
Bruno Bassetti
Kathy Bassière

Sandro Battini
Roger Baumgarten
Paolo Beccio
Eva Belik
Annie Benzeno
Jan Berger
François Bertolero
Alessandro Bianchi
Giorgio G Bianchi
Gianfranco Biggi
Grégoire Bignier
Germana Binelli
Judy Bing
Rosella Biondo
Jean François Blassel
A Blassone
William Blurock
Paolo Bodega
Marko Bojovic
Sara Bonati
Manuela Bonino
Gilles Bontemps
Andrea Bosch
Pierre Botschi
Marjolijne Boudry
Sandrine Boulay
Ross Brennan
Gaëlle Breton
Maria Cristina Brizzolara
Cuno Brullmann
Michael Burckhardt
Hans-Peter Bysaeth

Alessandro Calafati
Patrick Callegia
Maurizio Calosso
Michele Calvi
Nunzio Camerada
Danila Campo
Florence Canal
Andrea Canepa
Stefania Canta
Danila Capuzzo
Alessandro Carisetto
Monica Carletti
Elena Carmignani
Isabella Carpiceci
Gilbert Carreira
Emanuele Carreri
Mark Carroll
Elena Casali
Marta Castagna
Cristiana Catino
Maria Cattaneo
Enrica Causa
Dante Cavagna
Simone Cecchi
Giorgio Celadon
Ottaviano Celadon
Alessandro Cereda
Antoine Chaaya
Patricia Chappell
Patrick Charles
Jean Luc Chassais
Pierre Chatelain
Hubert Chatenay
Ariel Chavela
Laura Cherchi
Raimondo Chessa
Christophe Chevalier
Catherine Clarisse
Geoffrey Cohen
Franc Collect

Daniel Collin
Giulio Contardo
Philippe Convercey
Pier Luigi Copat
Michel Corajoud
Colman Corish
Monica Corsilia
Ivan Corte
Giacomo Costa
Raffaella Costa
Loïc Couton
Paolo Crema
Raffaella Belmondi Croce
A Croxato
Mario Cucinella
Irene Cuppone
Catherine Cussoneau
Lorenzo Custer

Stefano D'Atri
Catherine D'Ovidio
Isabelle Da Costa
Paul Darmer
Lorenzo Dasso
Mike Davies
Silvia De Leo
Alessandro De Luca
Simona De Mattei
Olaf de Nooyer
Daniela Defilla
S Degli Innocenti
Michel Denancé
Alessio Demontis
Julien Descombes

Michel Desvigne
Carmelo Di Bartolo
Ottavio Di Blasi
Maddalena Di Sopra
Vittorio Di Turi
Hélène Diebold
Brian Ditchburn
John Doggart
Olivier Doizy
Eugenio Donato
François Doria
Michael Dowd
Mike Downs
Klaus Dreissigacker
Klaus Drouin
Frank Dubbers
Susan Dunne
Jean Luc Dupanloup
Philippe Dupont
Susanne Durr
John Dutton

Mick Eekhout
Stacy Eisenberg
Ahmed El Jerari
Lukas Epprecht
Alison Ewing

Roberta Fambri
Roberto Faravelli
Giorgio Fascioli
Maxwell Fawcett
David Felice
Alfonso Femia
Jacques Fendard
Agostino Ferrari
Maurizio Filocca
Laurent Marc Fischer

Richard Fitgerald
Eileen Fitzgerald
Peter Flack
Renato Foni
M Fordam
Gilles Fourel
Gianfranco Franchini
Candy Fraser
Kenneth Fraser
Nina Freedman
Marian Frezza
Enrico Frigerio
Junya Fujita

Rinaldo Gaggero
Alain Gallissian
Andrea Gallo
Carla Garbato
Robert Garlipp
Maurizio Garrasi
G Gasbarri
Angelo Ghiotto
M Giacomelli
Davide Gibelli
Alain Gillette
Sonia Giordani
Alberto Giordano
Antonella Giovannoni
Marion Goerdt
Marco Goldschmied
Enrico Gollo
Anahita Golzari
Alessandro Gortan
Philippe Goubet
Françoise Gouinguenet
Robert Grace

Giorgio Grandi
Cecil Granger
Don Gray
Nigel Greenhill
Magali Grenier
Paolo Guerrini
Domenico Guerrisi
Alain Guèze
Barnaby Gunning

Greg Hall
Donald Hart
Thomas Hartman
Gunther Hastrich
Ulrike Hautsch
Christopher Hays
Eva Hegerl
Pascal Hendier
Pierre Henneguier
Maìre Henry
Gabriel Hernandez
Caroline Herrin
Christopher Hight
Kohji Hirano
Harry Hirsch
Andrew Holmes
Eric Holt
Abigail Hopkins
Masahiro Horie
Hélène Houizot
Michelle Howard
Jean Huc
Ed Huckabi
Frank Hughes

Filippo Icardi
Frediano Iezzi
Akira Ikegami
Djénina Illoul
Paolo Insogna
Shunji Ishida

Charlotte Jackman
Angela Jackson
Tobias Jaklin
Robert Jan van Santen
Amanda Johnson
Frédéric Joubert

Shin Kanoo
Jan Kaplicky
Elena Karitakis
Robert Keiser
Christopher Kelly
Paul Kelly
Werner Kestel
Irini Kilaiditi
Tetsuya Kimura
Laurent Koenig
Tomoko Komatsubara
Akira Komiyama
Misha Kramer
Eva Kruse
Betina Kurtz

Frank La Riviere
Jean Baptiste Lacoudre
Antonio Lagorio
Giovanna Langasco
Stig Larsen
Denis La Ville
François La Ville
Laurent Le Voyer
Jean Lelay
Renata Lello

Claudia Leoncini
Olivier Lidon
Lorraine Lin
Bill Logan
Johanna Lohse
Federica Lombardo
François Lombardo
Steve Lopez
Riccardo Luccardini
Simonetta Lucci
Rolf Robert Ludwig
Claudine Luneberg
Massimiliano Lusetti

Paola Maggiora
Domenico Magnano
Nicholas Malby
Milena Mallamaci
Natalie Mallat
Claudio Manfreddo
Flavio Marano
Andrea Marasso
Francesco Marconi
Massimo Mariani
Alberto Marre Brunenghi
Cristina Martinelli
Daniela Mastragostino
Manuela Mattei
William Matthews
Marie Hélène Maurette

Ken McBryde
Katherine McLone
Grainne McMahon
Nayla Mecattaf
Simone Medio
Barbara Mehren
Roberto Melai
Mario Menzio
Eveline Mercier
Benny Merello
Paul du Mesnil
Peter Metz
Marcella Michelotti
Paolo Migone
Sylvie Milanesi
Emanuela Minetti
Edoardo Miola
Takeshi Miyazaki
Gianni Modolo
Sandro Montaldo
Elisa Monti
Joost Moolhuijzen
Denise Morado
Nascimento
Gérard Mormina
Ingrid Morris
Jean Bernard Mothes
Farshid Moussavi
Mariette Müller
Philip Murphy
Andrea Musso

Hanne Nagel
Shinichi Nakaya
Hiroshi Naruse
Roberto Navarra
Pascale Nègre
Andrew Nichols
Hiroko Nishikama
Susanne Lore Nobis

David Nock
Elizabeth Nodinot
Marco Nouvion
Eric Novel

Anna O'Carrol
Tim O'Sullivan
Alphons Oberhoffer
Stefan Oehler
Noriaki Okabe
Antonella Oldani
Sonia Oldani
Grace Ong
Patrizia Orcamo
Stefania Orcamo
Roy Orengo
Carlos Osrej
Piero Ottaggio
Nedo Ottonello

Antonella Paci
Filippo Pagliani
Michael Palmore
Giorgia Paraluppi
Chandra Patel
Pietro Pedrini
Luigi Pellini
Danilo Peluffo
Gianluca Peluffo
Lionel Pénisson
Mauro Penna
Patrizia Persia
Gil Petit
Ronan Phelan
Paul Phillips

Alberto Piancastelli
Carlo Piano
Daniele Piano
Lia Piano
Matteo Piano
Enrico Piazze
Gennaro Picardi
Alessandro Pierandrei
Fabrizio Pierandrei
Fabrizio Pietrasanta
Marie Pimmel
Sandra Planchez
Bernard Plattner
Monica Poggi
Andrea Polleri
Roberta Possanzini
Fabio Postani
Nicolas Prouvé
Costanza Puglisi

Gianfranco Queirolo

Michele Ras
Maria Cristina Rasero
Dominique Rat
Neil Rawson
Judith Raymond
Antonella Recagno
Luis Renau
Tom Reynolds
Elena Ricciardi
Kieran Rice
Nemone Rice
Peter Rice
Jean Yves Richard
Gianni Robotti
Giuseppe Rocco
Richard Rogers
Renaud Rolland
Emilia Rossato

Bernard Rouyer
Lucio Ruocco
Joachim Ruoff
Ken Rupard
Antonella Sacchi
Angela Sacco
Jean Gérard Saint
Riccardo Sala
Maria Salerno
Maurizio Santini
Francesca Santolini
Paulo Sanza
Carola Sapper
Paul Satchell
Alessandro Savioli
Susanna Scarabicchi
Maria Grazia Scavo
Stefan Schafer
Helga Schlegel
Giuseppina Schmid
Jean François Schmit
Maren Schuessler
Andrea Schultz
Ronnie Self
Barbara-Petra Sellwig
Mario Semino
Patrik Senné
Anna Serra
Kelly Shannon
Randy Shields
Aki Shimizu
Cécile Simon
Thibaud Simonin
Alessandro Sinagra
Luca Siracusa
Jan Sircus
Alan Smith
Stephanie Smith
Richard Soundy
Claudette Spielmann

Adrian Stadlmayer
Alan Stanton
David Summerfield
Yasmin Surti
Antonella Sacchi [see note below]

José Luis Taborda
  Barrientos
Hiroyuki Takahashi
Norio Takata
Noriko Takiguchi
Hélène Teboul
Anne Hélène Téménides
Carlo Teoldi
Peter Terbuchte
G L Terragna
David Thom
John Thornhill
Cinzia Tiberti
Luigi Tirelli
Elisabeth Tisseur
Vittorio Tolu
Taichi Tomuro
Bruno Tonfoni
Graciella Torre
Laura Torre
Olivier Touraine
Alessandro Traldi
Renata Trapani
Renzo Venanzio Truffelli
Leland Turner
Mark Turpin

Yoshiko Ueno
Kiyomi Uezono
Peter Ullathorne

Colette Valensi
Maurizio Vallino
Mauritz Van der Staay
Antonia Van Oosten
Michael Vaniscott
Maurizio Varratta
Paolo Varratta
Claudio Vaselli
William Vassal
Francesca Vattuone
Bernard Vaudeville
Martin Veith
Reiner Verbizh
Laura Vercelli
Maria Carla Verdona
Eric Verstrepen
Silvia Vignale
Antonella Vignoli
Mark Viktov
Alain Vincent
Paul Vincent
Patrick Virly
Marco Visconti
Lorenzo Viti

Louis Waddell
Jean Marc Weill
Florian Wenz
Nicolas Westphal
Chris Wilkinson
Neil Winder
Martin Wollensak

George Xydis

Masami Yamada
Sugako Yamada
Hiroshi Yamaguchi
Tatsuya Yamaguchi
Emi Yoshimura
John Young

Gianpaolo Zaccaria
Kenneth Endrich Zammit
Lorenzo Zamperetti
Antonio Zanuso
Martina Zappettini
Walter Zbinden
Maurizio Zepponi
Massimo Zero

230 **Select bibliography**

Books

Piano, R, Arduino, M, Fazio, M *Antico è Bello*, Rome/Bari, Laterza, 1980

Donin, G *Renzo Piano, Piece by Piece*, Rome, Casa del Libro Editrice, 1982

Dini, M *Renzo Piano, Projects and Buildings 1964–1983*, London, Electa/Architectural Press, 1984

Nono, L *Verso Prometeo*, Venice, La Biennale/Ricordi Editori, 1984

Piano, R *Chantier Ouvert au Public*, Paris, Arthaud Editeur, 1985

Piano, R *Dialoghi di Cantiere*, Bari, Laterza Editrice, 1986

Piano, R and Rogers, R *Du Plateau Beaubourg au Centre Georges Pompidou*, Paris, Editions du Centre Georges Pompidou, 1987

Renzo Piano, Il Nuovo Stadio di Bari Milan, Edizione l'Archivolto, 1990

Renzo Piano, Buildings and Projects 1971–89 New York, Rizzoli, 1990

Exhibit Design: Renzo Piano Building Workshop Milan, Libra Immagine, 1992

Exhibition catalogues

Renzo Piano: the process of architecture London, 9H Gallery, 1987

Renzo Piano Paris, Editions du Centre Georges Pompidou, 1987

Renzo Piano Tokyo, Editions Delphi Research, 1989

Renzo Piano Building Workshop: selected projects P Buchanan, New York, the Architectural League of New York, 1992

Monographic issues of journals

AD Profile No 2, 1977: *Centre Georges Pompidou*

AA February 1982: *Renzo Piano Monografia*

A+U No 3, 1989: *Renzo Piano Building Workshop: 1964–1988* (includes article by R Banham, 'Making architecture: the high craft of Renzo Piano')

A&V No 23, 1990: *Renzo Piano Building Workshop: 1980–1990* (includes the following articles: 'The most beautiful craft in the world: Renzo Piano and the passion for building' by J Sainz; 'Between design and engineering: technology at the service of man' by P Buchanan; 'Desires and prejudices: the frugality of an industrial craftsman' by R Banham)

GB Progetti August–November 1990: *Crown Princess*

GB Progetti May/June 1991: *Columbus International Exposition*

Process Architecture January 1992: *Renzo Piano Building Workshop: 1964–1991, in search of a balance*

Articles

1966
Arts and Architecture August 1966, pp20–30: 'Structural plastics in Europe' by Z S Makowski

1967
Domus March 1967, pp8–22: 'Ricerca sulle strutture in lamiera e in poliestere rinforzato'

1968
Domus November 1968, p6: 'Nuove tecniche e nuove strutture per l'edilizia'

1969
Systems Buildings and Design February 1969, pp37–54: 'Plastic structures of Renzo Piano' by Z S Makowski

Techniques et Architecture May 1969, pp96–100: 'Italie recherche de structure' by R Piano

Domus October 1969, pp10–14: 'Uno studio–laboratorio'

1970
Architectural Design March 1970, pp140–145: 'Renzo Piano'

Architectural Forum March 1970, pp64–69: 'Rigging a roof'

Bauen + Wohnen April 1970, pp112–121: 'Structuren aus Kunstoff von Renzo Piano' by Z S Makowski

AA Quarterly July 1970, pp32–43: 'Architecture and technology' by R Piano

1971
Domus February 1971, pp12–15: 'Renzo Piano, per un'edilizia industrializzata'

Domus October 1971, pp1–7: 'Piano e Rogers: Beaubourg'

Industrial Design October 1971, pp40–45: 'Grand Piano'

AMC November 1971, pp8–9: 'Councours Beaubourg, "Est-ce un signe de notre temps?"' by M Cornu

1972
Techniques et Architecture February 1972, pp48–55: 'Projets des lauréats'

Casabella March 1972: 'Padiglione dell'industria Italiana all'Expo 70 di Osaka'

Domus June 1972, pp9–12: 'A Parigi, per i Parigini l'evoluzione del progetto Piano + Rogers per il Centre Beaubourg'

Deutsche Bauzeitung September 1972, p974–6: 'Paris Centre Beaubourg'

1973
Architecture d'Aujourd'hui July/August 1973, pp34–43: 'Centre Culturel du Plateau Beaubourg'

Domus August 1973: 'Centre Plateau Beaubourg'

Architecture d'Aujourd'hui November/December 1973, pp46–58: 'Piano + Rogers'

1974
Domus January 1974, pp31–6: 'Edifici per gli uffici B&B a Novedrate'

Architectural Design April 1974, pp245–6: 'B&B Italia factory'

Architecture Intérieure June/July 1974, pp72–7: 'Architecture et transparence'

Zodiac No22, pp126–147: 'Piano'

Architectural Review December 1974, pp338–345: 'Factory, Tadworth, Surrey'

1975
Acciaio February 1975, pp1–7: 'Una struttura tubulare per un nuovo edifico per uffici a Novedrate' by F Marano

Acciaio September 1975, pp3–15: 'Renzo Piano: la struttura del Centre Beaubourg a Parigi' by P Rice and L Grut

Domus April 1975, pp9–12: 'A Parigi musica underground'

Architectural Design May 1975, pp75–311: 'Piano + Rogers'

Acier. Stahl. Steel September 1975, pp297–309: 'Main structural framework of the Beaubourg Centre, Paris' by Peter Rice

Construction September 1975, pp5–30: 'Le Centre Georges Pompidou' by R Bordaz1976

1976
RIBA Journal February 1976, pp61–9: 'IRCAM design process'

A+U June 1976, pp63–122: 'Piano + Rogers: architectural method'

Architectural Design July 1976, pp442–3: 'Beaubourg furniture internal system catalogue' by Piano & Rogers

1977
Domus January 1977, pp5–37: 'Centre National d'Art et de Culture Georges Pompidou'

RIBA Journal January 1977, pp11–16: 'Piano + Rogers'

Architecture d'Aujourd'hui February 1977, pp40–81: 'Le défi de Beaubourg'

Bauwelt March 1977, pp 316–334: 'Frankreichs Centre National d'Art et de Culture Georges Pompidou'

Bauen + Wohnen April 1977, pp132–9: 'Centre National d'Art et de Culture G Pompidou ein arbeitsbericht von zwei architekturestudenten' by J Bub and W Messing

Architectural Review May 1977, pp270–294: 'The Pompidolium'

Domus May 1977, pp17–24: 'Piano & Rogers, 4 progetti'

GA No44, 1977, pp1–40: 'Centre Beaubourg: Piano + Rogers 'by Y Futugawa

Abitare October 1977, pp69–75: 'Intorno al Beaubourg'

Domus October 1977, pp1–11: 'Parigi: l'oggetto funzional' by P Restany, C Casati

Werk–Archithèse November/December 1977, pp22–29: 'Eiffel vs Beaubourg' by C Mitsia, M Zakazian and C Jacopin

Techniques et Architecture December 1977, pp62–3: 'L'opéra Pompidou' by P Chemetov and pp64–6: 'Ce diable Beaubourg' by M Cornu

1978
Industria delle Costruzioni February 1978, pp187–198: 'Il centro nazionale d'arte e cultura G Pompidou a Parigi' by A Paste

Domus June 1978, pp12–13: 'Tipologie evolutive'

Domus August 1978, pp25–28: 'Materie plastiche ed edilizia industrializzata' by G Biondo and E Rognoni

Casabella September 1978, pp42–51: 'Esperienze di cantiere tre domande a R Piano'

AA October 1978, pp52–63: 'IRCAM'

1979
Abitare January/February 1979, pp2–21: 'Da uno spazio uguale due cose diversissime'

Architectural Review August 1979, pp120–123: 'Heimatlandschaft' by L Wright

Bauen + Wohnen September 1979, pp330–332: 'Mobiles-quartier laboratorium'

Abitare October 1979, pp86–93: 'Per il recupero dei centri storici. Una proposta: il laboratorio mobile di quartiere'

Spazio e Società December 1979, pp27–42: 'Piano Rice Associates il laboratorio di quartiere' by L Rossi

1980
Toshi Jutaku February 1980, pp14–23: 'Free–plan four house group' by Toshi Jutaku

Architects' Journal 30 April 1980, pp852–3: 'Technology, tools and tradition' by Peter Buchanan

Design July 1980, pp58: 'Fiat's magic carpet ride'

232

AA December 1980, pp51–4: 'La technolgia n'est pas toujours industrielle'

1981
AA February 1981, pp92–95: 'C G Pompidou'

Domus May 1981, pp27–9: 'Sul mestiere dell'architetto'

Ottagono June 1981, pp20–27: 'Colloquio con R Piano' by P Santini

Building Design 31 July 1981 pp11–14: 'Pianoforte'

Architettura November 1981, pp614–662: 'Renzo Piano itineraio e un primo bilancio' by R Pedio

Casabella November/December 1981, pp95–6: 'Renzo Piano Genova'

1982
Abitare March 1982, pp8–9: ' Fiat vettura sperimentale e sottosistemi'

Cite August 1982, pp5–7: 'A clapboard treasure house' by S Fox

Building Design 20 August 1982, pp10–11: 'Renzo Piano: still in tune'

Architectural Review October 1982, pp57–61: 'Renzo Piano'

Casabella October 1982, pp14–23: 'Abitacolo e abitazione'

1983
Casabella April 1983 pp18–19: 'Parigi 1989' by P A Croset

Domus April 1983, pp10–15: 'La macchina climatizzata'

Modulo June 1983, pp20–33: 'Taller de Barrio: colloqio con Renzo Piano y Gianfranco Dioguardi'

Techniques et Architecture June/July 1983, pp51–61: 'Des technologies nouvelles pour l'habitat ancien'

Architectural Review August 1983, pp26–31: 'Piano machine'

Archi–Crée September 1983, pp118–123: 'Schlumberger à Montrouge'

Casabella September 1983, pp34–36: 'L'allestimento di Renzo Piano per la mostra di Calder' by M Brandli

Moniteur September 1983, pp60–67: 'Un chantier experimental à Mountrouge' by J P Robert

Spazio e Società September 1983, pp50–62: 'La cultura del fare' by L Rossi

Building Design 23 September 1983, pp32–34: 'Piano's progress' by Martin Pawley

Architectural Review November 1983, pp68–73: 'Piano rehab'

Domus November 1983, pp56–59: 'Calder a Torino'

Techniques et Architecture
November/December 1983, pp121–138: 'Artisan du futur' by R Piano

Architettura December 1983, pp888–894: 'Retrospettiva di Calder a Torino' by R Pedio

Modo November 1983, pp53–57: 'Instabil Sandy Calder' by M Margantini

Bouw December 1983, pp9–12: 'Recent werk van Renzo Piano' by R Rovers

1984
Arts + Architecture January 1984, pp32–5: 'Menil Collection'

Domus January 1984, pp22–7: 'Paris x Paris' by O Boisière

Omni January 1984, pp112–115: 'R Piano: sub-systems automobile' by G R Palffy

Acciaio February 1984, pp53–7: 'Una tensostruttura per l'insegna della mostra di Calder a Torino'

Spazio e Società March 1984, pp66–9: 'R Piano: sub–systems automobile' by M Fazio

Casabella May 1984, pp30–31: 'Venti idee per il Lingotto' by M Zardini

Building Design 18 May 1984, pp26–8: 'Lingotto Piano/Schein'

Architecture d'Aujourd'hui June 1984, pp14–23: 'Renovation du site industriel Schlumberger, Montrouge' by Y Pontoizeau

Techniques et Architecture June/July 1984, pp144–145: 'Exposition itinerante de technologie informatique'

A+U September 1984, pp67–72: 'IBM exhibit pavilion, Paris exposition'

Abitare September 1984, pp4–6: 'Una mostra itinerante per far conoscere il computer'

Rassenga September 1984, pp94–7: 'Beaubourg analogo'

Architecture d'Aujourd'hui October 1984, pp59–64: 'Projets & realisations' by Y Pontoizeau

Modo October 1984, pp36–40: 'Creativa e Progetto' by C Di Bartolo

Architectural Review November 1984, pp70–75: 'Arcadian machine'

Architettura November 1984, pp818–824: 'Exhibit IBM, padiglione itinerante di tecnologia informatica' by R Pedio

Casabella November 1984: pp38–9: 'Riflessioni sul "Prometeo"'

GA Document November 1984: 'L'expo IBM'

Architectural Review December 1984, pp53–7: 'Piano + Nono'

1985
SD January 1985, pp47–67: 'Renzo Piano and his methods'

Modulo March 1985, pp164–170: 'La grande nave lignea' by G Simonelli

Acciaio April 1985, pp166–170: 'Il Prometeo' by M Milan

Architectural Review May 1985, pp58–63: 'Piano pieces' by J Glancey

Techniques et Architecture May 1985, pp42–53: 'Restructuration d'un site industriel à Montrouge'

Forum No 29, 1985, pp138–144: 'The traps of technology' by P Buchanan

A+U June 1985, pp67–74: 'Music space for the opera "Prometeo" by L Nono' by R Piano, S Ishida

Archi–Crée August/September 1985, pp64–9: 'Natura, la revanche' by O Fillion

Daidalos September 1985, pp84–7: 'Il Prometeo'

Casabella October 1985, pp26–9: La Schlumberger a Montrouge di Renzo Piano' by J P Robert

Techniques et Architecture October 1985, pp101–111: 'Entretiens avec Renzo Piano' by A Pelissier

Werk, Bauen + Wohnen November 1985, pp23–8: 'Kunstliches und Naturliches' by E Hubeli

Architecture d'Aujourd'hui December 1985, pp12–15: 'Des chantiers permanents'

GA December 1985, p84–99: 'Urban conversion of the Schlumberger factories' by N Okabe

1986
Architettura April 1986, pp246–253: 'Reazione spaziale di Renzo Piano negli uffici Lowara a Vicenza'

Werk, Bauen + Wohnen April 1986, pp4–9: 'Eine mobile oper und ein "quartierlabor"'

Abitare September 1986, pp382–4: 'Houston, Texas, De Menil Museum'

Architecture d'Aujourd'hui September 1986, pp1–37: 'Piano de A à W' by D Mangin

Domus September 1986, pp29–37: 'Renzo Piano, progetto Lingotto a Torino' by M Pruisicki

Abitare October 1986, pp28–31: 'Progetto bambù' by F Zagari

Abitare November 1986, pp111: 'Vicenza, una mostra di Renzo Piano'

Arca December 1986, pp28–35: 'Il museo de Menil a Houston' by O Boissiere

Gran Bazaar December 1986, pp22–5: 'Conversando con Renzo Piano' by M Vogliazzo

Progressive Architecture December 1986, pp25–33: 'Piano and Palladio, virtuoso duet' by D Smetana

1987
Industria delle Costruzioni January 1987, pp27–33: 'Concorso per la sede del Credito Industriale Sardo' by B Galletta

Moniteur January 1987, pp58–59: 'Le Synchrotron de Grenoble'

Architects' Journal 21 January 1987, pp20–21: 'Piano lessons'

Building Design 23 January 1987, pp14–15: 'Piano solo'

Arca January/February 1987, pp29–37: 'Il forum industriale' by R Piano

Architectural Review March 1987, pp32–59: 'Piano practice' by E M Farrelly

Arca April 1987, pp59–65: 'La modernita secondo Piano' by R Piano

Gran Bazaar April/May 1987, pp47–54: 'L'architettura ritrovata' by B Nerozzi

Architecture May 1987, pp84–91: 'Simplicity of form, ingenuity in the use of daylight'

Detail May 1987, pp1–4: 'Trenward system aus glasfaserverstaktem beton'

Progressive Architecture May 1987, pp87–97: 'The responsive box' by P Papadanmetriou

Texas Architecture May/June 1987, pp40–47: 'Pianissimo, the very quiet Menil Collection' by R Ingersoll

Art in America June 1987, pp124–9: 'In the neighborhood of art', Reyner Banham (reprinted in A+U, November 1987)

Casabella June 1987, pp54–63: 'Renzo Piano, lo stadio di Bari e il Sincrotone di Grenoble'

Industria delle Costruzioni June 1987, pp6–23: 'Ristrutturazione e riuso di un'area industriale a Montrouge' by A Benedetti

Australia Architecture July 1987, pp63–7: 'The art of assembly' by M Keniger

Domus July/August 1987, pp32–43: 'Renzo Piano, Museo Menil, Houston' by E Ranzani

Architectural Review September 1987, pp70–80: 'The quiet game'

Ottagono September 1987, pp48–53: 'Piano: la basilica Palladiana non si tocca' by G K Koenig

Architecture d'Aujourd'hui October 1987, pp48–50: 'Piano retour près de Beaubourg'

Techniques et Architecture October/November 1987, pp146–165: 'Renzo Piano: la métamorphose de la technologie' by J F Pousse

Arca November 1987, pp80–85: 'Poesia e geometria per Bari' by A Castellano

A+U November 1987, pp39–122: 'Renzo Piano', Reyner Banham and Shunji Ishida

Domus November 1987, pp17–24: 'Renzo Piano: sovversione, silenzio e normalita' by V M Lampungani and E Ranzani

RIBA Journal November 1987, pp28–35: 'Piano's entente cordiale' by S Heck

SD November 1987, pp48–50: 'The Menil Art Museum' by Shunji Ishida

Baumeister December 1987, pp36–41: 'Sammlung in Houston'

Werk, Bauen + Wohnen December 1987, pp30–39: 'Konstructinen für das Licht'

1988
Abitare January 1988, pp192–197: 'Destinazione museo' by F Irace

Bauwelt January 1988, pp29–31: 'Umbau eines industriecomplex und landschaftgestaltung in Montrouge, Paris' by C Ellis

Detail May/June 1988, pp285–290: 'Menil Collection Museum in Houston, Texas'

Deutsche Bauzeitung June 1988, pp795–798: 'Menil – Sammlung in Houston'

Rassenga September 1988, pp110–113: 'Il Lingotto'

Werk, Bauen + Wohnen September 1988, pp48–55: 'Genua'

1989
Arquitectura Viva January 1989, pp15–19: 'Pianissimo – la discreta collecion Menil' by R Ingersoll

Spazio e Società January–March 1989, pp104–106: 'Quale Piano e per chi?' by R Radicioni

Building Design 20 January 1989, pp26–8: 'Flying high' by G Picardi

Architecture d'Aujourd'hui February 1989, pp42–53: 'L' Aéroport du Kansai à Osaka' by M Champenois

Japan Architect February 1989, pp191–7: 'Competition Kansai International Airport'

Techniques et Architecture February 1989, pp65–8: 'Kansai: le course contre le temps' by A Pelissier

GA Document February/March 1989, pp44–6: 'Football stadium'

Architectural Review March 1989, pp4–9: 'Piano's Lingotto' by Peter Davey

234

Casabella March 1989, pp22–3: 'Il consurso per il nuovo aeroporto di Osaka'

Architectural Design March/April 1989, pp52–61: 'Kansai International Airport'

Accacio April 1989, pp168–173: 'Arvedi space'

Architectural Review April 1989, pp84–8: 'Piano quays, Osaka airport' by D Ghirardo

Architecture d'Aujourd'hui April 1989, pp50–54: 'Musée d'art moderne à Newport' and 'Ensemble touristique dans la baie de Sistiana' by M Desvigne

Blueprint April 1989, pp52–4: 'Italy's Brunel' by A Nahum

World Architecture April 1989, pp72–7: 'Piano plays nature's theme'

Gran Bazaar April/May 1989, pp29–34: 'L'artificio assulto'

Domus May 1989, pp34–9: 'Il concorso per l'aeroporto internazionale di Kansai' by V Magnano Lampugnani

Building Design 22 September 1989, pp20–21: 'A gate for Malta'

Architectural Review October 1989, pp60–75: 'Piano quartet' by Colin Davies

Techniques et Architecture October/November 1989, pp114–119 and pp120–123: 'Raison de forme centre commercial de Bercy 2 à Charenton-le-Pont, and extension de l' IRCAM, Paris' by J F Pousse

Domus December 1989, pp14–16: 'Renzo Piano: allestimento al Lingotto' by E Ranzani

Rassenga December 1989, pp90–93: 'Una mostra al Lingotto'

Techniques et Architecture December1989/January 1990, pp144–145: 'Fusion horizontale'

1990
Domus January 1990, pp76–9: 'Renzo Piano: Libreria, Teso, Fontana Arte' by O di Blasi

Architecture d'Aujourd'hui February 1990, pp120–121: 'Stade de Bari, Italie'

Domus February 1990, pp38–47: 'Ampliamento dell' IRCAM a Parigi' by E Ranzani

Moniteur February 1990, pp76–9: 'Une usine modulaire en forêt' by F Lenne

Domus May 1990, pp33–9: 'Renzo Piano, stadio di calcio e atletica leggera, Bari' by E Ranzani

Moniteur Architecture June 1990, pp32–9: 'Le Stade de Bari'

Arca September 1990, pp72–81: 'La nave delfino' by A Castellano

Detail August/September 1990, pp395–398: 'Extension to IRCAM studios in Paris'

Architectural Review September 1990, pp71–3: 'Soft shore'

Werk, **Bauen + Wohnen** September 1990, pp22–9: 'Ort und stadium'

Arup Journal Autumn 1990, pp3–8: 'The San Nicola stadium'

Techniques et Architecture December 1990/January 1991, pp44–9: 'Le Grande souffle: stade de carbonara, Bari, Italie'

Rassenga December 1990, pp98–101: 'L'automobile, produzione e design a Milano 1879–1949'

1991
Abitare January 1991, p145: 'Fontana Arte: "Teso" '

Space Design January 1991, pp88–91: 'Bridge for the port of Ushibuka'

GA Document March 1991, pp60–95: 'Renzo Piano Building Workshop' by S Ishida and N Okabe

Space Design March 1991, pp74–6: 'The Menil Collection Museum'

Presenza Tecnica March/April 1991, pp10–23: 'Un nouva porto antico per Genova'

Techniques et Architecture April/May 1991, pp52–7: 'Lyon, Cité Internationale de la Tête d'Or'

Architectural Review May 1991, pp83–90: 'Eastern promise' by F Anderton

Deutsche Bauzeitung May 1991, pp64–7: 'Raumschiff'

Moniteur Architecture May 1991, pp51–61: 'Détail: Renzo Piano façades en briques et composites' by J P Menard

Domus May 1991, pp44–71: 'La transformazione delle citta: Genova' by E Ranzani

Architecture d'Aujourd'hui June 1991, pp162-6: 'Piano à Bercy'

Industria delle Costruzioni June 1991, pp22–30: 'Centro commercialle a Bercy II, Parigi' by R Morganti

Architectural Review July 1991, pp59–63: 'French connection'

Techniques et Architecture July 1991, pp38–47: 'Côté Jardin'

Domus July/August 1991, pp27–39: 'Complesso residenziale a Parigi'

Architecture d'Aujourd'hui September 1991, pp45–50: 'Renzo Piano, l'aéroport du Kansai à Osaka' by M-J Dumont

Arquitectura Viva September/October 1991, pp42–7: 'A flor de piel' by J Cervera

Architecture d'Aujourd'hui October 1991, pp9–13: 'Centre Cultural Kanak à Nouméa' by F Chaslin

1992
Architectural Review January 1992, pp56–7: 'Piano's magic carpet' by P Buchanan

Moniteur January 1992, pp84–5: 'Logements rue de Meaux, Paris XIXe'

Abitare March 1992, pp229–234: 'Renzo Piano, aeroporto Kansai' by A Castellano

Architectural Review March 1992, pp61–63: 'Pacific Piano' by P Buchanan

Progressive Architecture March 1992: 'Flights of fantasy' by T Fisher

Modulo March 1992, pp170–180: 'La nuova sede del Credito Industriale Sardo' by P Righetti

De Architect March 1992, pp60–65: 'Kansai International Airport'

Rassenga March 1992, pp114–117: 'Il Grande Bigo' by L Gelhaus

Progressive Architecture April 1992, pp94–95: 'The place of sports' by T Fisher

AU architetura urbanismo April/May 1992, pp54–63: 'Un aereoporto sobre o mar' by M Barda

Costruire May 1992, pp26–38: 'La scoperta di Genova' by F Bertami and G Salsalone

Modulo May 1992, pp488–491: 'Sotto le ali di una tenda' by M Toffolon

Werk, **Bauen + Wohnen** May 1992, pp54–57: 'Trompe l'oeil'

Abitare June 1992, pp133–136: 'Piano per Genova – La città sul mare' by F Irace

Architecture d'Aujourd'hui June 1992, pp78–85: 'Piano, renovation du port de Genes' by M Champenois

A+U July 1992, pp70–114: 'Renzo Piano Building Workshop: shopping centre Bercy: Bari soccer stadium; subway station, Genoa' by R Ingersoll and S Ishida

DBZ July 1992, pp1033–1035: 'Internationale Columbus Ausstellung, Genoa' by C F Kusch

Quaderni July 1992, pp19–24: 'Genova domani'

Progressive Architecture August 1992, pp78–85: 'Perspectives, Genoa's historic port reclaim' by Z Freiman

Baumeister August 1992, pp40–45: 'Colombo '92 in Genua' by R Maillinger

Sport & Città September 1992, pp10–16: 'Il Porto Vecchio' by C Garbato

Arredo Urbano September 1992, pp30–33: 'Berlino. Renzo Piano a Potsdamer Platz: l'eclecttico e il disciplinato dell' architettura' by A Valenti

Flare October 1992, pp4–13: 'Genova, le celebrazioni Colombiane' by N Baldassini

Modulo October 1992, pp1024–1033: 'Gli ex Magazzini del Cotone' by P Righetti

Architecture d'Aujourd'hui October 1992, pp92–97: 'Deux Etoiles Italiennes' by J C Garcias

Casa Vogue October 1992, pp 58–61: 'Il delfino bianco' by G Paci

GA November 1992, pp40–59: 'Unesco Workshop, Columbus International Exposition, Thomson CSF Factory' by S Ishida

Rassenga December 1992, pp94–97: 'Un sistema, illuminotecnico funzionale'

Domus December 1992, pp44–55: 'Progetti per l'area della Potsdamerplatz, Berlino' by P Rumpf

Archittetura December 1992, pp862–863: 'Esposizione Internazionale 1992 nel porto antico' and pp884–886: 'Dal bullone al territorio'

1993
Architectural Review January 1993, pp20–28: 'Cross roads Berlin' by D Cruickshank and pp36–41: 'Genoa drama' by D Cruickshank

Arca January 1993, pp48–53: 'Un parco culturale per la citta il Lingotto' by R Dorigati

Domus January 1993, pp52–9: 'Renzo Piano Aeroporto di Kansai, Osaka'

Werk, **Bauen + Wohnen** January/February 1993, pp41–8: 'Zwischen seelandschaft und piazza' by G Ullman

AD January/February, pp18–23: 'Potsdamer Platz – Leipziger Platz, Berlin 1991' by C Sattler

Casabella January/February 1993, pp 120–121: 'Sistemazione degli spazi esterni dell' industria Thomson a Guyancourt'

Interni January/February 1993, pp120–121: 'Crown Princess'

Architecture February 1993, pp22–3: 'Renzo Piano exhibit in NY' by D Albrecht

Progressive Architecture February 1993, pp19: 'Renzo Piano exhibit opens in NY' by P Arcidi

Detail February 1993, pp593–7: 'Elektronikfabrik in Guyancourt'

Arquitectura Viva March/April 1993, pp52–9: 'Mecanico e Organico' by P Buchanan

Domus April 1993, pp87–9: 'Renzo Piano' by E Morteo

Abitare April 1993, pp156–169: 'Unesco & Workshop' by E Regazzoni

Flare May 1993, pp26–8: 'La luce nell'architettura Hi-Tech' by N Baldassini

Mwa Vee May 1993, pp48–53: 'Le Centre Cultural Jean-Marie Tjibaou'

Arquitectura Viva May/June 1993, pp96–7: 'Hipergeometrias, el ordenador en el studio de Renzo Piano' by J Sainz

Techniques et Architecture June/July 1993, pp114–121: 'La grande vague' by M Tardis

Japan Architect Summer 1993, pp212–217: 'Ushibuka fishing port connecting bridge'

Werk, **Bauen + Wohnen** July/August 1993, pp20–25: 'Solitars in der periurbanen wurste' by R P Red

Detail August/September 1993, pp414–417: 'Haltestelle Brin in Genua'

Japan Architect Autumn 1993, pp54–69: 'Kansai International Airport, passenger terminal building'

Maiora December 1993, pp4–11: 'Un edificio residenziale a Parigi: rue de Meaux' by M Rognoni

Industria delle Costruzione December 1993, pp64–5: 'Progetti di Renzo Piano in mostra itinerante' by G Messina

Lapiz December 1993, pp45–9: 'Arquitectura en la confluencia de los limites' J M Alvarez Enjuto

235

236 **Index**

Page numbers in italic refer to illustrations

Agnelli, V G **150**
air conditioning, Beyeler Foundation **179**
airports see Kansai
Albini, Franco **69**
Alfa Romeo see 'Automobiles in Milan'
  exhibition
aluminium **60**, **155**
'American Art 1930–1970' exhibition **15**,
  162, *166*
Amiens see Jules Verne Leisure Park
Amsterdam see National Centre for Science
  and Technology
Amsterdam, map *134*
Andrews, John **85**
Ansaldo see 'Automobiles in
  Milan' exhibition
aquarium, Genoa **9**, *10*, **103**, *108*, **112–13**,
  114, **135**
Archigram **106**, **153**
art exhibitions, Lingotto Factory **162**, **164**
art galleries
  see Beyeler Foundation Museum
Arup, Ove & Partners **13**, **38**, **70**, **78**, **179**
Assisi church **182**, *183*
'Automobiles in Milan' exhibition, Ansaldo **9**,
  168–9

Banham, Reyner **85**
Barcelona, Church of Sagrada Familia **185**
Bardsley, Henry **22**
Barker, Tom **179**
Basle see Beyeler Foundation Museum,
  Lingotto Factory Renovation, J M Tjibaou
Basle Cathedral **173**
Bercy 2 Shopping Centre, Paris **10**, **12**, **13**,
  16–33, **34**, **78**, **132**, **215**
  plans *26–7*
  shell **16**, *18*, *19*
Berio, Luciano **117**
Berlin see Potsdamer Platz

Beyeler Foundation Museum, Riehen, near
  Basle **9**, **78**, **170–9**
  drawings *176–7*
Bianchi, Giorgio **117**
Bigo see Grande Bigo
Blassel, Jean-Francois **22**
boats see cruise ships; yachts
bonded warehouses, Genoa **126–7**
Brancusi, Constantin **71**, *72*, **84**
Brin station, Genoa *8*, **46**, **50–1**, *52*
building management system, Lingotto
  Factory **155**
  team members, photos *66–75*
  two centres in Genoa **76**
  internationalism **96**
  see also UNESCO Laboratory-workshop
business centre, Lingotto Factory **155**

Cagliari see Credito Industriale Sardo
Cambridge Seven Associates **112**
Canepari station, Genoa **46**, *48*
Carandente, Giovanni **162**, **164**
Caricamento station, Genoa **46**, *49*
Carpenter, James **114**
cases, J M Tjibaou Cultural Centre *10*, **12**,
  82, **192**, **193**, **194**, **197**, **198**, *198*, **199**,
  200, **201**, **203**, **205**, *206*, *209*
chaos-theory mathematics **13**
Charenton see Bercy 2
churches see Padre Pio Pilgrimage Church
Cité Internationale, Lyons **66**
cities see urban reconstruction schemes
cladding, metal panels **12–13**, *13*, **14**, **216**
  Bercy 2 **19–20**, **22–23**, *30*, *31*, *32*,
  33, **215**
  Kansai International Airport **12**, **23**,
  215, **220**, **224–227**
  National Centre for Science and
  Technology, Amsterdam **132**, **134**,
  135, **215**

Potsdamer Platz **215**, **216**
  Thomson Optronics factory **37**
cladding, pre-cast concrete
  aquarium, Genoa **112**
cladding, stone
  Credito Industriale Sardo **12**, *12*,
  143, *148*
cladding, terracotta
  Harbour Master's Office and service spine
  122, *122–123*
  IRCAM extension **12**, *12*, **122**
  Potsdamer Platz *216–218*
  Rue de Meaux Housing **12**, *12*
Codognato, A **162**, *166*, **167**
colour *39*, **40**, **127**
Columbus International Exposition,
  Genoa **8**, **9**, *10*, **12**, **14**, **94–131**
  site plan *99*
  historic relics *103*
  service spine **122**
  bonded warehouses **126–7**
  views **128–9**
  see also Grande Bigo
components see kit

computers
  building management system **155**
  and stone cutting **180**
  use in determining curves **12**, **13–14**
  Bercy 2 **21**, *22*
  J M Tjibaou Cultural Centre *204*
  Lingotto Factory renovation **155**
  National Centre for Science and
  Technology **134**, **135**
  Padre Pio Pilgrimage Church **180**, *188*
concert hall/congress hall
  Columbus International Exposition **118**,
  120
  Lingotto Factory renovation **154**,
  160, *162*

Contemporary Art Museum
  see Newport Harbor
Le Corbusier **73**, **85**, **150**, **184**
Corciano, Il Rigo Housing *192*, **194**
creativity, R P on **67–8**, **73**
Credito Industriale Sardo, Cagliari, Sardinia
  12, **55**, **140–9**
  plans *144*
Crown Princess **9**, **58**, *60*
cruise ships and yacht **9**, **58–63**

Daimler Benz **212**, **215**, **216**, *218*, *219*
Danish Naval Institute **60**
Darsena station, Genoa **46**, *48*
Design Museum, planned for Ansaldo,
  Milan **168**
design process, R P on **73–4**
Desvigne, Michel **37**
Dinegro station, Genoa **46**, **50**
dome, use in ship superstructure **60**
  Lingotto conference suite **154**
Drees & Sommer **78**

electronic communications **81**
electronic information systems **153**
electronic monitoring system, Lingotto
  Factory **15**, **155**, **158**
energy-saving claddings **78**
European Community funding for research
  78, **80**
evolution, R P on **68–9**
exhibition space **9**
  Columbus International Exposition *113*
  J M Tjibaou Cultural Centre **193**
  Lingotto Factory renovation **154**, **162**,
  164
exhibitions see 'American Art 1930–1970';
  'Automobiles in Milan'; 'Columbus
  International Exposition'; 'Galileo in Padua';
  'Russian and Soviet Art 1870–1930'

Exploratorium *see* National Centre for Science and Technology, Amsterdam

Expo '92, Seville **99**, **180**, *181*

Fabbrica della Chiesa, Padre Pio Pilgrimage Church **185**

factories *see* Lingotto Factory renovation; Thomson Optronics factory

Fiat VSS experimental car **58**

Fiat *see also* Lingotto Factory, Turin

Fincantieri shipbuilders **58**

flexibility, Thomson Optronics factory **34**, **36**

Flying Carpet, basic transport **58**

Foggia *see* Padre Pio Pilgrimage Church

Fontana Arte, Milan **92**

fractals **13**

funicular ride, UNESCO Laboratory-workshop **80**, *81*

furniture, glass **92–3**

'Galileo in Padua' Exhibition Project **130–1**

Gassman, Vittorio **106**

Genoa

archaeology **103**, **126**

historic cit **94**, **96–7**, **103**

see also

Columbus International Exposition;

Metro stations; Molo quarter;

UNESCO Laboratory-workshop

geometry **12–13**

Bercy 2 **22–3**, *31*, **221–3**

fractal **13**, **23**

toroidal **13**, *22*, *23*

glass, structural, Beyeler Foundation Museum **170**

glass furniture system **92–3**

glazing

Lingotto Factory Renovation **156**, **157**, *161*

Thomson Optronics Factory **37**, *41*

UNESCO Laboratory-workshop **77**, **79**, *86*, *87*

Il Grande Bigo, Genoa *2*, **103**, *104*, **106**, *107*, *108*, *110*, *117*

harbour and town, Genoa **96–7**, **99**, **103**

see also Molo quarter

Harbour Master's office, Genoa **103**, **122**, *123*

harmony, R P on **68**

helipads, Lingotto Factory **155**

high-tech movement **10**

R P on **64**, **113**

Hilmer & Sattler **212**

hotel, Lingotto Factory renovation **155**

Houston, Texas *see* Menil Collection

Hulten, Pontus **71**

IBM Travelling Pavilion *192*, **194**

'incubator units', Lingotto Factory **155**

internationalism **74–5**, **96**

IRCAM extension, Paris **12**, *12*, **37**, **55**, **94**, **122**, **194**, **218**

Italian pavilion, floating, Columbus International Exposition **9**, **112**, **113**, **116–17**

J M Tjibaou Cultural Centre, Noumea **9**, **10**, **12**, **68**, *82*, **190–209**

Jules Verne Leisure Park, Amiens *193*

Kanak arts and culture **190**, *196*, **197**, **203**

Kansai International Airport, Osaka **9**, **12**, **13**, **14**, **18**, **66–7**, **96**, **212**, **220–7**

cladding **23**, **134**

sculptures **106**

Kempinski Haus, Berlin **218**

kit of components, pre-designed

for Lingotto Factory **155**,

for Thomson Optronics Factory **37**

Kulturforum, Berlin **15**, **210**, **212**, **218**

landscape

Lingotto Factory **152**, *153*, **154**, **158**

Potsdamer Platz **212**

Thomson Optronics factory **36–7**

Lanterna, Genoa **117**

Lavarello, Mario and Matteo **117**

light fixtures, Lingotto Factory **155**

Lingotto Factory renovation, Turin **9**, **15**, **79**, **150–67**

history of Fiat factory **150**, *152*

louvres and blinds, CIS **145**, *146*

UNESCO Laboratory-workshop **79**, **80**

Lyons, Cité Internationale **66**

Macchi, Giulio **96**, **117**

Magazzini del Cotone, Genoa **103**, **118–21**

'A Manipulative Universe' exhibition **67**

Martorell Bohigas Mackay **180**, *181*

materials *see* natural materials; stone; timber

Matte-Trucco, Giacommo **150**

megastructure, Lingotto Factory renovation **150**, **153**, **158**

Menil Collection, Houston **113–14**, **135**, **136**, **170**, *172*, *173*, **194**

metal cladding **12–13**, **14**, **216**

Metro stations, Genoa **8**, **46–57**, *53–5*

map *48*

Mies van der Rohe, Ludwig **145**, **216**, *218*

Milan *see* 'Automobiles in Milan' exhibition

Millo building, Genoa **103**, *104*, **106**, **124–5**

Molo quarter, Genoa **8**, **94**, **98–9**, **127**

Monfalcone shipyards, Trieste **58**

monitors, glass, Beyeler Foundation museum **175**, **179**

Monte Carlo leisure centre **153**

museums *see* Beyeler Foundation museum; Design museum; National Centre for Science and Technology, Amsterdam

National Centre for Science and Technology, Amsterdam **9**, *10*, **13**, **14**, **132–9**, **215**

cladding **132**, **134**, **135**

exploratorium **134**, **136**, **138**

initial scheme *136*

final scheme *137*, *138*

National Library, Berlin **210**, **212**, *213*

'natural' architecture **6–15**, **23**, **55**

R P on **68**

J M Tjibaou Cultural Centre **190**, **192–4**, **205**

Lingotto Factory **158**

UNESCO Laboratory-workshop **84**

natural materials **10**, *12*

research into **76**, **80**

Nervi, Pier Luigi *182*, **184**

New Caledonia *see* J M Tjibaou Cultural Centre

Newport Harbor, California, Contemporary Art Museum **170**, *172*

Noumea, New Caledonia *see* J M Tjibaou Cultural Centre

Okabe, Noriaki **22**, **23**

operetta theatre and casino block, Potsdamer Platz **216**

organic architecture **6–15**

Bercy 2 **23**

Lingotto Factory **158**

by Scharoun **215**, **216**

Origoni, Franco **117**

Osaka *see* Kansai International Airport

Otranto *see* UNESCO neighbourhood workshop

Otto, Frei **106**

Ove Arup *see* Arup, Ove & Partners

Padre Pio Pilgrimage church, San Giovanni Rotondo, Foggia **10**, **12**, **13**, **73**, **180–9**

Padua

'Galileo in Padua' exhibition **130–1**

Palazzo della Ragione **130–1**

Palazzina, Lingotto Factory **152**, *162*, *167*

Palazzo San Giorgio, Genoa **97**, **99**, **103**, *104*

Paris *see* Bercy 2 Shopping Centre; IRCAM extension; Pompidou Centre; Rue de Meaux housing; Schlumberger renovation

Piano, Renzo

interview with Peter Buchanan **64–75**

Anglo-Saxon cast of mind **69–70**

'Open Site' television programmes **96**, **185**, **220**

and the sea **58**

Renzo Piano Building Workshop **10**, **74–5**, **96**

internationalism **96**

team members, photos **66–75**

two centres in Genoa **76**

Piano & Fitzgerald *see* Menil Collection, Houston

Piano & Rice Associates

Il Rigo Housing, Corciano *192*

UNESCO Neighbourhood Workshop **97–8**, *193*

piazza, internal, Potsdamer Platz **216**

Piazza Caricamento, Genoa **103**, **112**, **126**

Piazza de Ferrari station, Genoa **46**, *49*

Picasso, Renzo **46**, *48*

plants, studied at UNESCO Laboratory-workshop **76**, **80**

Plattner, Bernard **172**

Pompidou Centre, Paris *39*, **40**

237

238 Potsdamer Platz, Berlin **12**, **14–15**, **66**, **78**,
81, **210–19**
history **212**
competition scheme **213**
current scheme **214**
shells **215–16**
Principe station, Genoa **46**, **48**

railways see Metro stations, Lingotto Factory
Renovation
Ravenna, S. Apollinare in Classe **185**
Ravenna Sports Hall **12**, **13**, **182**, **184**
Regal Princess **58**
Reihen, Basle see Beyeler Foundation
museum
Renaud, Jean **21**
Resolute Lady yacht **63**
Rice, Peter **13**, **19**, **22**, **23**,
70, **73**, **106**
and the UNESCO Laboratory-workshop **76**
Padre Pio Pilgrimage Church **180**
Rice Francis Ritchie (RFR) **19**
Il Rigo Housing, Corciano **192**, **194**
Rome, Palazzo del Sport **182**
roofs
double layered, Bercy 2 Shopping Centre,
20, **20**, **30**, **31**
energy-saving **78**
glass, Beyeler Foundation Museum **170**,
171, **172**, **175**, **175**, **178**, 179
Credito Industriale Sardo **142**, **143**, 145,
145–147
Metro station **51**, **53–57**
J M Tjibaou Cultural Centre **200** **201**,
202, **204**, **208**
UNESCO laboratory workshop **76–91**,
77–91
Kansai International Airport **224**,
226–227, research into **78**
tented **10**, **106**, **152**, **153**

roof lights
aquarium **113**, **114**, 114
Bercy 2 Shopping Centre **21**, **21**, **22**,
25, **31**
Grande Bigo tent **106**, **107**, **111**
Rue de Meaux Housing,
Paris **12**, **114**, **218**
'Russian and Soviet Art 1870–1930'
exhibition, Lingotto
Factory renovation **15**, **162**, **164**

Saint Quentin en Yvelines see Thomson
Optronics factory
San Giovanni Rotondo **184**
see also Padre Pio Pilgrimage Church
Sardinia see Credito Industriale Sardo
Sarzano station, Genoa **46**, **49**
Savona, Paolo **140**
Scharoun, Hans **15**, **210**, **212**,
215, **216**
Schlumberger Renovation, Paris **94**, **152**,
153
sculpture see Brancusi, Constantin; wind
sculptures
sea **8**, **9**, **10**, **58**, **80**, **85**
celebrated in Columbus International
Exposition **117**
see also harbour
Seagram Building, New York **145**
Sedgwick, Andy **179**
Semino, Mario **96**
Seville see Expo '92
shells **12**, **14**
see also Bercy 2; Potsdamer Platz; Kansai
International Airport
Shingu, Susumu **106**, **108**, 110
ships, model, in Columbus International
Exposition **117**
shopping centres see Bercy 2
signage mast, Bercy 2 **19**

solar control see louvres and blinds
sopraelevata **48**, **96**, 97, **104**, 126
space
R P on **66–7**
in National Centre for Science and
Technology **136**, **139**
sports hall see Ravenna
stations see Metro stations, Genoa
stone **10**, **12**, **55**
artificial, Metro stations **50**, **55**
CIS **143**, **148**
Padre Pio Pilgrimage Church **180**
structure, concrete
Bercy 2 Shopping Centre **20**
Credito Industriale Sardo **143**
laminated timber
Bercy 2 Shopping Centre **10**, **21**, **21**, **22**,
25, **28–31**
Beyeler Foundation Museum **173**, **175**,
175–179
J M Tjibau Cultural Centre **190–209**,
191, **198**, **200–209**
UNESCO laboratory workshop **77–78**,
78, **83**, **85–89**
steel, aquarium **116**
Grand Bigo **106**, **106–110**
Harbour Master's office and service spine
122, **122**, **123**
Lingotto Factory Renovation conference
suite **154**
Kansai International Airport **220–227**
Metro station **51**, **52–57**
Thompson Optronics Factory **37–39**,
37–45
stone arches, Padre Pio Pilgrimage Church
180–185, **181**, **185–189**
structural shells **12**, **14**
Studio Piano, Office/workshop, Genoa **79**,
175
Sydney Opera House **22**

telecommunications, Lingotto Factory **155**
tented roofs see roofs
thermal experiments, UNESCO Laboratory-
workshop **80**
Thomson Optronics Factory, Saint Quentin en
Yvelines **10**, **14**, **34–45**
Tiergarten, Berlin **212**
timber **10**, **193**, **197**
Tjibaou, Jean-Marie **192**
see mainly under J M Tjibaou
Cultural Centre
torus, in geometry **13**
trade fair hall, Lingotto Factory **160**
Turin
University **155**
Via Roma **154**
see also Lingotto Factory

UNESCO, sponsor of research at Building
Workshop **76**
UNESCO Laboratory-workshop, Vesima
8–9, **10**, **76–91**, **86–91**
R P on **70–1**, **72**
functions **83–4**
UNESCO Neighbourhood Workshop, Otranto
193, **194**
UNESCO Travelling Workshop, Senegal **193**
University of Turin, facilities in Lingotto
Factory **155**
urban reconstruction schemes **14–15**
see also Columbus International
Exposition; Molo;
Potsdamer Platz
Utzon, Jorn see Sydney Opera House

Vesima see UNESCO Laboratory-workshop
Via del Mare, Genoa **112**, **114**, **116**, 117
Vicenza, Palladio Basilica **130–1**
Villa Berower, Basle **172**
Vincent, Paul **190**

Warhol, Andy, exhibition **162**, **167**
water, conduction of **20**, **36**
wind sculptures, Genoa **106**, **108**, **110**
Kansai International Airport Terminal **106**,
223
wind studies, J M Tjibaou Cultural Centre **204**
cruise ship design **60**
windows see glazing
Wisniewski, Edgar **212**
wood see timber

yacht, based on sponsor's posters **116–17**
see also Resolute Lady

Zeppelin airship **18**

Photographic credits

Unless otherwise indicated, all line drawings of projects are the copyright of the Renzo Piano Building Workshop.

Resi Accardi 63
Ove Arup (Jeppe Hundervad) 154, 182
Gabriele Basilico 8, 14, 113, 116, 128–129, 157
Roger Boulay 196
Peter Buchanan 183
James Carpenter Design 114
Mario Carrieri 92
Sergio Cigliutti 15, 160(x5), 166(x3), 167(x2)
Cinefiat 152(x7)
Mario Cucinella 62,
Michel Denancé 4-5, 10,(x2), 12(x2), 13, 14, 17, 18, 19(x3), 20, 30(x5), 31 32, 33, 35, 36, 37(x2), 38(x3), 39(x3), 40(x2), 41(x6), 42-43, 44, 45, 54(x5), 56-57, 104, 107(x3), 153, 171, 173(x2), 175(x2), 178(x2), 179, 200(x4), 201(x5), 202, 203, 208, 209(x4), 212, 213(x5), 214(x2), 215, 216, 217, 219(x2), 223, 224, 226-227
Focchi 157
Kenneth Fraser 181, 185(x3), 186, 188
Fregoso and Basalto 65, 77, 83, 84(x2), 86, 87, 89, 90–91
Gianni Berengo Gardin 8, 12, 15, 19(x2), 28(x6), 29(x2), 30, 31(x2), 32(x3), 50, 51(x3), 53(x7), 54(x4), 59, 60(x2), 61, 62(x3), 67, 69, 70, 72, 74, 82, 88, 142, 143(x5), 146(x2), 148(x7), 95, 96, 97, 99(x4), 102(x2), 103(x3), 110(x4), 111, 112(x2), 115(x2), 118(x2), 119, 120, 121(x2), 122(x2), 157(x2), 123,124(x5), 126(x5), 127(x3), 151, 162(x3), 163(x2), 164, 192, 193, 222(x3), 223(x5), 224(x3), 225(x3)
Stefano Goldberg 81(x2), 86
I Guzzini 155(x2)
Roland Halbe 141, 142, 145(x2), 146(x2), 149
Donald Hart 66, 67(x2), 68, 69, 70, 71, 73, 74, 79, 96(x2), 97, 102(x2), 103(x2)

Yoshio Hata 13, 224
Paul Hester 240
Shunji Ishida 9(x2), 11, 51(x2), 52, 54(x2), 62(x2), 66(x3), 68, 69(x2), 70(x3), 71(x3), 72(x4), 73, 74(x5), 75(x3), 78, 80(x6), 81(x4), 82(x2), 84(x4), 85(x4), 86(x3), 88(x2), 143, 148(x2), 97, 106, 107(x2), 113, 115, 116(x2), 117(x3), 118, 125, 127, 131(x2), 157, 160, 162, 166, 168, 169(x4), 182, 183(x2), 184(x2)
Kinumaki 223, 224(x3)
Lupo 153, 158
Gerard Martrom 208
Gabrielle Maschietti 157(x3), 160, 161
Emanuela Minetti 52, 53(x3), 106(x2), 107, 111(x2), 121, 127, 185(x3)
Olaf De Nooyer 106(x2)
Noriaki Okabe 223(x2), 224(x2)
Renzo Piano Building Workshop Archives 78, 181, 194(x3), 195(x8)
Renzo Piano Building Workshop, Japan 66, 223(x2)
Publifoto 15, 60, 63(x5), 78(x2), 79, 135, 136, 138, 96(x2), 97(x2), 98(x2), 100-101, 106, 109, 112, 113(x3), 117, 130, 166(x2), 216(x2)
Réunion Des Museés Nationaux 197
C Rives/M Folco Editions Du Pacifique 196(x4), 197(x2)
Hickey Robertson 172
Rotta 152
Philippe Ruault 20, 21, 25, 28, 29, 30(x3), 31(x4)
Vàclav Sedy 164, 165
Sky Front 221
Luciano Soave 92(x2), 93(x4), 167
Tabiana Taccone 85
Mauro Vallinotto 153(x2), 156
William Vassal 207(x3)

240

Volume One contents

Aluminium Research Institute, Novara **166–73**

B&B Italia Offices, Como **50**

Calder Retrospective **80–3**

Contemporary Art Museum, Newport Harbor **164**

European Synchrotron Radiation Facility, Grenoble **200**

Fiat VSS Experimental Car **64**

'Flying Carpet' Basic Vehicle **65**

Free-plan Houses, Cusago **51**

Genoa office–workshop **44**

IBM Ladybird Pavilion **132–3**

IBM Travelling Pavilion **110–30**

IRCAM Extension, Paris **202–13**

Italian Industry Pavilion, Expo 1970 **49**

Kansai International Airport Terminal **20–5**

Lowara Offices, Montecchio Maggiore **134–9**

Menil Collection gallery, Houston **140–63**

Mobile Structure for Sulphur Extraction **47**

'The Open Site' **66–7**

Palladio Basilica Rehabilitation, Vicenza **177**

Piano & Rice Associates **64–77**

Piano & Rogers **50–63**

Pompidou Centre, Paris **52–63**

Prometeo opera, setting for **84–9**

QB Housing, Genoa **44**

Reinforced Polyester Space Frame **47**

Rhodes Moat Development **176**

Il Rigo Housing, Corciano **18–19**

Rue de Meaux Housing, Paris **214–27**

San Nicola Stadium, Bari **179–99**

Schlumberger Renovation, Paris **90–109**

Shell Structural System for the Fourteenth Milan Triennale **48**

Sistiana Tourist Resort, Trieste **201**

Studio Piano **46–9**

Tensile Steel and Reinforced-Polyester Structure **48**

Twombly (Cy) Pavilion, Houston **165**

UNESCO Neighbourhood Workshop, Otranto **68–77**

Valletta City Gate **174–5**

Woodwork Shop, Genoa **47**